Praise for *Real Life, Real Funny*

"The distinguished Mainers contributing to this book are pillars of a time when our politics were more respected and much more respectful. Reading the stories is like a trip down memory lane to a time when policy differences didn't make political enemies. It's gratifying to think that Maine is unique in the way it governs its body politic—with humor and mutual understanding of the human condition we all share. This book should give you optimism that it might always be so. Kudos to Chris, Dave, and Dennis for collecting stories that remind us all that Maine is a unique and special place."
—**Kay Rand, former campaign manager and chief of staff for Governor and Senator Angus King**

"A hysterical—and historical—glance over our collective shoulder at Maine life. I literally could not put it down, reading nearly the entire book in one sitting! As a humorist, I have always known that the funniest tales are those that emanate from real life. The contributors to this book have proven me correct. If laughter truly is the best medicine, keep this volume next to your medicine chest!"
—**Gary Crocker, author of *The Best of Gary Crocker: Maine Humorist Comedy***

"A big thumbs-up. A very funny reminder of Maine's true political life and times and a wonderful look at our fascinating and unique Maine history. I found it both humorous and illuminating."
—**Gerard Dennison, founder of the Franco-American Heritage Center**

"Highlights prominent Mainers who have forged Maine's political leadership from Bill Cohen to Dana Connors and underscores a political axiom that you cannot take yourself too seriously in Maine politics. A must-read for anyone who wants to be a political professional and everyone who needs a good laugh."
—**Patrick Woodcock, president and CEO, Maine Chamber of Commerce**

REAL Life, REAL Funny

REAL Life, REAL Funny

THE WAY MAINE HUMOR SHOULD BE

EDITED BY CHRIS POTHOLM, DAVE EMERY, AND DENNIS BAILEY

Down East Books

Essex, Connecticut

Down East Books

An imprint of The Globe Pequot Publishing Group, Inc.
64 South Main St.
Essex, CT 06426
www.globepequot.com

Copyright © 2026 Chris Potholm, Dave Emery, and Dennis Bailey

All rights reserved. No part of this book may be reproduced in any form or by any electronic or mechanical means, including information storage and retrieval systems, without written permission from the publisher, except by a reviewer who may quote passages in a review.

British Library Cataloguing in Publication Information available

Library of Congress Cataloging-in-Publication Data

Names: Potholm, Christian P., 1940– editor | Bailey, Dennis M. editor | Emery, David F., 1948– editor
Title: Real life, real funny : the way Maine humor should be / edited by Chris Potholm, Dennis Bailey, and David Emery.
Description: Essex, Connecticut : Down East Books, 2026.
Identifiers: LCCN 2025041274 (print) | LCCN 2025041275 (ebook) | ISBN 9781684752836 paperback | ISBN 9781684752843 epub
Subjects: LCSH: Maine—Social life and customs—Humor | American wit and humor—Maine | BISAC: HUMOR / Form / Essays | HISTORY / United States / State & Local / New England (CT, MA, ME, NH, RI, VT) | LCGFT: Humor | Essays
Classification: LCC PN6231.M18 R43 2026 (print) | LCC PN6231.M18 (ebook)
LC record available at https://lccn.loc.gov/2025041274
LC ebook record available at https://lccn.loc.gov/2025041275

To the Great State of Maine

"Maine: The Way Life Should Be"

David Swardlick

and

Jed Lyons,

Publisher Extraordinary and

Friend to Authors Everywhere

Editors' Note: See also page 229 for another Jed vignette from Kevin Delehanty, the registered All-American Cool Guy.

CONTENTS

Foreword xiii
Introduction 1

Part I. Back When Politics Was Fun 11

On the Road 12
William S. Cohen

A Hair-Raising Incident 18
Dave Emery

Henry Kissinger Channels Jesus of Nazareth 22
Chris Potholm

My Rookie Year and the Events That Followed 26
Tony Payne

Mocking the Mock Convention 32
Chris Potholm

And . . . Don't Forget the Key! 38
Dave Emery

"He's Still Dead" 42
Angus King

Prediction Follies 44
Dennis Bailey

Fun with Wireless Microphones: Give Me a Hug 47
Pat Callaghan

ix

CONTENTS

Feeling the Heat 51
Don Carrigan

Underdogs Welcome: Political Oddballs Find Fertile Ground 56
Pat Callaghan

Amusing Incidents at the Front Door to History 61
John Baldacci

Going to Heaven After All 65
Bill Diamond

Read the Signs More Carefully Next Time! 69
Dave Emery

A Cardinal Trumps a Bishop . . . and a Dr. Demento 72
Chris Potholm

The Court Jester 78
Dennis Bailey

Stories We Don't Usually Tell 85
Ethan Strimling and Phil Harriman

Arrest the Jesus Lady? 94
Larry Benoit

Finding Leg Room on the Campaign Trail 100
Spiros Droggitis

Good Clean Fun at the Maine State House 106
Maria Fuentes

Everybody Needs Help on the Campaign Trail 110
Janet Mills

Politics 101 113
Ruth Foster

A Bull, a Bush, and Some Fried Dough 118
Rob Caldwell

CONTENTS

Maine and Mitchell, Guns and Pigs. 122
Corey Hascall

A Walk, a Ride, and a Possible Retirement Home. 131
Chris Potholm

Part II. Living and Laughing in the Pine Tree State 135

Land of the Disappointing Toys. 136
Dennis Bailey

Charlie's Bull. 140
Keith Brown

The Tale of the Bat Boy and the President 145
Juliana L'Heureux

The Curse of a Weak Stomach. 149
Dave Emery

The Birds and the Bees and the Sonny Newcomb Word 153
Dennis Bailey

COVID Capers 157
Will Davis

The Brothers Strike Back 165
Bob Whelan

Mistaken Identity 170
Dana Connors

Deah Pahts. 175
Scott Hood

Investor Blues 178
Chris Potholm

Ode to Brother George 183
Edie Smith

CONTENTS

Jimmy 189
Bobby Reynolds

Gerry, Gerry 192
Bill Nimitz

And He Liked the Ladies 197
Paul Mills

Dating High Jinks in DC 201
Dave Emery

The Last Patrol. 205
Chris Potholm

Gun Running for a Good Cause. 210
Jordan DeCoster

Acknowledgments 217
About the Editors 221
About the Contributors 223

FOREWORD

Maine humor is not an oxymoron whereas Utah humor is. Maine humor is droll and understated. Americans generally get it when someone attempts a Maine accent when telling a joke. The Down East dialect is widely recognizable across the nation in much the same way that Brooklynese is recognized. Both stand out for their regional authenticity.

Like many Americans, I first encountered Maine humor by listening to the wildly popular *Bert and I* records in the 1960s. When I arrived in Brunswick, Maine, as a freshman at Bowdoin College in 1970, my fellow classmates and I were intent on repeating the *Bert and I* stories, usually employing a very poor imitation of a Down East accent. When the fraternity parties wound down late at night, we often drove down to nearby Freeport where L.L.Bean was open twenty-four hours a day. There we sat and listened transfixed to the retired Maine Guides who worked the night shift and enjoyed telling their own Maine jokes and stories.

Chris Potholm arrived in Brunswick the same year I did. He and his beautiful wife, Sandy, moved there so that Chris could begin his fifty-year teaching career in Bowdoin's Government Department. Seeing Sandy on campus that year, I struck up a conversation and asked her for a date, not knowing that she was married to my gov professor. Over the years, we became very close friends. My book publishing company, Rowman & Littlefield, published a dozen books for Chris as well as an oral history of the 1972 Bill Cohen for Congress campaign that Chris managed and for which I served as an advance man.

I was also fortunate to meet Bob Bryan—half of the *Bert and I* duo—when our Down East Books imprint published Bob's autobiography in 2014. Down East also published several collections of *Bert and I* stories.

FOREWORD

Bob was a lovely man, an ordained Episcopal minister who flew his own plane to remote Labrador to tend to a small congregation there. He was a Yalie from Locust Valley with an accent to match his upper-crust background. He learned Maine stories summering on a lake in Maine as a boy. One memorable day, Bob and I met another famous Maine humorist, Tim Sample, in a recording studio in Portland. The two seasoned storytellers proceeded to crack each other up retelling their favorite Maine tales. It was a magical afternoon.

When Chris suggested that we publish this collection of original Maine stories, I jumped at the chance. As the leading expert on Maine politics and polling for the last fifty years, Chris knows everyone in the state and where to find the gems you will enjoy in this collection. His co-editors have had distinguished careers in Maine and know the state's nuances and eccentricities better than most. Dave was a three-term Congressman from Maine's First Congressional District and served as deputy director of the U.S. Arms Control and Disarmament Agency before founding Scientific Marketing and Analysis in Maine. Dennis was a reporter for the *Lewiston Daily Sun*, the *Maine Times*, and the *Portland Press Herald* and served as Governor Angus King's press secretary and communications director, later creating Savvy, Inc., a public relations firm.

Together they have assembled a marvelous bouillabaisse for us to enjoy.

Jed Lyons, Publisher

INTRODUCTION

MAINE IS A UNIQUE STATE IN MANY WAYS.

It's the only state with just one syllable.

It's the only state bordered by only one other state.

And we would argue also that it's unique in its homegrown humor, storytelling, and way of life. Certainly, lots of Mainers think so.

Mainers are born storytellers. At any gathering—wedding, funeral, bowling alley, bean supper, hunting lodge, or local tavern—you'll hear wild, unique, mostly humorous tales about life in Maine, some of them true, many of them embellished, and many repeated over and over for effect.

Many of our jokes and life stories have a bucolic, rustic, small-town flavor, capturing innate wisdom from the Maine coast and inland. Our humor also talks of Mainers living lives of note, struggle, and triumph. The accounts at once underscore and appreciate the denizens of those areas and treat folk wisdom as a treasure to be appreciated in the retelling.

For example, in a long-running popular joke, a reporter asks an old Maine farmer, "What is the greatest invention of the twentieth century?" The farmer replies instantly, "The thermos." The reporter is quite incredulous and says, "Well why do you say that?" The farmer counters, "Because it keeps hot things hot and cold things cold."

"So?" follows up the reporter.

The farmer grins, "Well, but how do it know?"

There is lots of humor in everyday life in Maine that you can hear if you listen to the conversations of others as you are going about your business.

For example, listen the next time you are out and about and you might hear some oft-heard, native Maine bons mots.

INTRODUCTION

When encountering an old friend in a Hannaford or Shaw's supermarket or even the small corner store, you might hear them exclaiming in a loud voice, "Hey, good to see you, so you're out on bail?"

This greeting is usually good for a laugh from the friend and strange looks from bystanders.

Or vice versa.

Another formerly widespread staple for greeting friends and neighbors alike was this salutation in the Great North Woods of Maine during the fall: "Got *your* deer yet?"

Note the accent on "your" since it is assumed that you have worked all year long to protect that particular deer from coyotes and other creatures of the wild so that you might slay it yourself.

Over the years, the most likely location for this salutation was north and west of Augusta. Unfortunately, in the Maine of today, you are now probably more likely to hear this greeting in the towns of York or Cape Elizabeth where there are five times as many deer per square mile as in the North Country. Affirmative answers today in that part of the world also probably mean you ran into *your* deer with *your* car.

Another very widely—and certainly overused—phrase, thankfully finally beginning to fade due to over and often strained usage, is "You can't get thay'a from he'ah." Three or four generations of Mainers have waited with bated breath for some rube from away to ask how to get to X so they could gleefully explain that it is impossible.

Marshall Dodge and later Tim Sample made that phrase a staple, and its enduring character even shows up unscripted from time to time and place to place in real life. For example, when Bill Cohen was first campaigning in Lubec some time ago, he looked quizzically across the sparkling water toward Eastport where he was due in twenty minutes—his campaign manager first shrugged and then asked one of the residents, "How can we get there from here?" pointing to that beloved town to the north. Laughingly, that fine voter said, "You can't get there from here. You have to flip backwards, turn around, and drive all the way back around through Whiting and Dennysville." Thus was the candidate forty-five minutes late for his talk in Eastport and thereafter took over the job of driver for himself, someone "who knew how to get there from here."

INTRODUCTION

Maine, throughout its long history, has produced much humor and some topnotch humorists and comedians. For example, Bangor native Richard Golden, playing the lead role as *Old Jed Prouty* in his widely acclaimed 1889 play of the same name, is credited by many historians with creating and nationalizing Downeast humor.

The late nineteenth and early twentieth century saw another major humorist in action. Holman Day authored numerous popular books about Maine's Great Woods and its ever-demanding coast, including *King Spruce*, *Blow the Man Down*, and *The Rider of King Log*. But it is his highly regarded and often overlooked humor in such works as *Kin O'Ktaadn* and *When Egypt Went Broke* that provide considerable humor and pithy insights delivered in regional far-fetched yarns:

> I went up to the Skowhegan Fay'ah last summah. There was stock caa racin,' divin' from the high platfo'm, and teams uv hosses pullin' against each uth'aa. The fea'cha attraction on the last day of the fay'ya was the releasing of a light'a than a'ya b'loon, and I won the chance to go along for the ride. In a few minutes, we wuz up over the tents, and in an hour, we wuz up in the clouds. We decided to let out some a'ya (pssssssch) so we could come down to see just way'ah we wuz. We saw a faa'ma plowing in his field, so I leaned ovah the side and holla'd, "Where aaah we?"
>
> "In a b'loon, ya damned fool!"

or,

> *Kenneth Fowl'a had had an awful season. Everything he planted was eaten by blackbirds* as soon as he scatta'd the seed, fy'ah destroyed his blu'bry grounds at ra'kin time, and termites ate up his ice house. On top of that, a stray cat drowned in his well. So long 'bout Octobah, he decided he better go out hunt'n and stock up on food for the wintah. So he took his gun, the one with the side-by-side barrels and headed out for th' woods. He maa'ched along all day without firing a shot, till long 'bout sundown, when he spied a fox about two rods distance and took careful aim. Just

INTRODUCTION

as he pulled the trigga, he spied another fox about twenty feet from the first. The shot hit a rock, splitted in two, and killed both foxes; the kick from the gun knocked him into the stream behind him; and when he come to, his right hand was on an otta's head; the left hand was on a beava's tail; and his trousa pockets was so full of trout that a button popped of his fly and killed a paatridge.

The magic is almost entirely found in the oral presentation, occasionally reinforced by vocal sound effects and onomatopoeia; simply reading these stories as prose is a nearly worthless endeavor and perhaps even a little frightening to some (as seen below!) because the flavor and atmosphere is entirely missing.

We think an appreciation of this humor also requires having some context, such as knowing something about Maine and possibly knowing a few authentic Maine characters as well. Dave remembers that when he was first elected to Congress and moved to DC, he tried out a few *Bert and I* stories with his own Maine accent, and they fell flat because his DC audience had no frame of reference. Consequently, he gave up.

We still love these stories and (purely by mental osmosis) have committed many of them to memory. So these stories live on. Sadly, Marshall Dodge was killed in a hit-and-run accident while vacationing in Hawaii in 1982. We still miss him.

However created by talent "from away" and surely stereotyped over time, the humor of Dodge and Bryan conveyed an underlying love of the state and its people and underscored many of their colloquialisms and oddments.

Twenty years after the advent of the *Bert and I* record's first appearance (which was followed by *More Bert and I* and *The Return of Bert and I*), they published a book, *Bert and I and Other Stories from Down East.*

It was a big success.

Interestingly enough, revisiting this historic tome as we were putting together this volume, your intrepid editors were struck—overwhelmed, actually—by the surprising amount of mayhem, danger, and death that abound in that beloved work. Indications were that life on the frontier was dangerous! In one vignette, for example, a moose is shot in the leg on purpose and then exhibited to townspeople as a wonderment; in another,

INTRODUCTION

Bert and his captain friend are run down by the Bangor Packet and their lobster boat sunk; in another, an unidentified body is found in the kelp. There's also a story in which a game warden is run over by the village librarian.

Say what?

There are even more disasters elsewhere in the short, whimsical tome: a faithful dog is shot dead by his owner; a beloved wife's coffin is misplaced; and an aunt dies on route from California while an untidy lobsterman is pulled to his death by his own warp line.

Talk about strange.

Where *did* they get these stories?

As occasional Maine resident George W. Bush once said upon hearing Donald Trump's first inaugural address, "That was some weird s***."

Upon revisiting these stories today, they do seem to reflect surprisingly dark humor indeed.

At least dark subject material.

From our perspective today, one can only wonder about the mindscape of the authors at the time these were all put to pen.

Their Maine, one now realizes, was apparently experiencing a most dangerous period, but reading their account, at least we can be thankful that war with Canada and an outbreak of the bubonic plague were avoided during the period the authors were chronicling.

And no one was stoned to death for blasphemy either.

But, for sure, a lot of locals shuffled off their mortal coils in their telling.

For his part, Tim Sample (who today always seems so much more cheerful and upbeat and positive on TV selling hearing aids in competition with Joe Namath) seamlessly slipped into that humorous Down East world. After Dodge's death in Hawaii in 1982, Sample paired up with *Bert and I* co-founder Bob Bryan to make a record called *How to Talk Yankee,* which they described as the first and only "Downeast Foreign Language Record."

Then, for the next forty years, Sample toured Maine and New England, and for eleven years, provided Charles Kuralt and the *CBS Sunday Morning* show with vignettes about the Pine Tree State for a segment called *Postcards from Maine.* Sample has also had a long, long career in

INTRODUCTION

standup comedy, and his beloved books include *Saturday Night at Moody's Diner*, *Born in Maine*, and *Answers to Questions Nobody Was Askin'*.

Another important humorist is Kendall Morse, both as a singer and a writer, as well as a beloved raconteur. In the 1970s, he hosted *In the Kitchen* on Maine Public Television. He published several collections of his stories: *Father Fell Down the Well* and *Stories Told in the Kitchen* (which features the tongue-in-cheek warning on the cover, "C'mon in! If my coffee don't kill ye . . . my stories might!").

Among the Maine humorists he featured on his show were Marshall Dodge, Bruce McGorrill (*Saturday Night in Dover-Foxcroft*), Joe Perham, Don Taverner, Henry Hatch, Bill Gagnon, and Edward "Sandy" Ives (*George Magoon and the Down East Game War*).

And who can forget the WCSH weatherman and later general manager Lew Colby (real name: Lewis Bowlby), who in the 1960s and 1970s provided listeners and viewers with humorous and often preposterous weather forecasts from his mythical town of Hannibal's Crossing in central Maine? Colby is also credited with creating the station's "Storm Center" and "Coats for Kids" special programs. His outreach efforts were usually accompanied by droll humor.

Of course, no retrospective on Maine humor and storytelling would be complete without noting John McDonald and his books such as *A Moose and A Lobster Walk into a Bar*, *A Maine Dictionary*, *Ain't He Some Funny*, and *Moose Memoirs and Lobster Tales: As True as Maine Stories Ought to Be*, which capture additional dimensions of the Maine political and cultural scenes, especially the humor found in small-town events and characters.

McDonald's long-running WGAN call-in talk show was a must for politicians and listeners alike, and he toured Maine from one end to the other, performing comedic routines that delighted people of all ages. He also was a founder of the Maine Storytellers Festival.

Moreover, in his introduction to *A Moose and a Lobster*, McDonald gives us an excellent description of traditional Maine humor:

> The sheer velocity of life in Maine is slower than other places, so our humor tends to be unhurried; it's allowed to take its time and develop unimpeded as it should—the way we've always liked it.

INTRODUCTION

Also of long duration center stage on the Maine humor front was Robert Skoglund, who, as "The humble Farmer," provided newspaper columns, radio programs, books such as *Chicken Poop for the Reader's Soil*, and podcasts. Skoglund, who died in 2024, was sometimes referred to as "New England's answer to Garrison Keillor" (although that was fortunately before the latter's MPBN talk show host ran afoul of the #MeToo movement).

Skoglund continued the long tradition of Maine humor with rural echoes, although occasionally with a bit more of an edge than the likes of John Gould, but fortunately, quite a bit less dark material from the dark web of their imaginations than found in *Bert and I and Other Stories from Down East*.

Another important humor writer in Maine is Don Levesque, the longtime columnist and eventual editor and publisher of the *St. John Valley Times* in Madawaska. His weekly column, *Mes Cinq Sous* (My Five Cents), captures the spirit and community of Acadia as well as the Maine of today in the St. John Valley and was instrumental in bringing the World Acadian Congress to Northern Maine. His dictionary of Franco-American patois, *Le Parler de Chez Nous* (The Language of Our House), blends words from Franco-American Atlantic Canada and Maine and is an important guide to the 85 percent of the population of the St. John Valley, whose native language is French.

For other "Maine humor" by Maine celebrities, interested readers can tap the long and often droll running commentary of John Christie and such contemporary comics as Emma Willmann, Andrea Martin, the ever-edgy Bob Marley, Joe Perham, Dennis Fogg, Ian Stuart, Jason Brett Hodgdon, Karmo Sanders, George Hamm, Brett Somers, Ben Roy, Jessica Delfino, Ryan Gaul, (the late) Charles Rocket, Ian Harvie, John O'Hurley, Justin Timothy Kimball Morse, Gary Crocker, Lisa Belise, Connor McGrath, and Theo Von.

This is indeed an impressive list for those looking for "Maine humor" in the past and the present. If you'd like to read more rural Maine vernacular and its concomitant patois check out our very own *Tall Tales from the Tall Pines*, the hunting and fishing adventures of Snappy and Gus by one of your intrepid editors, Chris Potholm.

INTRODUCTION

But your faithful editors have long believed there is considerably more, essentially untapped, everyday humor in Maine, especially in the conduct of its politics and the process of growing up and life in the Pine Tree State with all of its marvelous dimensions.

We also think Maine is unique in its living as well as its laughing: what Governor (now Senator) Angus King has termed our "flinty self-reliance," how Maine people cope with the demands not only of our rugged coast and vast inland forests but everything in between as well. This aspect is innately tied to our sense of the antic and the humorous in the Pine Tree State.

Thus "The Maine Way" of living *and* laughing is the focus of this work as we seek to capture the enduring spirit of the place.

We laugh as we live. We live as we laugh.

Hence, we have assembled a wide-ranging collection of Maine voices from many walks of life to share their humorous and insightful vignettes. While we can assert that not only are the authors included of absolutely no threat to the above-mentioned standup comics—although the wiser ones among those stand-ups still standing tall might well wish to sign up some of our contributors as writers—we believe they bring a much wider spectrum of points of humorous tales and life views, even if many are more softly and sometimes indirectly presented. Many of them also capture that "flinty self-reliance" as a theme as they ponder their growing up and living in the Pine Tree State.

What follows in this work are thus many different voices capturing that Maine, featuring its idiosyncratic nature and its truly unique nature.

We celebrate life in Maine with:

Tales of humor in Maine and Maine humor.

Tales of real fun—and often irony—in Maine life without pretension.

We have high hopes that the authors included have captured so much of the uniqueness that is Maine.

In fact, we go considerably further, believing as we do that this work—including its editors—represents the finest collection of ne'er-do-wells, touts, brigands, local yokels, wags, jockapoos, truants, dubs, lay-a-bouts, desperados, malingerers, rubes, lollygaggers, eccentrics, oddballs, bozos, miscreants, posers, yakabees, under-achievers, mooncalves, mutton heads,

INTRODUCTION

yahoos, bumpkins, loafers, wackadoodles, misfits, mavericks, free spirits, dweebs, and rejects from the cool kids' table they so eagerly sought to join in high school ever assembled in one place.

Dip into this collection and you will, no doubt, be forced to agree, even if that conclusion seems likely to run against your better judgment as you read this fulsome introduction.

The vignettes in this volume include contributions from the print and electronic media, the political realm of consultants and participants, as well as from an overall variety of Mainers who just tell funny and insightful stories that we have captured here for the first time.

Stylistically, this work is divided into two principal parts (which can and do overlap in some themes as well), those from the political realm, "Back When Politics Was Fun," and the nonpolitical realm "Living and Laughing in the Pine Tree State."

The contributions provide a wide variety of topics and settings.

For example, mistaken identity and its humorous aspects are captured by a number of contributors, including Bill Nimitz (*Gerry, Gerry*), Dana Connors (*Mistaken Identity*, which includes Dave Emery's brief addition, *Je Ne Sais Quoi*), and Ruth Foster (*Politics 101*).

The joys, trials, and tribulations of the campaign trail and those who trod it as well as those who chronicle it are underscored by Janet Mills (*Everybody Needs Help on the Campaign Trail*), Pat Callaghan (*Fun with Wireless Microphones* and *Underdogs Welcome*), Rob Caldwell (*A Bull, a Bush, and Some Fried Dough*), Angus King (*He's Still Dead*), Don Carrigan (*Feeling the Heat*), Tony Payne (*My Rookie Season*), John Baldacci (*Amusing Incidents at the Front Door of History*), Bill Diamond (*Going to Heaven After All*), Dennis Bailey (*The Court Jester*), William C. Cohen (*On the Road*), Chris Potholm (*Henry Kissinger Channels Jesus of Nazareth, A Cardinal Trumps a Bishop, Mocking the Mock Convention,* and *A Walk, a Ride, and a Possible Retirement Home*), Dave Emery (*Read the Signs More Carefully Next Time!*), Corey Hascall (*Maine and Mitchell, Guns and Pigs*), Ethan Strimling and Phil Harriman (*Stories We Don't Usually Tell*), Ruth Foster (*Politics 101*), Spiros Droggitis (*Finding Leg Room on the Campaign Trail*), and Dennis Bailey (*Prediction Follies*).

INTRODUCTION

Growing up in Maine and some of its true indoor as well as outdoor adventures also prove to be enduring themes in the writings by Dennis Bailey (*Land of the Disappointing Toys*, *The Birds and the Bees and the Sonny Newcomb Word*), Will Davis (*COVID Caper*s), Keith Brown (*Charlie's Bull*), Scott Hood (*Deah Pahts*), Bob Whelan (*The Brothers Strike Back*), Dave Emery (*The Curse of a Weak Stomach* and *Dating High Jinks in DC*), and Chris Potholm (*Investor Blues* and *The Last Patrol*).

Loving portraits of those formerly on the Maine scene, which also illuminate our uniqueness, are also captured by Edie Smith (*Ode to Brother George*), Maria Fuentes (*Good Clean Fun at the Maine State House*), Bobby Reynolds (*Jimmy*), Paul Mills (*And He Liked the Ladies*), and Dave Emery (*A Hair-Raising Event*).

Irony and that flinty self-reliance—some of it worth its weight in carefully mined gold—also abounds in many of the contributions, such as Larry Benoit (*Arrest the Jesus Lady?*), Juliana L'Heureux (*The Tale of the Bat Boy and the President*), Jordan DeCoster (*Gun Running for a Good Cause*), and Dave Emery (*And . . . Don't Forget the Key!*).

Maine people sharing stories that made them smile and laugh and/or give you a sense of true life in Maine are included as we remember the earlier words of Kendall Morse, who once wrote, "Humor is the opiate of the melancholy."

Your faithful editors hope you will enjoy this wide-ranging collection with its examples of humor in daily Maine life from those who live in our beloved Pine Tree State. We dedicate this work to the sturdy people of Maine.

We hope that you will have as much fun reading these vignettes as we did writing and assembling them dedicate this volume and that it provides mirth for, as Stephen King has written, "You can't deny laughter; when it comes, it plops down in your favorite chair and stays as long as it wants."

Chris Potholm, Dave Emery, and Dennis Bailey
2025

PART I

BACK WHEN POLITICS WAS FUN

OF COURSE POLITICS IS OFTEN ABOUT SERIOUS MATTERS AND NEEDS TO be dealt with accordingly. Yet an intrinsic and important dimension is the humor that it can—and we would argue, should—produce.

Especially politics in Maine.

Included in this section are a variety of vignettes devoted to the fun of politics in both campaigns and in governing. We Mainers have always prided ourselves in our ability to laugh at our many examples of humor on the campaign trail.

In this section, the colorful people who run for office and run political campaigns, share their most memorable experiences.

Your editors laughed, often out loud, when they first read these pieces.

We hope you will too.

ON THE ROAD
William S. Cohen

IN 1972, I DECIDED TO RUN FOR A SEAT IN CONGRESS AND CALLED UPON my Bowdoin classmate and dear friend Professor Christian Peter Potholm to manage my campaign, an endeavor for which we both lacked foreknowledge of the hazards we were likely to encounter.

At the time, I was a lean lad of thirty-two and open to both reasonable and mildly insane suggestions. Chris exploited the latter vulnerability and proposed that in my quest to capture the hearts and minds of voters I strike out on a 650-mile walk across Maine's Second Congressional District, the largest political land mass east of the Mississippi.

Highly ambitious but equally skeptical of the merits of this uber marathon, I worried that I might twist an ankle on the rocky, soft shoulders of the secondary roads that lay ahead. I donned a pair of heavy-soled, thick leather boots at the very edge of the "Live Free or Die" state at Gilead, Maine with the hope that the boots would last until I crossed the finish line at the border of what was (then) our closest geopolitical ally.

The hike was an epic but dangerous undertaking, as Canadian citizens from Toronto and Montreal hurtled along Route 2 at 70 to 75 mph on their way to the sandy delights offered at Old Orchard Beach, Ogunquit, and points south.

While most vacationers honked and waved at what they assumed was a sunstruck homeless man or lost asylum seeker, a few tossed an empty Coke or beer bottle my way as a non-vulgar gesture of their disapproval.

It was mostly a joyous experience, though, and far less stressful than enduring root canal surgery without the benefit of Novocain or nitrous oxide.

Along the way, I met thousands of people in their homes, small shops, shoe factories, textile mills, and paper companies. I was not only able to relate to future constituents in a deeply personal way but also learned some important lessons about what not to do as a candidate for political office.

Rule #1: Never wear a pair of construction boots if you plan to walk an average of twenty miles a day unless you are willing to tolerate blisters the size of silver dollars and be forced to make emergency stops at local hospitals for what could be euphemistically called a surgical pedicure.

Rule #2: Avoid barrooms before (and after) noon.

While halfway along the Appalachian Trail, I passed through a small town with one traffic light that seemed to be permanently stuck on green, which I took as a subliminal signal for strangers to avoid stopping.

There were a few scattered buildings, but one that appeared to be a gathering place for local residents had flashing neon lights in the window promoting Budweiser.

As I intrepidly opened the door, I stepped into a dark room that contained a few small tables that were occupied by some rather large men. The lights from the bar managed to provide the only illumination in the room. One man was sitting on a stool facing the brightly, back-lit bottles of bourbon, gin, vodka, and scotch stacked in front of a smoky mirror. He was dressed in worn jeans and a red flannel shirt. He had shoulders the width of an aircraft carrier flight deck.

As I approached the bar, I gingerly introduced myself saying, "Hi! I'm Bill Cohen and I'm running . . ."

Before I could finish my practiced salutation, the man said in a tone that was not inviting, "I know who you are."

"Oh. Have we met before?"

"Sure have."

"Where was that?"

"Courthouse in Bangor."

"Did I represent you?" I thought he might have been a former client of one of my law firm partners, as I couldn't recognize his reflection in the mirror behind the bar.

"You're the son of a bitch who put me in jail."

There was menace in his voice, and I could feel a rumbling in my chest (which I came to know in later years as atrial fibrillation). I had served as an Assistant Penobscot County Attorney for three years, and my memory was instantly jarred into recall. He had battered his wife (presumably now his ex-wife) and I had recommended that his anger management treatment include some prison time.

It would have been prudent for me to call for backup. The problem was that cell phones had not been invented and I had no backup to summon as I had insisted upon making the trek alone. The synaptic gaps started firing off in my brain and the thought came (and quickly went) that I should reach for the .357 Magnum that I used to carry as a summertime constable at Chris Potholm's (a brother-in-arms policeman) neighborhood in Old Lyme, Connecticut. Except . . . that I had decided that carrying even a less lethal Dirty Harry firearm (Harry's was a .44 Magnum) as a political candidate would reflect either a certain lack of confidence in my physical prowess or that I had a penchant for violence rather than diplomacy.

Nervously, I said, "Well, I hope that it was a short sentence and . . ." as I eased toward the exit door and made as fluid a departure as my pride and the situation allowed.

Rule #3: If courting women's votes, beware of No Trespassing signs, even those not posted.

While trudging along the last fifty or so miles of my walk, with my ace fieldman Jed Lyons, I decided to enter a small beauty shop in Presque Isle. I assumed that the lady patrons would welcome a smiling young man stopping in to pay them a compliment during their beautification sessions.

When I stepped inside the entrance door, I inhaled the scent of industrial-grade hairspray and saw five women, some of whom seemed to be wearing helmets designed by Elon Musk (I'm time shifting here) for interplanetary travel.

Immediately, all gaiety ceased and the room went silent.

Ever the optimist, I launched into my radio-voiced "elevator speech." "Hi, I'm Bill Cohen and—"

I got no further. The owner of the establishment, in a voice that produced that now-familiar rumbling in my chest, said, "You really shouldn't be here Mr. Cohen. These women are entitled to their privacy and you . . ."

My legs had turned from walk-muscled to overcooked linguini. I pivoted around (not quite ballerina-graceful) and eased my way out the front door, thankful that the proprietor did not hurl a lead-handled brush at my head.

Rule #4: Never lose control.

Eager to participate in local events that would persuade citizens that I, having inhaled the big city helium that lifts small-town boys to dizzying heights, had not "gone Washington."

Unwisely, I agreed when my (I thought!) faithful field man Jed Lyons got me to ride a horse in a popular parade. My riding credentials consisted of driving cars powered by three-hundred horsepower engines, not riding horses that weighed nine hundred pounds.

I did my best to project the self-confident stature of Roy Rogers or Lash LaRue to the several hundred residents who had gathered along the parade route with their children.

I waved and smiled at the faces in the crowd trying my best to project competence in the saddle when an antique car backfired and let loose the sound of a rifle shot. The horse I was riding (or sitting on) rose up. I dropped the reins and suddenly I was racing down the highway wrapping my arms around the horses neck vainly shouting for him to stop—I didn't know whether to call "him" Trigger or Black Diamond at that moment but didn't think calling out his or its name would have slowed down what was a full gallop.

Fortunately, a fourteen-year-old girl, who just had to be related to Calamity Jane, raced after me, catching up after the length of a football field, and brought the aspiring Kentucky Derby wannabe to a halt.

Chiding me mildly (she had to be a future presidential candidate), she said, "Mr. Cohen, you should never drop the reins of a horse. Never."

She led me back to the parade to the rousing applause and laughter of the local crowd while I smiled as if I had enjoyed that little excursion and silently vowed to "rein in" my horse for the rest of the parade—and fire the staff member who thought it was wise to put me on that horse. I couldn't seem to find Jed at the moment.

Rule #5: Never trust a pinniped.

My experience with sea life would have been classified as nonexistent—that is, until I met Andre the seal. My campaign activities were generally limited to terra firma, but on one occasion while making my way up the Maine coast, I paid a visit to Rockport to meet the local hero who had achieved movie fame.

Andre was an orphan pup harbor seal that had been raised by Harry Goodridge, Rockport's harbormaster. Andre was known as a friendly and fun-loving soul who performed various tricks for the local community. Andre spent winters in a Boston aquarium and upon being released in the spring, he would make his way back to Rockport just about the same time each year.

While attending a summer event in Rockport I thought it might be good for me to shake "hands" with the local hero whose name was far more popular than mine.

As I cruised around the harbor in a fishing boat, Andre decided to join the ride as a passenger. All went smoothly, although my attempts to make conversation with Andre were awkward.

Finally, when we neared the end of the cruise and approached the dock, Andre's mood shifted. While my gaze was fixed on those standing at the dock to welcome us back, Andre launched a sneak attack and bit me high on my buttocks.

I reached back and could feel that my exquisitely tailored jeans (actually just Wranglers) had been ripped. I looked accusingly at Andre and was prepared to utter a spate of expletives. But a reporter aboard, armed with a dangerous recorder and Nikon camera, deterred me from taking retaliating action even if it was only verbal.

I gave Andre my best Clint Eastwood stare. "Are you feeling lucky punk?" ("I mean pup. Don't bite me again").

Andre just stared back. He wasn't playing, and he looked as though he might go for seconds. Fortunately, we arrived safely at the dock and I made my way out of the boat trying to shield my backside as much as possible for fear that the reporter aboard would write a headline that said "Lovable Andre Bites Cohen! Shreds Cohen's clothes and casts doubt over his political future."

There are other such lessons I could pass on, such as, "Never enter a stockcar race at the Spud Speedway in Aroostook County with a driver called the Flying Frenchman of Madawaska."

Or, again at the suggestion of the—you guessed it—the ever-intrepid Jed Lyons, "Never knock on car windows at a Houlton drive-in theater playing an XXX movie called Boxcar Bertha."

But those, dear reader, must await Volume II of *Real Life, Real Funny*.

A HAIR-RAISING INCIDENT
Dave Emery

HATTIE BICKMORE, A WIDOWED MOTHER OF FIVE AND A MARINE Corps veteran, was the Republican State Chair as well as District Administrator for my First District Congressional office during my eight years as Congressman. A resident of Cumberland, her presence was felt from one end of the state to the other, and the various factions in the party: conservative, moderate, and whatever passed for progressive in those days felt comfortable with her.

Hattie was fun-loving and gregarious and made friends very easily. She was also fearless when in the company of powerful figures. I remember the time she met Henry Kissinger and called him "sweetheart." Kissinger had come to Maine for a Republican State Committee fundraiser, as I recall, in Portland.

Amid the horrified expressions on the faces of the assembled dignitaries, and to their great surprise, her unorthodox introduction elicited a broad smile from Kissinger, a former Secretary of State and former National Security Advisor, and one of the world's most highly respected and influential diplomats despite his numerous detractors, especially opponents of the Vietnam War.

"Why thank you, Hattie" he replied.

Hattie could always laugh at herself, a characteristic that made her popular and welcome wherever she went. And there were plenty of occasions that called for self-effacing humor.

A lot of them.

I remember several with great fondness.

A HAIR-RAISING INCIDENT

There was a time during the 1970s when women's wigs were much in vogue and a woman could easily change her hairstyle or hair color simply by adorning herself with the wig of her choice. Many women in politics did. So Hattie bought one and wore it proudly to dinner one evening at a popular Portland restaurant.

The problem was, Hattie wasn't quite used to that wig. Although it was a fashion statement, the wig was hot. And it itched. And it didn't seem to fit just right. I guess said wig had not been vetted, politically or otherwise! So Hattie couldn't resist the temptation to try to adjust it occasionally with her fingers, just to be sure it was properly arrayed over her *real* hair. She fiddled with it through the salad and the soup, but it never seemed to stay where she put it for very long.

Now, this particular wig was held in place with a strip of elastic, and as any high school freshman knows, elastic bands are lots of fun in study hall because you can snap them across the room at your buddy or significant other or someone you'd like to eventually be your buddy or significant other.

So it was with Hattie's wig.

After one finger-twitch too many, across the dining room the wig suddenly flew like a stylishly coiffed flying squirrel. It zipped through the air with the greatest of ease and then landed squarely on the full dinner plate of an astonished patron. Yes, across the room and onto his food, which was meatballs and spaghetti as I remember. He and his party looked—as you might imagine—surprised, horrified, and incredulous, in that order.

A profuse apology was made and gracefully accepted, and a new, un-coiffed dinner was eventually provided for the gent in question. But it is not known *to this day* whether or not that particular gentleman has ever dined on angel hair pasta again!

I do know that Hattie was never again seen in public wearing that particular wig. One presumes that when she did wear other wigs, they were more securely fastened.

The era I have been describing had its pros and cons, of course, as well as its strengths and its weaknesses, in fashion and in other ways. But it is safe to say that it was an unmitigated boon to Hattie that in that restaurant at that particular time, there were (1) no cell phones, (2) no internet availability (in fact, no internet at all), and (3) no YouTube voraciously looking for fresh content.

Can you imagine the mirth the incident would have caused had it gone viral?

I can.

Another noteworthy incident with Hattie involved a ride in my little red MGB convertible one warm spring morning. We were on our way to a constituent meeting in Old Orchard Beach and were enjoying the sunshine and fresh air as we zipped down the Maine Turnpike through Scarborough. We were positive, upbeat, and concentrating on what we were going to say and do at the meeting.

We even looked to be ahead of schedule.

Everything was well in hand.

We thought.

Suddenly, out of the clear sky flew a massive payload of seagull excrement, as expertly targeted as if it had been guided by a Norden bombsight or some newer sensory homing devices. The bird mess hit the windshield just in front of poor Hattie's face and smeared the entire passenger-side viewing area with impenetrable whitish goo.

Hattie yelped in surprise, and for a split-second, I thought we had been hit by a rock or some other dangerous projectile. I pulled over for a few minutes to regain our composure and clean off the windshield as best we could before continuing on our journey.

It was at that point that we realized how lucky we had been.

Had I been going as much as a small fraction of a mile-per-hour faster, poor Hattie would have been hit squarely in the face!

We both laughed it off and soon agreed that it is a very good thing that cows don't fly.

Also of import, she was not wearing a wig at the time or that might have flown off as well or have been hit by splatter.

Hattie was very proud that she had served in the Marine Corps and was quick to correct anyone who referred to her as a *former* Marine; "Once a Marine, always a Marine!" she'd say. The subject came up one

A HAIR-RAISING INCIDENT

day during a meeting with constituents when someone said to her, using barracks terminology, "So you were a Broad-Ass Marine?"

She snapped back, "That's Beautiful American Marine to you, buster!"

Campaigning with Hattie was fun.

She knew everyone in Cumberland County and was as comfortable in barrooms as in boardrooms. Of course, we would frequently encounter Democrats who were not inclined to vote for me and said so to our faces, and whenever we did, Hattie's retort would be, "Oh come on . . . you don't want to put a widow out of work, do you?" And that would at least bring out a quizzical smile, if not entirely break the ice.

Hattie caught a lot of flak for me, did an amazing amount of first-class constituent work and did so with style and verve. She certainly deserves the (spontaneously provided) good ink she gets from three different authors in this collection. She remains a Maine legend and deservedly so.

HENRY KISSINGER CHANNELS JESUS OF NAZARETH
Chris Potholm

As Bill Cohen's "political guy" in Maine, I often went to a variety of places to meet with people and groups—sometimes ones not his favorites or if he was already booked—in order to show the flag. Sometimes though, he asked me to go to other events where he was participating just so I could share his joy—or the pain, as the case might be.

One such event occurred when the Maine Republican State Committee invited Henry Kissinger, former National Security Advisor and subsequent Secretary of State under Richard Nixon, to come to Maine in early November 1979 and hawk his new book and also to get some newly invented for his benefit "Rockefeller Award" from the Republican Party. Imagine the chances of naming it that today!

The then-chairwoman of that august group, Hattie Bickmore, called and asked if I would come when she picked him up at the airport. At the time, I taught international relations at Bowdoin with the popular and distinguished Professor Allen Springer, so I guess she thought I could chat Kissinger up on weighty matters such as ICBMs—intercontinental ballistic missiles—if things got dull. I tried to duck the invite as it was to be followed by one of those truly horrible political dinners (to this day, the smell of Sterno takes away my appetite) that seem to go on and on and on forever.

However, Bill thought I should attend. In light of subsequent events, his inkling seems prescient indeed. He was flying in later so he couldn't (luckily) be in the limo picking up "HAK" (which we quickly found out was in lingo for the former Secretary of State). In the limo were (1) the driver, (2) Hattie Bickmore, (3) yours truly, (4) an initially bemused and later very annoyed HAK, and (5) Robert A.G. Monks (aka "RAG"), the godfather of the modern (i.e., post–Margaret Chase Smith) Republican Party.

Now Hattie and Bob were of robust size and stature in those days, and Henry was in his most portly phase, so they were really, really jammed together in the backseat. This was not a stretch limo, you understand, but only a modestly sized Lincoln town car! Wisely, I slid in beside the driver and began chatting him up.

As soon as we pulled away from the airport, however, Bob Monks lit up a huge Cuban cigar. A massive stogie. He began smoking it very purposefully, blowing that smoke directly at HAK. An astonished HAK began wildly waving his arms to dispel the smoke and looked frantically around for his two security guys who were in the chase car following us. Like General George Pickett's division on the second day of the battle of Gettysburg, though, they might just as well have been on the dark side of the moon for all they could do to help at that moment. RAG had HAK right where he wanted him.

Coughing, an alarmed HAK motioned for Monks to roll down the window at least. Grinning maniacally, Monks did so, but continued to blow smoke directly at HAK, the rush of air thus now carrying all the smoke in his direction. Upon later examination, this errant behavior proved to be Monks' strange protest against Kissinger, Nixon and the Vietnam War now mercifully concluded. Who knew?

A belated but heartfelt gesture no doubt.

At this point, Hattie began frantically kicking the bottom of my seat, an action I took as a sign she wanted me to talk to HAK and thereby distract him from the carcinogenic cloud surrounding him. I awkwardly twisted around and began babbling on and on about F-105's fighter bombers ("Da Thud," HAK replied as the plane was dubbed by the pilots who survived its many crashes) and about how many B-52 payloads from which sites were dropped on Cambodia ("More from Thailand than Guam," Kissinger asserted and I figured he should know, truly).

We finally arrived at the beautiful downtown Portland Holiday Inn and I was able to escape the still-smoky limo. The security forces in the chase car (better late than never) finally arrived and helped carry in the many, many books HAK had brought to be hawked at the dinner.

Now usually at these dinners, I would go in, make a cameo appearance, make sure THE SENATOR (every senator is "THE SENATOR" to her or his staff) was well taken care of by other staffers and then quietly sneak away. But this time, of course, I wasted a lot of valuable time telling others such as Dave Sparks, who was Olympia Snowe's Chief of Staff, about the great adventure I had just had in the middle of the oddest anti-war demonstration I had ever seen—and I'd lived through the 1960s on the campuses of Dartmouth and Vassar!

The dinner began, and the honored guests, including then–three-term Congressman Dave Emery and the newly elected Congresswoman Olympia Snowe, who were served first, started to eat. They were up on a raised dais and everything looked in order. A radiant and recovered HAK occasionally looked up, smiled, and waved briefly to adoring members of the crowd. Off to the side was a table with huge piles of books and his security and sales team.

Book buying was in full swing.

Thinking all was well and in hand, I began inching my way toward the rear doors. I got to the last row of chairs where all the other staffers for Dave Emery and Olympia Snowe, both Congressional and Maine, were standing when one grabbed my arm. "The Senator wants you." I looked up and my good buddy Bill Cohen was indeed waving for me to return to the raised head table. He had a concerned look on his face, so I did not stop to chit chat with Republican faithful on my way to the dais.

So I looked very serious and determined as well, as if only I could solve whatever the weighty problem was, and as I approached the dais, I saw a line forming of people with books in their hands. There was now quite a melee as they were beginning to come directly from the buying table to have HAK sign their books midmeal. It was as if he was only going to sign ten copies and they didn't want to be left out!

Cohen pointed at the line and said simply, "Stop that." I then looked around hopefully, but he indeed meant for me to do the deed. Taking command like the superb flack catcher I was in my prime, I strode over to the head of the line, held up my arms, and said, "Please, please, folks let the Secretary finish his meal first."

Whereupon a certain Republican State Rep from Down East who was second in line said with some vigor, "F— off." Other guests in line nodded their approval of that admonishment. I held my ground, however, repeating for several minutes, "You must wait. You must wait."

Whereupon behind me a full-throated, booming voice, full of vibrancy and command, countermanded my admonishment:

"Let them come Chris, let them come."

HAK was smiling and gesturing with open arms like he was Jesus of Nazareth at the Sermon on the Mount but on a raised dais instead of a hill.

"Let them come, Chris, let them come."

Hopeless outnumbered and out-gunned, I looked plaintively at Bill Cohn as if to say, "What do I do now, Chief?" Bill gracefully shrugged and immediately and earnestly began chatting to the person next to him.

Beaten and humiliated and now truly and totally superfluous, I walked to the back of the room. Dave Sparks, always good for a cheery word and a fine laugh, said loudly, "That went well." The other staffers laughed gleefully at my abject failure.

Much later, I was having dinner at my own house, a strong vodka tonic in my hand, thinking "The Republic is in good hands—although no thanks to me."

And to think I had missed a no-doubt engaging and entertaining faculty meeting for all that painful fun.

MY ROOKIE YEAR AND THE EVENTS THAT FOLLOWED
Tony Payne

IN 1977–1978, I SERVED AS THE EXECUTIVE DIRECTOR OF THE MAINE Republican Party. Fresh off staffing the not-so-successful but highly spirited U.S. Senate campaign of Bob Monks versus incumbent Ed Muskie, I was simply an unemployed twenty-three-year-old cheerleader for all things Republican with little experience in the management of much of anything. Nevertheless, with the help of good friends such as Monks, my predecessor Don Bourassa and Senate President Chief of Staff Bobby McKernan to vouch for my character, I undertook the task of administering Maine's Grand Old Party and executing our strategy to recapture control of the Maine Legislature.

The duties of the state party apparatus include conducting the party's bi-annual platform hearings across the great expanse of the State of Maine. A political party's platform is a written declaration of its values and policy positions. Often a consensus document that is debated, amended, and voted upon at the bi-annual conventions, its drafting begins with platform hearings that start in January and end in the spring.

From the liberal-to-moderate areas of southwestern Maine to the far more conservative regions that begin about five miles north of Greater Portland, it is the job of the state party to convene the faithful in regional meetings so people can express their many views about the issues of the day and the underlying philosophies that inform those opinions.

My job was to organize and promote these events while engaging the news media to amplify the proceedings. This essentially was a public relations campaign with a goal of getting as much free news coverage as possible.

So it was that the Eastern Maine platform hearing was promoted and generously covered by the media—television, radio, and newspaper reporters all were present for this airing of aspirations articulated by both the articulate and the enthusiastic. The finer points of free enterprise, foreign relations, education, and a sound economy would all be addressed.

This particular platform hearing was chaired by the croaky-voiced state senator from Hancock County, Cecil McNally, whose portfolio included the chairmanship of the legislature's Transportation Committee. A true son of Maine, McNally was born in 1899 in Pittsfield and earned a degree in civil engineering at the University of Maine. The Senator had a somewhat well-earned reputation for being unpredictable. With him presiding, I crossed my fingers and held my breath.

Once all those who had shared their thoughts and opinions were through, the senator declared the proceedings complete for the evening. I was so relieved and looked forward to a relaxed drive back to Augusta.

While the television cameras were being dismantled, the microphones packed away, and the newspaper reporters' notebooks folded and stowed, the senator said, "I have just one more thing I want to say...."

I cringed. What could have gone unsaid that needed everyone's attention?

"I just want to say that I think the Maine Legislature should be 99 percent Republican!"

I regained my breath and relaxed. Heck, who could argue with that pronouncement? However, the good senator from Hancock County then continued, "But, I think we need one percent of the Maine Legislature to be Democratic, because they do the things that are good for people."

Today, as a former Republican no longer enrolled in a party, I've come to believe that government should, indeed, do what's good for people, though that requires relative parity and consensus between the two parties. We can only hope—and vote.

In the meantime, I content myself with fond memories and quiet chuckles at past events and characters of the Maine GOP, few more colorful than Hattie Bickmore.

Maine, it seems, has always fought above its weight in the national political arena by sending sharp, sensible, and often outspoken leaders to the halls of Congress: Speakers of the House of Representatives James G. Blaine (R) and Thomas Brackett Reed (R); Senator Margaret Chase Smith (R); Senator and Secretary of State Edmund S. Muskie (D); Watergate star, Congressman, Senator, and Secretary of Defense William S. Cohen (R); Democratic Senate Majority Leader George Mitchell; and noted moderate Congresswoman and U.S. Senator Olympia Snowe (R).

Maine has also made its mark for referenda and party politics. For example, in 1978, with its stable of modern-day icons such as Cohen and Snowe at the top of the ticket, the Maine GOP recaptured numerical control of the State Legislature, briefly bucking the rising tide of victories by Muskie-inspired Democrats. As a footnote, I like to think the single vote plurality was furnished by my mother, Nancy Payne, a moderate Republican who won an unlikely victory in the newly redistricted and solidly Democratic stronghold of Portland.

The stars had aligned for the Maine GOP victory in 1978 with good candidates and money in the bank that had been bolstered by the appearance of former California Governor Ronald Reagan who headlined a major and successful fundraiser earlier that year. Nevertheless, every election means starting at zero, and the Maine Republican coffers needed to be replenished for the next campaign cycle.

Enter Hattie Bickmore, a tall ex-Marine with the instincts of a middle linebacker, widowed mother of five and a personality that enveloped everyone in her sphere. In addition to being a staff member for a Congressman, Hattie had advanced in the GOP ranks from three tours as the party's state Vice Chair to leading the show as Chair for the 1980 presidential election cycle.

Knowing that New Hampshire's first-in-the-nation presidential primary was the official kickoff for voters, it was Hattie's idea that Maine should host one of the first gatherings of presidential aspirants. She intended to conduct a straw poll months prior to New Hampshire in which registered Maine Republicans could make a reasonable donation to come listen to the contenders and cast their preferential ballots. While it seemed audacious, Hattie was determined.

It also was her idea that a keynote speaker, perhaps of equal notoriety as Reagan, should headline the event, so off she went to Washington in search of a sure-winner personality. Obviously, none of the presidential contenders could be given the keynote spotlight, so the field seemed rather narrow.

There, at a Republican National Committee meeting, however, was none other than former U.S. Secretary of State Henry Kissinger. Whether notable or notorious, he fit the bill for Hattie's desire for a global headliner to come to Maine's kickoff event. The middle linebacker went in for the tackle.

She sidled up to the diminutive diplomat, put her arm around him, and said, "Henry, sweetheart, do you want to come to Maine?" How could he possibly refuse her charm and determination?

The date was set, the keynote secured, and invitations sent to all the major (and not so major) candidates. The venue would be the Portland Exposition Building, the site for nearly every major sporting event in the region. From high school basketball and indoor track to the spectacles of professional boxing and Big Time Wrestling, the Portland Expo was perfect for the first of an elimination bout among the presidential wannabes of 1980.

The building was erected in 1915. Besides its vaulted ceiling, its other distinctive quality was the decades of odors that stuck to the walls and rafters ... dewy sweat and the acrid stench from pallets of smoked cigars, the more palatable aromas of buttered popcorn and grilled hot dogs. The stage was set.

Though candidates ranged from Harold Stassen, John Connolly, Jack Kemp, and John Anderson to Bob Dole and Howard Baker, it was Maine's notable summertime resident, George H. W. Bush, who had to make his mark in this contest as the hometown favorite ... or risk being left behind.

Despite overtures from Bush, Maine's junior U.S. Senator Bill Cohen had thrown his time and energy to his Senate colleague and minority leader Howard Baker of Texas. Having the state's highest-ranking Republican and Cohen's formidable network on Baker's side, it seemed as though the die was cast Maine's first-in-the-nation beauty contest would surely go to Baker.

Before the speeches and floor demonstrations, Dr. Kissinger took the stage to share his worldview and recite the challenges to be faced by the eventual party nominee. His dry sense of humor was on full display. "Thank you to my good friend Hattie," said Kissinger with his signature German-born accent. He continued, "Vell, but for a small problem with the U.S. Constitution, you could have the best qualified candidate as your nominee."

While the audience was still laughing in appreciation, young Neil Bush was picking up his Dad. On the way to the event, Neil shared the news that the house seemed packed for Baker, so by the time Bush the elder reached the Portland Exposition Building, he was fully fired up and ready to fight. Word had spread among the audience that Bush was on his way. The atmosphere began to crackle.

The otherwise unflappable former Ambassador to China and one-time CIA Director came loaded for bear and delivered one of his best speeches of the 1980 campaign cycle. The event made him a contender in a crowded field.

As reported by the *New York Times* with a Portland, Maine date line:

> Mr. Bush, the former United States representative to the United Nations, came out ahead today at the party's informal convention here, pitting rousing oratory against Mr. Baker's first serious organizational effort.
>
> Mr. Bush, who got a standing ovation when he arrived, was loudly cheered when he told the audience that the United States needed more confidence and that [it] was time to "stop wringing our hands and apologizing for our country."

Though Bush bested Baker and the rest of the field that day, it would be Ronald Reagan, a no-show in the Maine Straw Poll parade, who would become the party's nominee. Some felt certain, though, that the

Bush come-from-behind-victory positioned him for his eventual selection as Reagan's vice-presidential choice.

In Maine's finest fishing tradition, Hattie Bickmore had baited the trap, set her buoy, and hauled in a catch that any Maine lobsterman would have been proud to claim . . . and the rest is history.

MOCKING THE MOCK CONVENTION
Chris Potholm

WANT TO KNOW A TRULY BAD POLITICAL IDEA?
Have a mock political convention that chooses no real delegates and stage it right next to and before the New Hampshire presidential primary.

That's my view anyway. And probably Maine's (then) junior senator as well. But as you'll read elsewhere in the volume, it was loved by many people and a high point of some political lives.

1979 was the year. Maine was the place.

The Maine Republican Party decided that such an extravaganza would put the state on the political map, and since Maine's favorite son, George H. W. Bush, would be in the mix and here anyway, the other candidates would have to come and make at least a show of it before the (then) all-important and even more significantly, *real* New Hampshire one.

Even before it began, the Republican presidential race had already caused me a lot of angst and heartburn. Bush was serving as the Republican national chairman and was traveling around the country drumming up support for his presumed run for the presidency. He very much wanted to get Senator Bill Cohen to support him. He was in Augusta one fine day and didn't want to drive to Portland. For his part, Cohen was in Portland but didn't want to drive to Augusta.

For *my* part, I was in Brunswick, happily sitting in my office at Bowdoin College, meeting with students, and I didn't want to drive to either place. So, when asked about the situation, I suggested the two principals meet in—you guessed it—Brunswick. I even found a hopeful venue, the Bowdoin Civil War gothic-style chapel. Please, dear reader, do not think we ever fouled that sacred ground itself with a crass political event; we actually met in a small room behind the altar and organ. I did vainly hope that the soaring towers would inspire peace and love and political melding.

We could have used some divine intervention, though, that much I do know. I thought Cohen supporting Bush would be a natural, as Congresswoman Olympia Snowe already had done and Bush was our Down East neighbor. But—and this is a monumentally big "but"—Senator Howard Baker, the Republican leader in the U.S. Senate, was also running. Bill Cohen's Chief of Staff Tom Daffron and Bill thought he should support Baker because, win or lose, Bill would have to work with him no matter what, and Bill really thought he would make an excellent president. And besides, Ronald Reagan was most likely to win the nomination anyway.

But I didn't fully appreciate these dynamics at the time, thinking Bill and George H. W. might well work things out at some point. So I was hoping a cozy meeting at Bill's alma mater (a smaller one than Bush's, no doubt, but a much loved institution nevertheless) between the two of them would do the trick and support would be eventually asked for and eventually given.

Quite wrong was I.

On both counts.

Thus ensued one of the most awkward meetings of my political life. Small talk abounded. Kind words were exchanged. Memories shared. More awkwardness ensued. Great awkwardness. The meeting faded into nothingness.

I don't remember much of the actual conversation, but I do remember Bush patting me on the back as I escorted him out of the chapel. He didn't yell or show anger at his rebuff. "Bad staff work that," he said as he smiled somewhat ruefully. Fast forward a few years and he would again show the same kindness and grace under pressure. It was August 2001 and Colin Powell and others were in Kennebunkport planning the U.S. response to the Iraqi invasion of Kuwait.

Our family was down there for a fundraiser, and I was struck at how Bush could balance all these different aspects of the presidency. He even paused the reviewing line to make sure my teenage children, Erik and Heather, got an extra photo of them with the president for themselves. Grace under pressure and a most gentleman courtesy from someone with undoubtedly a very lot on his mind. Incidentally, the Gulf War is the only war the United States has won since World War II, a salient fact much overlooked by many military historians and political junkies, but true nonetheless.

But back to the mock election.

Many others thought it was a great idea and that it turned out to be a great success, but for me, it went downhill fast and got worse.

Much worse.

Cohen later publicly endorsed Baker, and Baker decided to come to Maine for the November mock convention along with a flock of national, big-foot reporters. One was David Broder of the *Washington Post*, one of my all-time favorites. I interacted with him quite often over the years and found him very smart, very professional, and very honest. Even more importantly, he never burned me when I spoke off the record, quite an unusual modus operandi for most political print reporters who would "hide" my identity by describing me as "an unidentified Republican professor at Bowdoin whose office is in Hubbard Hall said off the record...."

Anyway, Broder shocked me when he said that he'd heard Baker was definitely going to win the mock convention. When I diffidently asked where he'd heard that, he said "Howard Baker told me."

Huh?

Say what?

Oh boy.

Nothing like setting the bar very high and calling your own victory ahead of time. *Who was advising this guy anyway?* I thought. It seemed a totally bizarre thing to do, especially to a Big Rolodex national reporter.

More strangeness followed. Some Maine Republican wag had seen a picture of Baker somewhere, sometime, eating a handful of those little goldfish crackers that somebody foisted on American consumers. So nothing would do but the convention site had to become replete with hundreds and hundreds of little goldfish in dishes and as Baker went around at it, people would bring him to the bowls and offer him some.

After this happened five or six times, he asked, "Why do they think I like these awful crackers?" Minions were then hastily dispatched to remove the crackers, but the goldfish fiasco would thus become something of a metaphor for the Baker campaign—and the mock convention overall, at least from my point of view.

Other than that, the convention was something of a heavy slog. And a huge burden for the senior senator from Maine. Bill faithfully and diligently told one and all why he admired Baker and why he would make a great president. There was a long, long line at Bill's hospitality suite that night, and Baker stayed for most of it, although Bill outlasted him. Even after Baker went to bed, Bill continued making his case.

The next morning after breakfast, more delegates came to Bill to meet Baker. That was now impossible. Baker had already hived off to New Hampshire to campaign where he and his staff thought his presence really mattered. Talk about awkward. Not only did Bill have to labor to explain why Baker should be their choice, he now had to labor even more to explain why Baker wasn't even there. I remember one delegate getting quite put out when told that: "He has a funny way of asking for my support."

Baker did finally deign to return to give a speech at the end of the day right before the vote. At least it was billed as a speech. Whatever it was supposed to be, it was awful. He droned on in a monotone. Dull, boring, and with no fire or oomph.

Disaster City.

Historical footnote: This is where we in Maine first noticed the sharply dressed duo of Paul Manafort and his partner Charlie Black (readers probably know more about the former than the latter), eyeing how the local yokels did things. They stood in the back of the room with supercilious smiles on their faces although Young Charles did seem to be the sharper of the two as he occasionally circulated around the Bushies imparting Washingtonian wisdom. At least I don't believe he ever went to the slammer.

You can guess how the vote finally came out.

Ironically, Bush, who apparently expected to lose (again, bad staff work that) had left for Boston right after his rousing speech (which got a standing ovation), so he wasn't even there when he received 35 percent of the vote compared with 33 percent for Howard Baker. John Connally got 18 percent, and Ronald Reagan, who had not yet announced—but would do so a few days later—got 7 percent.

I've always thought it was a minor miracle and a testament to the powers of persuasion of one William S. Cohen that Baker finished that close second to Bush. Who knows how it might have turned out if Baker, who was actually quite impressive one-on-one and a fine senator with lots of legislative and bipartisan accomplishments, had put his best foot forward. He probably would have made a good president—later he brought much-needed order out of chaos in Reagan's second term as Chief of Staff. What if he had stayed and actually campaigned that day or at least given even a halfway decent speech? He might have thus lived up to his own-inspired hype.

In any case, Bush won the Maine mock—and mocked—convention, but his margin was so small there had to be another winner.

Of course there was. The real winner was one candidate who wasn't even there. The one who finished last, lasted. Ronald Reagan did not bother to attend but eventually ended up as the Republican nominee for president in 1980, picking George Herbert Walker Bush as his Veep, no doubt on the strength of his success at the Maine mock convention!

Do you remember Ronald Reagan? Yes, that one, the friendly, positive, upbeat chap who loved America so much? He would probably not win a single primary in today's Republican weird presidential hot house and Crazy Town politics.

His opposition to the Soviet Union alone would be enough to disqualify him for many, if not most, Republicans today. So too would his free trade policies. And his "live and let live" personal philosophy. And his positive view of America and its future. And his bipartisan approach to public policy—remember his productive friendship with Democratic Speaker Tip O'Neill?

And last, although certainly not least, The Gipper would not ever say the moon was made of green cheese—even if an orange-haired spawn of Satan told the American people it was and many, many strange acolytes believed him.

AND . . . DON'T FORGET THE KEY!
Dave Emery

FOR EVERY FRESHMEN CONGRESSPERSON, THERE IS A TRIED-AND-TRUE DC institution colloquially known as the *Tuesday through Thursday Club*. You see, the leadership of each party drills into their newest members the absolute necessity of firming up their political support at home, knowing that a freshly minted Congressperson is most vulnerable in his or her first reelection campaign. Accordingly, by unspoken agreement, little work of substance is scheduled on Mondays or Fridays, at least during the first few months of the session. This allows the freshmen to leave DC at a reasonable hour on Friday, spend a long weekend in their home districts meeting with constituents, and return to DC at a reasonable hour on the following Monday.

So it was in the spring of 1975 during my first few months in office. And since the Delta Airline schedule included late Friday afternoon flights from DC to Portland and early Monday morning flights from Portland back to DC, I was able to maximize both my time on the job in Washington as well as to maintain the requisite district schedule as well.

At the time, I was renting a home in a comfortable middle-class neighborhood in Alexandria, Virginia, just eight miles or so south of the Capitol that I was sharing with George Smith and Dave Sulin. George had been my campaign manager, and Dave had taken a leave of absence from the Merchant Marine to become my legislative assistant for the Merchant Marine and Fisheries Committee during consideration of the 200-Mile Limit bill. We were close friends, so the decision to share living quarters was an easy one. Now, folks who like to watch made-for-TV

AND . . . DON'T FORGET THE KEY!

dramas might have an image in mind for the typical DC bachelor pad. But this was more like *Animal House* than *Real Bachelors of Washington, DC*. We didn't have much furniture in the house other than an old beanbag chair we found somewhere, a bumper pool table, and a circa-1950s kitchen table with chairs that were in the house when we arrived. We didn't decorate, hang tasteful paintings on the walls, or match curtain fabric to the décor; in fact, there were no curtains at all, as I remember. And Sulin didn't even have a bed; he slept in a sleeping bag on the floor.

So one particular Monday morning, I flew back to DC from a typically busy weekend in Maine, went directly to my office in the Cannon Building, travel bag in hand, to begin my usual workday. This consisted of a morning staff meeting, committee hearings, meetings or lunch with visiting constituents, and beginning at 10 a.m., the day's session on the floor of the House, which often coincided with hearings throughout the morning and afternoon. All was going along as usual until about 4:30 p.m., when I got an urgent (read: panicked) message to call my office *immediately*.

What the hell?

When I called in, I was greeted by a breathless and hyperventilating staffer saying something about a break-in, stolen property, the Alexandria Police, and a ladder. Needless to say, I hurried back to the office to see *what in the dickens* this was all about.

As soon as I got there, I was greeted with the following story:

An Alexandria patrolman on his usual beat noticed a ladder up against the house under a partially open second-floor window, and he knocked on the door to see what was going on. When there was no answer, he peeked in the window and determined that "the house appeared to have been ransacked, there was no furniture or paintings on the wall, and there were fresh-looking tire marks in the driveway." The patrolman then dutifully reported his findings to his superiors, who then quickly discovered that the house was being rented to a Congressman . . . and with that, all hell broke loose. Cop cars and detectives were dispatched, the grounds were searched, canines were brought in to detect a trail, fingerprints were taken, and my office was notified.

I flew south along Shirley Highway (that is, as fast as *anyone* could fly in the midst of 5 p.m. DC traffic), and when I arrived at the house, I was greeted by the Alexandria Chief of Police who was wearing more gold braid than the Chairman of the Joint Chiefs of Staff and who assured me that his best men would get to the bottom of it and recover my belongings.

Something didn't feel just right.

One of the detectives asked me to put together an inventory of the missing property, but from where I was standing in the entry hall, everything looked normal.

"Just a minute," I said. "Let me take a quick look around."

Hmm . . . nope. Nothing missing that I can see. Beanbag chair is still there. So's the bumper pool table. Sulin's red camping tent was set up in the living room to dry, and his sleeping bag was in its usual place. Nobody took the 1950s dinette set . . . God knows, nobody would want that anyway. No one had stolen the beer from the refrigerator. And the pile of dirty laundry was exactly where I had left it on Friday.

"Nope! Nothing missing," I said to the perplexed gendarmes.

"What happened to all the furniture?" the detective inquired.

"This is all we have," I said. "We just moved in and can't afford to outfit a house of this size, so we haven't bothered to buy any."

"But how do you explain the ladder up against the house? Did you put it there?" asked the Chief.

"I haven't the foggiest idea," I said.

"Maybe someone did try to break in, but saw it wasn't worth the effort," he suggested. "Do you want to report this as an attempted break-in?"

"No, that won't be necessary," I said.

The *last thing* I wanted was to have my name associated with a crime scene investigation, even as the *victim!*

"Wrap it up," he ordered.

So after the Alexandria Police left with a good story to pass around the precinct, I asked George and Dave what they might know about all this . . . I was pretty sure they would have the answer. And I was right!

AND . . . DON'T FORGET THE KEY!

It seems that over the weekend, while *I* was back home in Maine on the rubber chicken circuit, *they* had decided to go out on the town to do what single twenty-somethings like to do . . . after forty-four years of a very happy marriage, it's hard to remember exactly what that might have been . . . but it obviously displaced other considerations in their minds. You see, when they arrived back at the house at whatever o'clock in the early morning, they couldn't find the house key; apparently they had left it inside on the counter. So after a few minutes, one of them remembered the ladder in the garage. In hope of finding a nondestructive way in, the ladder was hoisted to my bedroom window, which happened to be unlocked. George slithered in through the bedroom window, unlocked the front door for Dave, and without giving another thought to the ladder or its possible implications, off they went to sleep!

And the rest is history, as they say, having provided countless laughs among ourselves over the years . . . and without a doubt, having been told, retold, and embellished in the annals of the Alexandria, Virginia Police Department ever since.

"HE'S STILL DEAD"
Angus King

SERVING AS GOVERNOR AND THEN IN THE U.S. SENATE, I ACCUMULATED a few experiences that both provided humor and kept me grounded.

In one of my favorites, I was having breakfast with a group of my motorcycle buddies in a diner in Kingfield, when a female server made a beeline for our table, pulling her phone out of her pocket on the way.

"Oh, Bill Green!" she said, excitedly. "I'm a huge fan—can I have a picture?"

"Actually, I'm your Senator, Angus King," I replied, perhaps a little too proudly.

"Well," she said, obviously disappointed, and slid her phone back into her pocket as she headed for another table.

That's just the kind of encounter that will put things in perspective and keep you grounded, even if you occasionally believe your own press releases!

Another grounding experience happened when we were in Machias after an unpleasant motorcycle ride down the coast in the rain and pulled into the motel parking lot next to Helen's restaurant. I noticed a couple getting out of a car nearby with two kayaks on the roof and Maryland license plates. So I went into my tourism promotion mode and walked over to welcome them to Maine.

"Great to have you come to Maine," I said, "I hope you have a great visit; I'm the Governor."

"HE'S STILL DEAD"

The lady took a step back, eyeing me encased in soaking wet bike-riding leather gear from head to toe, and said, "Yeah sure, and I'm Queen Elizabeth."

Another time we were riding motorcycles along the route of the Androscoggin River and stopped at a rest area where we met a couple on bikes who were from Massachusetts. Again, I did my usual "Welcome to Maine, I'm the Governor" routine, but our new friends looked at me with somewhat puzzled expressions.

When I returned to my buddies, Chief Justice Dan Wathan leaned over and reminded me that we were in New Hampshire. He wryly suggested that it would be best if the Governor of Maine knew *what state he was in* at all times.

But I would have to say that my all-time favorite political humor story from the campaign trail came to me from Al Gamache.

I began my political career working for Senator Bill Hathaway. Hardworking and dedicated to the people of Maine, he was an inspiration to me. I also appreciated the example and advice of Al Gamache, Bill Hathaway's longtime Chief of Staff ("Administrative Assistant" in those days) and campaign manager who often told the story of one of the perils when meeting voters and/or constituents on the campaign trail.

Al told me one such story that I remember to this day. It seems that Peter Kyros, incumbent First District Congressman, was touring a factory in southern Maine and, as he was shaking hands with the employees, met a guy whose family he knew. "How's your Dad?" asked Peter.

"He died last year," came the reply.

After expressing his condolences, Peter continued through the factory, shaking hands as he went. Finally, at the end of the tour, he ran across the same guy. "How's your Dad?" asked Peter, again. The guy responded, "Still dead."

Ah, the joys and challenges of the campaign trail.

PREDICTION FOLLIES
Dennis Bailey

POLITICS IS UNPREDICTABLE. EVEN THE MOST EXPERIENCED CAMPAIGN veterans and commentators get it wrong a lot of the time, some even most of the time. It's impossible to predict the unpredictable. But they do try.

Laughter soon follows.

I know.

In 1979. I was a young, twenty-something reporter at the Biddeford *Journal Tribune* when the editor came up to my desk one day with an assignment. Ronald Reagan had just announced his candidacy for president and was making his first stop in nearby New Hampshire. He told me and a staff photographer to run down to Portsmouth and attend the candidate's press conference.

At the time, I was not actually a political reporter. I covered car crashes and city hall meetings. So when I got to the hotel in New Hampshire where Reagan was holding his press scrum and saw all the big national political reporters I recognized from the nightly news shows, I felt like I had just joined the big leagues.

I didn't know much about Reagan. A former actor, former governor of California, that's about it. I was not closely following the ins and outs of GOP politics at the time, so I had no sense if Reagan was a frontrunner, a longshot, or a has-been. But after he entered the room, walking by within inches of me, I got a good look at him and instantly made my forecast: Not a chance. I thought it was obvious for sure.

PREDICTION FOLLIES

For one thing, I was shocked by his heavy makeup—rouge and powder—that gave him an almost clown-like appearance. Plus, he was old. Really old. Of course, at my age at the time, everyone seemed old. But Reagan was creaky. After almost every question that was lobbed at him, Reagan cupped his ear, leaned forward, and asked for it to be repeated. "What?" he must have said a dozen times to the reporters. Maybe it was the poor acoustics in the room, but he seemed hard of hearing, like an elderly grandfather who has to be reminded to wear his hearing aid. His age was already an issue in the campaign. He was sixty-eight.

If he were running today, they'd call him "the kid."

Back at the office, I was telling all of this to my editor, chuckling and shaking my head, thinking Reagan's campaign was surely a joke, when the photographer dropped his photos of the event on the desk. Again, I was shocked. Reagan looked great, like a million bucks. Healthy, ruddy, strong, alert. Nothing like the creaky, very old clown I saw. From his years in Hollywood, Reagan clearly understood the transformative magic of good lighting and makeup.

A year later, after Reagan's landslide victory over Jimmy Carter, I understood it too. That and how first impressions are not always the best ones.

Jump ahead a few years later, I had moved on to the *Maine Times*, the state's renowned alternative weekly. Still not a real political reporter, I was assigned to cover the 1982 Maine Democratic Convention. Most of the weekend was taken up with key legislative races and the governor's race featuring party stalwart Joe Brennan, who faced reelection. But there seemed to be only minor interest in another race between the sitting U.S. Senator George Mitchell and Republican House incumbent Rep. David Emery.

At the time, it was Emery's race to lose. Polls had him more than 30 points ahead, a daunting lead. He was seen as a young, down-to-earth political outsider despite years of Washington experience. He was hugely popular in his district, which returned him to Washington four times. Mitchell, on the other hand, had never won elected office. He'd even lost his bid for governor eight years earlier (a *lifetime* in politics) to an unknown independent, Jim Longley. After that, he served as U.S.

Attorney for Maine and later as a federal judge. He was appointed—not elected—to the U.S. Senate by Brennan after Ed Muskie resigned to become Secretary of State.

In other words, despite his impressive resume, Mitchell was seen as a bookish, rather dull elitist who got his Senate seat from party connections, not from the hard work of winning over Maine voters at bean suppers and hunters' breakfasts. It was evident to me that the Maine reporters at the convention had bought into the early polls (as they usually do) along with other political prognosticators, and even some of the delegates themselves, and weren't giving Mitchell much of a chance against the better-known Emery.

In fact, when it came time for Mitchell to address the convention, all the reporters were back in the press room filing their stories from the advance copy of his speech handed out by Mitchell's campaign. It was a much faster way to get their job done and head to the after-parties and cocktail bars than sitting through the speech. Those were the "must attend" affairs for many. I'm pretty sure I was the only print reporter on the floor actually watching Mitchell address the delegates.

What they missed was a new, energized George Mitchell, a surprising departure from his reputation as a straight-ahead sober judge. He was uplifting, inspiring, and the crowd ate it up. There's one axiom I tell anyone thinking of becoming a candidate: You have to really, really want it. Mitchell wanted it. I remember thinking, "Where did this guy come from?" Unfortunately, old issues of *Maine Times* aren't online, but I recall writing that the press had missed a new George Mitchell who seemed like he was ready and able to rise to the considerable challenge of overcoming a 30-point deficit in the polls. I don't think I predicted he would win, but I knew then that this was going to be a real race.

And it was, with Mitchell ultimately trouncing Emery with 61 percent of the vote in what at the time was the most expensive campaign in Maine history. His convention speech wasn't why he won—there were plenty of other reasons for his upset. But it was probably the first real indication that Mitchell *could* win, and the press missed it.

But I bet the cocktails were great. I missed out on those.

FUN WITH WIRELESS MICROPHONES: GIVE ME A HUG
Pat Callaghan

IN THE TV NEWS BUSINESS, WIRELESS MICROPHONE TECHNOLOGY CAN really bring a story to life, creating intimate moments for viewers. But the mic that's switched *on* when you think it is *off* can be problematic.

The first lesson any aspiring broadcaster must learn is that "all microphones are hot"—meaning, you never know who might be listening, even when you think you are off air.

Sometimes this lesson is driven home the hard way. I recall a friend hosting a candlepin bowling show in Bangor in the early 1980s who, when the show was in a commercial break, could be heard using expletives about how boring that day's contest really was. It got him a week's unpaid "vacation."

It's not uncommon for politicians to get caught speaking their truth when they don't know anyone can hear them. In 2010, then–Vice President Joe Biden was overheard enthusing to President Barack Obama that the signing of the Affordable Care Act was "a big f—king deal!" In 2017, Maine Republican Senator Susan Collins was chatting with her Democratic colleague Senator Jack Reed of Rhode Island after a budget hearing when Reed said of President Donald Trump, "I think he's crazy," and Collins replied, "I'm worried." According to the *Washington Post*, they continued talking on that still-open mic for more than a minute about Trump's ignorance of the federal budget.

In the early days of radio, microphones were quite large. They were placed on mic stands or on a table and attached to a sound board with thick cables. As television began to take hold in the late 1940s, you could see these bulky devices clearly. The development of smaller mics that could be worn around an announcer's neck was a step forward, allowing someone such as NBC *Today Show* host Dave Garroway to walk freely around his set, though still attached to a bulky cable. And they were still far larger than our modern microphones.

Wireless microphone technology was developed in the late 1950s and proved its worth at the 1960 Democratic and Republican National Conventions, when reporters could move about the floor freely to speak with delegates.

This useful tool has become more and more refined and unobtrusive, with small transmitter packs that fit in a pocket or on a belt, with a mic that can be attached to a lapel or necktie. They began being widely used by field reporters at Maine TV stations in the 1980s and '90s

What we record with these mics can often be quite useful.

For example, in 1997 I was covering former Maine Senator George Mitchell's adventures in Belfast, Northern Ireland, for WCSH TV, the NBC affiliate in Portland. He'd been named chairman of the multi-party talks that were aimed at bringing an end to the sectarian violence known as "The Troubles."

We fitted Mitchell with a wireless mic so we could record our conversation as we walked the streets and learned about what was at the root of the problems that Mitchell and the negotiators were trying to solve. He showed us where large bonfires would be set each summer by Unionists who fought to remain part of the United Kingdom—annual events meant to provoke the Republicans who want to see the entire island of Ireland made whole again.

After we had all we needed of the Q&A, photographer Scott Wernig jogged on ahead about a block to catch some wide shots to be used as "B-roll" as we call it in the biz—the pictures you see with the reporter's narration. Mitchell and I kept walking and chatting, as natural as can be. A couple of local gents walking toward us did not see the camera but recognized Mitchell. They stopped him to thank him for his work there

FUN WITH WIRELESS MICROPHONES: GIVE ME A HUG

and called him a very brave man for walking the streets of Belfast openly and without security. It was a nice little genuine moment that I knew would help me tell Mitchell's story to the folks back home.

Mitchell asked me if we had set up that encounter, but I told him I was not that clever—it just happened naturally. By the way, I had asked Mitchell about that very subject raised by the passersby, whether he felt safe doing this job. He replied that while there was always the chance of random violence in Northern Ireland in those days, he felt he was not important enough to become a target.

That's an example of a serendipitous moment that illustrated an important point. Not all such encounters are so enlightening.

We often used wireless mics on political candidates as they were out greeting potential voters. Some seem to forget they had them on.

A guy named Chipman Bull was one of the tomato cans (a sports metaphor for opponents who are easily knocked over!) that Democrats tended to put up to run against Rep. Olympia Snowe when she was firmly ensconced in Maine's Second Congressional District seat, people such as Harold Silverman and Jim Dunleavy.

Chip Bull's turn for a candidate profile was in 1984. A photographer put the wireless mic on him and stood at an unobtrusive distance as Bull looked for supporters to woo in downtown Bangor. When a passerby would give him the brush off, Bull would mutter an obscenity under his breath while still smiling for the cameras and the people. Needless to say, the editor of that story had to be very careful about using that audio, lest we hear from the Federal Communications Commission.

Bull managed to get almost 23 percent of the vote against the unbeatable Congresswoman. Snowe was elected to Congress eight times before moving up to the Senate, and only Patrick McGowan, who ran against her in 1990 and '92, ever really gave her a run for her money.

A favorite wireless mic moment came in 1988 when Senator Mitchell was running for his second full term. For part of my candidate profile, he wore a wireless mic as he shook hands inside a donut shop in Biddeford. Mitchell was the only candidate I recall who would warn each person he spoke with that he had a hot mic on, thereby preventing any embarrassing encounters. Perhaps it was the federal judge in him that was concerned about due process.

Then we went outside to conduct the interview.

As we were about to begin, the embarrassing moment he hoped to avoid thrust itself upon Mitchell. A gentleman who looked to be in his mid-50s or so wandered up. He wore a rainbow colored knit hat and carried what may have been a Bible. It quickly became clear that this fellow was not selling anything or looking for a handout.

With a big grin on his face, our visitor looked at the camera, looked at Mitchell, and leaned into that mic and proclaimed "This is not being recorded . . . but . . . Give me a hug, boy! Don't be an asshole!"

He then proceeded to wrap Maine's junior U.S. senator in a bear hug for a good ten seconds, with Mitchell, clearly knowing that this was indeed being recorded, looked our way with a frozen smile, helpless to do anything but hope the moment would pass quickly.

That particular video clip never made it into a news story. It would have been a little unkind and embarrassing for all concerned. (Though I believe the late great reporter and storyteller extraordinaire Bob Elliot may have used a bit of it without audio when reporting on Mitchell's retirement from the Senate.) Mitchell managed to get reelected with 81 percent of the vote, proving that he was loved by lots of Mainers, even those who never got to embrace him physically.

In fact, Mitchell beat Republican Jasper "Call Me Jack" Wyman—a very nice guy who liked and respected Senator Mitchell. For all I know, Wyman may have voted for Mitchell himself after doing his duty to raise GOP priorities during the campaign. Mitchell actually carried every town in Maine with the exception of a tie in one Aroostook County community and a loss in one in Washington County. But George being George, he visited both of those communities the day after the election to ask what he had done to lose their support.

And for years, we had a new catch phrase with which to greet one another in the newsroom: "Give me a hug, boy! Don't be an asshole!"

FEELING THE HEAT
Don Carrigan

As a twenty-three-year-old TV reporter in Bangor, I was paid very little, but the experience was worth it. And it was exciting to be out gathering the news, sometimes talking to big-time people. One of them, one night, prevented *me* from becoming the story.

At the time, Bill Cohen was the Representative to Congress from Maine's Second District. He was young, well liked in his hometown of Bangor, and had gained national recognition for his role in the Watergate hearings and the impeachment of former President Richard Nixon.

Most Friday evenings, Cohen would come back to Bangor for the weekend, a schedule that typically included Friday evening availability for interviews.

On this one night, he was meeting with a group at the popular Miller's Restaurant. As the night reporter and anchor, I was sent to interview Cohen about some issue of the day and was lucky enough to have a photographer with me to film it.

In those days, we were a very small newsroom, with only one full-time news photographer, so often I would run the camera myself. But this time I was lucky, and the photographer hung around to help me get "the big interview."

We shot all our stories then on 16mm film, which required a significant amount of light to get a good image for indoor shoots. The big sound camera would be set up on a tripod, the audio amplifier plugged into the camera and hung on one side with the microphone cable plugged into the amp.

The light, which was 650 watts (yes, we needed a lot of light then), was clamped to the camera a little above the lens. It was tough for the person being interviewed, who had that light blasting into his eyes from about six feet away. Of course, if we remembered to bring it, we might have clipped a filter onto the light to make it a little less intense.

As mentioned earlier, I wasn't paid much then and only had a couple of suit coats and neckties. And nothing was of high quality. That night I was wearing a blue blazer, which I think I had bought at the Kmart. A polyester blue blazer, in fact. You may see where this is headed.

We set up the camera and everything else inside the lobby between Miller's Restaurant and its banquet space, called the Red Lion. The photographer took a light meter reading, adjusted the f-stop on the lens accordingly, and we were ready. Congressman Cohen came out and we began the interview.

When a reporter does a TV interview, he normally stands in front of, and back to the camera, which essentially shoots over the shoulder. This we did.

About a minute into the interview, I noticed Cohen's eyes shifting a little bit from side to side and he seemed to lose his sentence.

"I think you're on fire," he said.

"What?" I asked.

"I think you're on fire."

He pointed toward my left shoulder. I looked around and, sure enough, smoke was rising from my back! The heat from that high-powered camera light was about to ignite my coat, with me in it!

I handed Cohen the microphone and quickly tore off the coat. The polyester had melted, and luckily it was noticed before actual flames broke out.

What to do then?

What else, but hang the coat on a nearby chair, take back the microphone and finish the interview. Rep. Cohen was typically gracious about it. We had a good laugh, as did the photographer. A hot story of a different sort!

I was unhappy about the coat, of course—remember, I couldn't afford many of those. Fortunately, the damage was on the back, so I could still wear it to anchor the news that night and for months thereafter, always rubbing the half-melted fabric before I put it on.

I finally was able to save up enough for a replacement, but no more polyester for me. And for a long time after, I may have done all my indoor interviews without a jacket.

Covering politicians, after all, can be a risky job. Covering them can also be surprising, as well.

Another Bill Cohen story follows:

When you cover politics in a small state and community, you can get closer to the officeholders than one would expect. I remember what happened to me on America's Bicentennial Day, the Fourth of July, 1976.

That huge day of celebration began very early. The Chamber of Commerce in the northern Maine town of Mars Hill was having a flag-raising event at dawn on top of Mars Hill mountain. Mars Hill is one of several spots in Maine that claim to be the first spot in the United States to see sunrise. It actually depends on the time of year, but Mars Hill was claiming it for that July 4, and no one was disputing it. They would be the first place in the country to see the sun rise on America's two hundredth birthday.

The celebration included several speakers, some music, and a flag-raising. The most prominent speaker was Maine's Second District Congressman, Rep. Bill Cohen, then in his second term and running for a third.

The Chamber wanted some TV coverage and invited us to come up, even offering to pay for a plane to fly us from Bangor to Presque Isle and provide transportation from that airport to Mars Hill.

We said yes. Heck, we didn't have to pay for the plane! At that time, the boss of the station would likely have not been willing to buy us a plane ride to Aroostook County.

There would be two of us flying up, myself and a photographer, but three flying back. Rep. Cohen, who was already planning to be in the County campaigning, needed to get back to Bangor to march in the city's Fourth of July parade. A flight back to Bangor would make that possible.

Early on the morning of July 4, around 2 a.m., we boarded the small charter plane and flew north. We landed and were driven to Mars Hill and up the mountain, where people were steadily gathering. It was a beautiful morning. People spoke, music played, the flag was hoisted, and the sun rose. Success! And a good story to start a long day of Bicentennial coverage.

We headed back to the airport, and all climbed into the small plane for the trip back to Bangor, getting there in the early morning light, around 6:30 a.m. We had left our car at the airport, but Cohen had none.

"Can you guys give me a ride home?" he asked.

We looked at each other, surprised, and naturally said yes. We were both just twenty-somethings and never expected to be driving a member of Congress around.

Cohen was a legal resident of Bangor at the time but didn't have a home of his own in the city.

"Take me to my mother's house," he said.

So of course we did.

It was 6:30 on a holiday morning, with little traffic or people moving around the city. Cohen's mother and father had a house on a side street, maybe a mile from our TV station.

So, on that morning, we pulled up in front of the house, Cohen got out, grabbed his bag and headed up the steps to the door.

As we pulled away, I saw him standing there, in the early morning, waiting for someone to open the door and let him in.

My first thought was: "I wonder, back in his high school days, how many *other* early mornings did he get dropped off on his mother's doorstep?"

My next thought was something like, *He's this big, important, nationally known Congressman and rising Republican star. How many of those big-time guys get left standing at their mother's door this time of day?*

Cohen, of course, went on to become a significant U.S. Senator in the 1980s and '90s. I even went to work for him for three years, before returning to journalism. Later, Cohen would serve as America's Secretary of Defense.

It's been close to fifty years since that early morning doorstep dropoff, but the image of it is still clear in my memory. You can take the reporter out of the story but you can't take the reporter out of the story!

FEELING THE HEAT

In hindsight, it might have been an important lesson for a young reporter covering politics. Deep down, they are people pretty much like the rest of us. People who, despite having important jobs, really never know when they, too, might need a ride home.

UNDERDOGS WELCOME: POLITICAL ODDBALLS FIND FERTILE GROUND
Pat Callaghan

Mainers have an independent streak, and they're damned proud of it. It shows in their politics. The state was historically known for its rock-bound coast and its rock-ribbed Republicans until the Ed Muskie era arrived in 1954.

Over the last sixty years, at least one-third of voters have been unenrolled, and no party has been able to hold the governor's office for more than eight years at a time. Look at the history of gubernatorial elections since 1962 when the term for Maine governors was expanded to four years:

1962 – Republican John Reed
1966 – Democrat Ken Curtis
1974 – Independent Jim Longley
1978 – Democrat Joe Brennan
1986 – Republican John McKernan
1994 – Independent Angus King
2002 – Democrat John Baldacci
2010 – Republican Paul LePage
2018 – Democrat Janet Mills

UNDERDOGS WELCOME: POLITICAL ODDBALLS FIND FERTILE GROUND

Given that history, it should come as no surprise that underdog or fringe candidates should find Maine welcome territory. We don't mind people with quirks.

One of them ran as regularly as folks line up for lobster rolls at Red's Eats.

A man named Plato Truman ("Two Great Names, One Great Candidate!") from Biddeford won a seat in the legislature in 1964, served one term, and then ran for other public offices and lost ten times: three times as an independent, four times as a Democrat, and three times as a Republican.

You cannot fault the man for a lack of perseverance.

In my time covering politics for Maine's NBC TV stations, I saw presidential candidates who might have seemed out of step with Maine surprise a lot of people and fare pretty well.

For example, civil rights leader Rev. Jesse Jackson wouldn't necessarily be a good bet in a state with such a small minority population and a lot of rural conservatives. But in the 1988 presidential cycle, Jackson's populist message connected with a lot of students and with blue-collar working people who felt marginalized. He visited the town of Jay to support paper workers on strike against International Paper, and the mostly white voters there and in other mill towns helped Jackson finish second in the Maine Democratic caucuses.

Jesse Jackson has another virtue—a sense of humor.

During that '88 campaign, Jackson complained about his media coverage by telling a story that goes like this:

"Jesse Jackson and the Pope are in a little boat on the ocean. A wind gust blows the Pope's hat off his head. Jesse gets out of the boat, walks across the water and retrieves the hat and brings it back. There is another boat filled with reporters watching this unfold. The headline in the next day's paper reads 'Jesse Can't Swim.'"

I had a memorable encounter with Reverend Jackson in New Hampshire in '88. I was part of a gaggle of reporters and photographers waiting for Jackson to arrive at his campaign headquarters in Manchester. We stood on the sidewalk, with a 10-inch snowbank between us and the street.

His car pulled up, and as he climbed out we all surged toward him and jockeyed for position, with some shouting questions at him. Jackson climbed on top of the snowbank and said, "Before you alligators in the media make me fall down and cause an international scene, where should I stand?"

My photographer Josh Bradford was not the tallest guy in the bunch, but he was in a perfect position to have a great shot of the candidate. With Jackson looking straight down into his lens, Josh snapped in his most commanding voice "Stand there! Stand there!" Jackson paused a moment, smiled and quietly said, "I'll stand here." Everyone got what they needed—media alligators and candidate alike.

Four years later in 1992, another outsider candidate made a strong showing in Maine's Democratic caucuses. Once and future governor of California Jerry Brown finished first, barely edging out our New England neighbor Senator Paul Tsongas. The eventual nominee, Arkansas Governor Bill Clinton, was roughly tied with "uncommitted" in third place.

Brown delivered a strong message here including an emphasis on environmental issues, and opposition to nuclear power, a very hot topic in Maine then.

Brown is a smart and interesting guy, and he surprised me when I was sitting down to do an interview with him. As we were about to begin, he pulled out a nasal inhaler and took a couple of sniffs in each nostril.

"It's saline," he explained. "It feels like diving into a wave."

Then he held it out to me and asked if I wanted to try it—a very generous gesture, but one I declined.

Though some called Brown "Governor Moonbeam," I took him at his word that the bottle contained only saltwater. But there is such a thing as too much sharing.

As for Bill Clinton, he did put some time into courting Maine voters. He was booked to do a live interview on our 6 p.m. newscast on a Saturday, when the building was largely deserted. The campaign asked if they could come early and use a conference room to take care of some business, and we agreed.

Around 5:30, the doorbell rang. A pizza delivery guy was there with food for the always-hungry candidate and his team. Producer Erin

UNDERDOGS WELCOME: POLITICAL ODDBALLS FIND FERTILE GROUND

Crowley stuck her head into the conference room, where one of the staffers—I wish I could say it was the "Ragin' Cajun" James Carville or one of the other guys who became famous when Clinton was president, but I don't remember—asked if she would pay the tab. Erin was young and feisty and wasn't going to be told what to do by these White House wannabes. She told them in no uncertain terms that they would be paying for their own dang pizza.

I also spoke with Clinton the night before the 1988 New Hampshire primary, when he was scrambling to overcome various scandals that seem awfully tame compared with what we have seen since 2016. Knowing he was speaking to a reporter from Portland, Clinton demonstrated his knowledge of political history when he compared himself with Maine Senator Ed Muskie, whom he said had suffered from unfair press coverage when running for president in 1972, just as Clinton claimed he himself had twenty years later.

The most successful also-ran in presidential politics in Maine was Texas businessman Ross Perot. He was a grassroots phenomenon in the 1992 election cycle, running as an independent against President George H. W. Bush, who had been softened up a bit by challenger Pat Buchanan in the Republican primaries and by Democratic nominee Bill Clinton.

Perot, who had never run for any elective office, was a true political outsider with an odd, folksy style that appealed to a lot of voters, though he often came off as prickly and short-tempered. And as former Congressman Dave Emery points out, "Ross Perot often said, 'I'm all ears,' and he was."

Perot was a real thorn in the side of the New England/Texas hybrid George Bush.

As he neared the end of his term, Bush had extraordinarily high approval ratings fueled by his success in building a coalition to force Iraqi leader Saddam Hussein and his army out of Kuwait.

But a lot of Republicans turned on Bush for breaking the explicit "Read my lips! No new taxes" pledge he had made in 1988.

Maine was one state that Bush probably felt he could rely on, given that he had spent every summer of his life apart from his service in World War II at his family's Walker's Point estate in Kennebunkport. Bush was a neighbor and a Republican in the moderate New England mold, something that has since become virtually extinct. He won the general election in Maine with more than 55 percent of the statewide vote.

Yet in the 1992 general election, Bush finished third in his summer home state behind Clinton and Perot. The political neophyte Perot won more than 30 percent of Maine's general election vote, coming within about 4 percentage points of taking an electoral vote in the Second Congressional District.

That had to sting. But maybe not for long.

In 2012 I was working on a documentary on the life and career of Senator Olympia Snowe, who had decided not to seek another term. Among the people I spoke to were former President Bush and his wife Barbara. They weren't doing news interviews anymore at that point, but because they were so fond of Snowe, they wanted to be part of the program.

When we finished the interview, the three of us were chatting while the photographer shot cutaways and wide shots. I told President Bush that I was one of those who believed that he likely would have defeated Bill Clinton and won a second term if Ross Perot hadn't been in the race. I asked if he agreed, but Bush simply shrugged it off, not caring to rehash ancient political history. But Mrs. Bush's eyes flashed, and she said she also believed, in no uncertain terms, that Perot had cost her husband a second term. And she was clearly still steamed up about it.

It was then that I realized something about the dynamic between the former First Couple: Barbara Bush held the grudges so George Bush didn't have to.

AMUSING INCIDENTS AT THE FRONT DOOR TO HISTORY
John Baldacci

When I was on the Bangor City Council, in the State Legislature, and in Congress and as governor, I always tried to reach across the aisle and make common cause with the opposition, whoever they might be. Sometimes it was easy, and sometimes it was hard, but I thought it was always worthwhile. My political philosophy has been that we simply need problems solved no matter whose idea the solution may come from. And *compromise* is a good word, not a bad one. We have to work together; politics is not an all or nothing proposition.

This approach also produced a fun ride along the way for I found there was a lot of humor to be encountered in our political process.

When I was in Congress, for example, there were many more friendships across party lines than there are now. One I remember with great fondness was Sonny Bono. For us as two Italian-American boys, both of whom were intimately familiar with restaurants (his upscale, mine working-class), Sonny and I got along very well even though he was a Republican from California and I was a Democrat from Maine. We also both liked Sonny and Cher's music.

We joked and laughed a lot together. Once when we were interviewed together by CNN, the moderator brought up his headline-breakup with Cher, his former wife and duet partner. I don't remember all the details, but Cher came on the interview and railed against Sonny. They went back and forth, and at one point the host asked me about men and women and who was right. Not wanting to get drawn into an even longer round of future couples' therapy played out on the front page of the *Bangor Daily News*, I demurred saying "I'm siding with Cher on this, women always know more than men about this subject." And added for more distancing, "Sonny and I only worked to help feed congresspeople numerous lobster rolls and spaghetti."

In addition to finessing questions with the media, I always enjoyed going to the country fairs in Maine. As a city slicker from Bangor, I always found them fascinating. I never did too well at them, however. The Fryeburg Fair, for example, always seemed to have a lot of livestock manure around the place, and it was hard not to step into some if you weren't very careful. It was not unusual to keep a change of shoes for the way home.

One time at the Springfield Agricultural Fair, they got even more creative with manure and had a contest for the political figures in attendance. I was there and asked to participate. I was quite surprised when I found out the "contest" was to see who could throw a cow pat the farthest down the racetrack.

Strange, I thought, but as I was in pretty good shape, I grabbed a shovel and began warming up as if I were in the on-deck circle in the baseball World Series. I flexed and stretched and whirled the shovel around and around before we began. The other contestants looked a little askance at me, but I didn't care, I was going to win.

Or so I thought.

All my warming up seemed to knock me off-kilter, because when it was my turn to throw, I whirled around this way and that but when I actually went to toss the cow pat, it simply slipped off and fell to the ground. Everybody laughed and had a fine time at my expense.

I had the last laugh, though, telling the crowd, "I never was good at slinging the bull!"

Another time I was dining at the Capitol Grill in Washington, a famous watering hole for political and media types, with Anthony Weiner and seven or eight other congressmen. This was, of course, before Congressman Weiner had taken to sending screen shots of his private parts around the internet.

AMUSING INCIDENTS AT THE FRONT DOOR TO HISTORY

We were joined by a couple of reporters from *Vanity Fair* magazine. Everybody seemed to be thinking that the conversation would be "off the record," and somehow the subject got onto interns, and some of the lads, especially Weiner, got carried away with their stories. Luckily, I remembered the old press dictum "Nothing is ever really off the record" and became quite attentive but silent.

Listening to that still small voice paid dividends, because the resulting *Vanity Fair* article reproduced the conversations in living technicolor, making the congressmen and their comments look very bad. Entitled "Meanwhile Back on Capitol Hill," the story touted "A worm's eye look at the nexus of lust and power" and declared "Idealism has a short shelf life."

It was not a positive piece.

The next day the *Bangor Daily News* picked up the story and there was much criticism from all sides about the attitudes and actions of the congressmen. It was a minor, although brief calamity, and I was subject to a lot of teasing and questions back in Maine, all of which made me happy I had been circumspect and careful.

But you can't please everybody!

My good friend and longtime supporter Severin Belliveau soon called and advised, "Next time *Vanity Fair* or anybody else is doing a piece on scandals, do something—give them a good story. You don't want to seem dull."

Conflicting advice, however, came from my dear mother. Her statement was at once most trenchant and telling of the responses. It was also the most filled with menace. Mama Baldacci said simply, "Do you need me to come down to Washington and clean things up?"

Case closed.

Speaking of Severin Belliveau, for any readers not familiar with his name, Severin has been a very potent force in Maine politics for over sixty years. So I took his advice seriously, but not, of course, serious enough to follow it in this case. My beloved mother let me know the true path I was to follow.

Incidentally, while Severin is known in some political circles as "The Wolf" for his ability to kill and eat even the biggest of game in the political realm, I have always thought that his animal totem should be the crocodile. If you have ever seen those *National Geographic* specials showing the Okavango swamp slowly drying up, you know that as the water pools gradually recede, crocodiles congregate and eventually start eating each other until there is only one huge, very clever, very powerful survivor.

That would be Severin.

I was surprised when he even claimed in 2025 that he was retired.

But I don't believe him.

Maybe from practicing law perhaps, but not from politics.

As I was writing this, I remembered watching him operate at a high level. A lifelong champion of Franco-Americans as well as Maine, Severin was a natural to be brought along when I was governor and on a promotional tour of France. His presence turned out to be something of a mixed blessing, however.

On the one hand, with his impeccable command of French and his take-charge attitude, he was much in demand by our hosts as we moved from city to city. Severin played an important role in our proceedings and seemed to be everywhere front-running our operation and explaining my remarks at considerable depth. Sometimes it sounded like he was expanding on them at considerable length.

But, of course, on the other hand, as the tour progressed, more and more French officials seemed to think that *he* was the governor and I but a diffident staffer. And although my knowledge of French was, and remains, rudimentary, I can attest that he didn't seem to be denying very strenuously their assumptions that he was governor. What good fun!

All in all, whenever and wherever you are in politics (or life for that matter), it's probably best not to take yourself too seriously, because there is always a banana peel lying around waiting for you to step on it or a cow pat to step into.

GOING TO HEAVEN AFTER ALL
Bill Diamond

THE FIRST TIME I RAN FOR THE MAINE STATE SENATE WAS IN 1982 after serving three terms (six years) in the Maine House of Representatives. My opponent was the incumbent Republican Senator David Huber from Falmouth. Dave was well-known and believed to be politically secure in the overwhelmingly Republican district made up of a dozen communities spreading from Falmouth Foreside to the town of Baldwin.

Dave was highly respected in the legislature and throughout state government as he served as Senate Chair of the Appropriations and Financial Affairs (AFA) Committee, the most powerful committee in the legislature. This was especially true in the financially fraught 1980s. To make matters even more interesting and challenging, his wife, Sherry Huber, had served in the House with me at the same time, and she was also highly respected and his obviously strong supporter.

In short, the team of Dave and Sherry Huber were the royalty of the legislature at that time. Sherry would even run for governor in 1986 as an Independent. She and another Independent, John Menario, split 30 percent of the vote, only somewhat less than the total amassed by the eventual winner, Republican Jock McKernan, who got 40 percent of the vote.

Dave was also one of the principals of the massive Huber land industries in northern Maine. One day in committee, someone snarled at him and accused him of being a millionaire. Dave retorted with a big smile, "That's absolutely not true, I'm a multi-millionaire!"

Everyone just broke up laughing.

Having served with Dave on the AFA Committee as a House member, I grew to know and respect his abilities and knowledge. Besides, he was "my senator" since my hometown of Windham was one of the twelve towns in the district. When I decided to run for "his" seat, the decision was based on many things—none of which was common sense! I just felt—win or lose—it was time for me to try to move up from the Maine House to the Maine Senate.

Running for the Senate is much different than running for the House primarily because a Senate district is five times larger than a House district. In addition, our area was 90 percent rural, and the houses that we were trying to reach were spread throughout the hinterlands.

One such rural community, New Gloucester, presented all such challenges, including access to voters and, more worrisome still, a large array of highly protective animals such as dogs, geese, roosters, goats, turkeys, and many more ranging from pets to varmints.

My goal was to have our team reach as many houses as possible, knowing that's the best way to beat a well-entrenched incumbent. I attempted to get as many volunteer door knockers as I could, which wasn't easy because of the challenging nature of the task, especially for first-time volunteers. Two of my most loyal "go anywhere, do whatever is needed" volunteers were my mother- and father in-law, Stan and Emma Estes. They were both in their midsixties, and campaigning door to door was a totally foreign concept to them. However, they never wavered.

Stan and Emma were true troupers.

They were relentless and fearless as they trudged on through the long, muddy driveways, not always receiving friendly receptions from suspicious homeowners who had never seen campaigners come to their house, especially people in their sixties. The most difficult challenges for my in-laws, however, were the overprotective animals in the district.

Stan and Emma were bitten by dogs, chased and pecked by geese, whose pinches are much worse than a dog's bite, pecked by pursuing turkeys and roosters, and butted by goats. Talk about hazardous duty!

Yet they persisted.

Attempted escapes from the various attacks required fancy footwork, stepping around discarded deer heads, hoofs, and other assorted animal remains that lay scattered around various yards. On one occasion my determined father-in-law, after spending a four-hour stint in what became known by our volunteers as "The Deliverance Expedition," proudly displayed several new goose bites on his butt and backs of his legs and a puncture from a goat horn that just missed scoring a fantastic and painful hole in one.

This is campaigning in rural Maine. Not for the fainthearted.

My favorite remembrance of that race follows:

I had a lot of fun going door to door across the district, including staunchly Republican areas. Once while campaigning in Dave's hometown of Falmouth knocking on doors and introducing myself to the locals—most of whom were Republicans—I happened to stop by this house and an elderly lady came to the door. She was very kind and welcoming and, after a couple of minutes, invited me in for a cold drink on what was a very hot July day. She was one of those nice voters who make campaigning a joy rather than a task.

After chatting for a while I could see we were actually connecting and she was becoming more comfortable with me notwithstanding the fact that I was a Democrat! I'm not sure she'd ever had a Democrat stop by to do some politicking.

That realization that I was a D did seem to bother her a great deal. She hemmed and hawed and said she was a lifelong Republican as were all of her family generations before her.

She finally reluctantly confided that she would like to vote for me but, frankly, was afraid that if she died after having voted for a Democrat it would greatly affect her chances for going to Heaven. "They might not take me in."

Talk about a "wedge issue."

Talk about something that was above my pay grade! I wasn't even in the Maine Senate yet and this kind of celestial challenge had arisen.

I realized I just couldn't crack her final concern or take over the responsibility of her afterlife.

So, after seeing how seriously she was worried about the ramifications of voting for a Democrat at her older age, I finally urged her to vote for Dave, who was a good Republican. I said, "Honestly, there was no reason for you to take a chance losing your spot in Heaven!"

"Dave's always been a good man and I've enjoyed serving with him," I added as I bid her farewell, wondering why I'd spent so much time on what had probably been a lost cause voter from the very beginning.

But I felt better about my conclusion and certainly so did she. She was visibly relieved at receiving absolution from such an unlikely source.

"Thank you, you seem like such a nice young man."

Her smile was worth the lost vote.

And she would be going to Heaven after all.

Despite all of our difficulties and unique experiences, the campaign finally came to an end on Election Day, November 2. One of our most gratifying accomplishments was the fact we won New Gloucester . . . by one vote!

As we watched the results dribble in, it became clear we were losing—with Falmouth, Cumberland, and Baldwin all supporting Senator Huber. In fact, with all of the towns in except Windham, I had lost. Then my hometown, Windham, reported their results around 3:30 a.m. where I won by a large margin, making an overall victory obvious.

The next morning Dave called to congratulate me, and the first words out of his mouth were "Well, you caught the bucket of shit!"

I loved Dave Huber.

And I've never forgotten his grace and good sportsmanship.

And I guess I benefited from good karma from him—and the nice Republican lady—going forward. For despite the vicissitudes of term limits and changes in the political landscape, I'm still the senator from the district forty years later, even though it covers fewer towns today.

READ THE SIGNS MORE CAREFULLY NEXT TIME!
Dave Emery

An incident of note that did not involve the ubiquitous Hattie Bickmore took place immediately following my 1978 reelection campaign. I had been scheduled to address a statewide meeting of the VFW Auxiliary, held at the Samoset Resort in Rockport two days following the election that year.

Naturally, I was very exhausted from the campaign and really would have preferred to go somewhere to relax for a few days, but you *never* turn down an invitation to address veterans, especially during a campaign or right after. You *do not* want to disappoint the veterans *ever*; they don't deserve to be disappointed. You always want to go the extra mile to show veterans your appreciation for their service and all they have done for our country.

So a political operative from Washington, DC, whom I will refer to as Carl, and a longtime friend, Skip Pease, who was my Rockland-area campaign chairman, accompanied me to the meeting.

Now, these things usually follow a predictable course, the main speaker taking the podium after dinner, say, at 9 p.m. or so, in which case the event is usually over and done with (for the main speaker, at least) by 9:30 or thereabouts. But this event was an outlier. The dinner was late, and the business meeting, the requisite introductions of visiting veterans, officers, and presentation of awards droned on and on. It was frankly a nightmare. It would have been excruciating in normal times, but at the end of the campaign with its draining demands, it was close to deadly.

There I sat at the dais, trapped, bored, and tired, powerless to move things along. I could see Carl and Skip in the rear, checking their watches—sometimes hitting them thinking they had stopped—and as ready to leave as I was.

It was about 11 p.m. when I was finally called to the podium. Looking around, I could see empty chairs and more than a few who had visited the bar a couple of times. So I truncated my remarks to only five or ten minutes and attempted a hasty retreat.

But where was Carl?

He had disappeared. Vanished into thin air (or rather, into air as thin as air *could* be at a VFW convention prior to smoking bans). A quick search determined that he was not at the bar nor in the men's room. We checked the hall, reception rooms, lobby, and everywhere else we could think of, but he wasn't anywhere to be found.

Skip and I eventually went out to our car, thinking he might be there waiting for us. Nope . . . not there either. So we sat and waited: Had he been abducted by a lonely conventioneer? Not *Carl* . . . ? We laughed at the myriad possibilities for his disappearance, from space aliens to a gorgeous girl smitten with his powerful political persona?

It was almost 11:30 when we saw him suddenly fly out of the door with a deer-in-the-headlights look. As he got into the car, we both pummeled him with the obvious question . . .

Wherethehellhaveyoubeen?

With a sheepish expression, he stammered, "I—I—I was trapped in the men's room . . . well, not exactly . . . I was trapped in the *ladies room*!"

"Whatthehellhappened?" we demanded.

"Just as you started to speak," he blurted, "I went to the men's room, thinking I'd be back in plenty of time. But you only spoke for a few minutes, and just as the event concluded, everyone made a mad dash for the restrooms, and just as I was about to leave the stall, the bathroom door opened, and some woman came in."

"Ahhhh," I thought. "Won't *she* be embarrassed when I come out of my stall and she sees that she went into the men's room by mistake. But then, another woman came in. And then another. And another. *Then* I realized that *it was I* who had gone into the wrong bathroom!"

There I was, trapped in a flimsy stall in the middle of a crowded ladies room, with no graceful way out. What would they say when they discovered me? What would *you* say when they announced that one of your associates had been caught lurking in the ladies room? And just as I began to contemplate my fate, a rough-sounding woman started shaking the stall door and demanded, "Hurry up in there. I've got to piss real bad."

"I didn't say a thing but grabbed the latch and held it in place with all my might so it wouldn't shake loose. Then I thought to myself, "What if one of them looks under the stall door and sees men's shoes?" So I immediately climbed up onto the flimsy seat rim, crouching and uncomfortably balanced, trying not to either fall *off* or fall *in*, one hand holding onto the toilet paper dispenser for support, the other holding down the door latch."

"Thus I sat on my precarious perch like a frightened hoot owl for at least twenty minutes, my mind numbed by a sensory overload of potty language, flatulence, flushing, foul odors, and primal fear. Finally, when I believed I was alone at last, I dethroned, burst out of the stall and ran out of the ladies room as fast as I could run, hoping you guys hadn't left without me."

Skip and I laughed a long time before we started the car and drove away. "That's one for the record books," Skip opined.

And ever since the fateful incident just related, I am told that Carl has learned to read restroom door signs in several languages, including Braille, for good measure.

A CARDINAL TRUMPS A BISHOP ... AND A DR. DEMENTO
Chris Potholm

SOME OF THE MOST HUMOROUS AND IRONIC MOMENTS IN POLITICS CAN occur when campaign integrity and planning are breached by forces beyond the campaign. Often, the true humor of the moment is lost at the time in the wave of frustration and anger if those breaches look to be decisive. But later one can laugh at how outside forces stumble and bumble their way into campaigns with hard-to-predict results.

A prime example follows.

In 1986 the Christian Civic League of Maine led by Jasper Wyman collected enough signatures to put on the Maine ballot a referendum that would ban "obscene" material and called for fines for its possession and/or dissemination. The exact wording was harsh: "To make it a crime to make, sell, give for value, or otherwise promote obscene material in Maine." The proposal, which would have penalized "prurient" content with up to five years in jail, was ultimately defeated. Yet despite the draconian tone of the measure, initially public polling showed that a large majority of Mainers supported such a ban, at least in the abstract.

At that time, I was called on by the Roman Catholic Diocese in Portland to evaluate the likelihood of the measure passing as the Diocese was actually more concerned about another possible measure, one that would permit assisted suicide in the State of Maine. "We probably don't have enough money to do both," said Mark Mutty, public affairs director of the Diocese, "and we need advice and guidance on where to put our focus."

We did an extensive poll and examined both issues, and in fact we created imaginary campaigns for and against both, complete with authority figures and influence vectors that would work for both sides, to judge probable outcomes from the initial cut to a second one at the end of the poll. The Catholic Church was against the concept of assisted suicide and in favor of a ban on obscene material, all of which made for a complex situation.

The pornography proposal did in fact start with very widespread support, I think 63 or 62 percent, and the one favoring assisted suicide even higher with 65 percent (one public poll had it at 70/28 percent). But when you duplicated the mock election campaign for each, giving respondents both sides of the two issues and a sampling of authority figures pro and con, the results flipped dramatically.

In other words, with the right campaign, assisted suicide could be defeated despite the very widespread support in the initial polls, but the ballot measure banning porn would probably lose no matter what, even though it was way ahead in the initial polling. But both would require considerable funding to get the various movement messages out and duplicate the efforts that we tested in the mock polls.

In the case of the porn referendum, the model poll showed that librarians were the most important authority figures on this issue, and if they presented a message of "no censorship," a majority of Maine voters, probably a large majority, would vote against the ban. I concluded that the porn ban was dead on arrival, although I was still somewhat suspicious by the ease with which voters had flipped.

The shift in sentiment captured by the beginning favorability and the subsequent unfavorability was striking, so striking in fact that I mistrusted the results; the size of the shift seemed too massive. So I insisted on doing a focus group to see if the results could be duplicated. Now, focus groups are based on science (you have to properly select the target audience very carefully) and art (as moderator, you have to do performance art and see if in the first forty-five minutes you can swing the group one way and, after a short break, see if you can swing the group another way).

I chose a focus group of fifteen, all women who were either undecided or leaning toward voting for the ban. As I remember it, half of them were women who worked at home; the rest worked outside the home.

In the first half of the session, using the authority figures from the poll and the best of the influence vectors ("If you knew . . .") I tried to duplicate a possible election sequence. Once I brought in the librarians and themes such as "some people say that while porn is bad, it shouldn't be banned and certainly should be punished"), the group voted decisively against the ban.

After the break, I couldn't get the group to move back toward favoring the ban, even after I had my assistant go to a nearby smoke shop and buy four or five raunchy examples of locally available porn. Surely these would flip the group back to supporting the ban I thought. Some women were appalled, some refused to look at the material, and some shrugged as if to say "no big deal." But they would not budge. I think the final vote was something like ten or eleven against the ban to four or five favoring it.

The porn referendum was indeed dead on arrival, I concluded.

By contrast, the overwhelming initial support for the concept of assisted suicide would melt away under a barrage by the best authority figures (doctors, nurses, hospice officials, the American Medical Association) and themes (to accomplish the suicide, you had to take a lot of pills, these pills could come through the mail and get into the wrong hands, and palliative care at the end of life was already available).

But hardcore support for the assisted suicide law remained firm and did not melt away as it did on pornography. It would take a hard, well-financed campaign to break that proposal close enough to make a statewide NO vote possible. Positions on assisted suicide were simply harder to move than on a ban on pornography with concomitant penalties.

So, the Portland Diocese faced a dilemma requiring the Judgment of Solomon.

When I asked the Diocese which referendum they cared about most, Mark, like Solomon, didn't split the baby in half. He was adamant that assisted suicide was far more important.

A CARDINAL TRUMPS A BISHOP . . . AND A DR. DEMENTO

I replied then, the choice is simple, don't put any money into trying to pass the porn referendum and keep your powder dry for the assisted suicide campaign. "You'll need all your resources for that one."

Perhaps a hard sell, but the correct call I believed.

Just how hard a sell I had no idea.

First, after convincing the chancellery staff and public affairs people, there had to be a meeting with the big Catholic lay donors, people who cared about a variety of public church issues and would donate considerable sums to make it happen.

Imagine if you will, people wanting to donate money for their causes and seeing polling numbers that showed one of their issues, the ban on porn, way ahead and the other one, assisted suicide, way behind. All well and good. But then they were told by some weird college professor and pollster with the nickname "Dr. Demento" *not* to get involved with the one that looked like they would win for sure and to put all their resources into the one that was behind 3-1. "Stay out of porn, it's going to lose big-time, but don't give up on defeating assisted suicide."

Incredulity reigned.

I don't think I've ever seen a group so stupefied.

I thought one man was going to faint, shaking his head this way and that. Another looked so quizzical I thought he would have a seizure.

Put simply, the big donors were nonplussed. Palpable doubt filled the air and the room.

One even ventured,

"But professor that's insane," one donor ventured. "We're way ahead" in the porn referendum. "We can put it over the top."

Much more shaking of heads.

Much more whispering and more shaking of heads.

The lead donor then stood up, his face showing marked disbelief and said incredulously, "So you're saying avoid the one we're leading 3-1 and go for the one we're behind 3-1? That makes no sense."

"Well, the internals of the polls tell us exactly that," I shrugged. "These issues are very fluid and both will flip in opposite directions if there are real campaigns. Of course, you are free to disregard the findings.

But my professional opinion is don't waste your effort on porn if you really care about assisted suicide."

End of meeting. Very disgruntled donors filed out the door still muttering about the need for new consultants.

Mark called the next day, indicating that while the donors were still bewildered and chagrined, his boss, Bishop Joseph Gerry, understood his arguments on the need to follow the polling results, and the Diocese would not be funding the anti-porn referendum. They cared too much about assisted suicide and knew that would be a much harder campaign.

I believed that was the right decision. I felt we had done a professional job projecting the forthcoming referendum and that the conclusions of the poll, while counterintuitive, were the correct ones.

Sometimes, in politics as in life, "Do Nothing" is the best advice possible even though very few clients ever appreciate that advice. Some even may ask "Why should we?" to which sometimes one can only reply, "Because I told you to."

So the summer arrived and unfolded. Mark and the other Catholic operatives seemed pleased to be keeping their powder dry for the other issue as the Christian Civic League ran with the campaign.

But then like a bolt of the proverbial lightning, something changed dramatically.

With some ominous results.

I blame the heat.

It was a warm summer in Boston and apparently Cardinal Law, the senior-ranking prelate of the Catholic Church in all of New England, came to Maine for some cooling relief in the Kennebunkport area. While enjoying himself in that fair city, he was accosted by an important Catholic woman who came up to him and harshly chided him and the church for not getting involved financially in the race to ban porn in Maine. By all accounts, the Cardinal was not pleased. Either by her tone or by the new knowledge as to what was brewing north of the Piscataqua River.

What are the odds?

A random meeting.

An irate parishioner.

A major authority figure accosted while on holiday.

A CARDINAL TRUMPS A BISHOP . . . AND A DR. DEMENTO

Who could have predicted the results that followed?

Not knowing anything about the issue or any of the polling or the reality of the situation—or not caring or having other much more important things on his mind—the Cardinal then called the Bishop and insisted that the Diocese get involved and put up funds for commercials and make a major effort from the pulpit to pass the anti-porn referendum.

I've always wondered if Bishop Gerry ever tried to talk the Cardinal out of that course of action. Probably not. I don't think you get to be a bishop unless you understand the iron law of hierarchy already and accept its many simple dictates.

All of that Church involvement of course was in vain.

The anti-porn measure ended up being truly crushed in November by the margin of 72 percent to 28 percent after, as predicted, all the librarians in the state rose as one to attack censorship, calling the proposed ordinance a threat to our free society. The focus group had foretold the future!

Somewhat later, the Cardinal resigned and went to live in Vatican City.

I do not believe the two events were linked by anything but happenstance.

A few cycles later, a grateful and exuberant Bishop Gerry flew down to Washington to receive a standing ovation from the other American bishops for his upset victory in Maine over assisted suicide, 51 to 49 percent—what those of us in the political biz call "too close for comfort."

We probably could have used another 1,000 gross rating points of TV in that one just to be on the safe side. But that money was long gone in the unsuccessful struggle against the state's librarians.

THE COURT JESTER
Dennis Bailey

It was the day before the 1994 Democratic Primary, and I was sitting in my office at the Tom Allen for Governor campaign when a staffer came in with a quizzical look on her face and said, "Dennis? Angus King is on the phone for you."

I said a silent hallelujah.

It was baffling to the staffer that Angus, who was running what was essentially a rival campaign for governor as an independent, would be calling his potential opponent's office the day before the election. But I was pretty sure I knew what the call was about. It meant that after tomorrow, in which Tom was expected to lose the nomination to Joe Brennan, I might still have a job.

I knew Angus only slightly. When I was a reporter at *Maine Times*, the state's renowned alternative newspaper, Angus was the paper's lawyer. I would sometimes see him at office get-togethers and parties, and he would call me occasionally for background when a story I had written was going to be featured on *Maine Watch*, the public television show he hosted. Later, I got to know his wife, Mary Herman, when I was a reporter for the *Portland Press Herald* covering the Maine Legislature and she was working as a lobbyist.

When it was announced in the fall of 1993 that I would be leaving my job as communications director for Congressman Tom Andrews after three years, Angus was the first of several candidates who were gearing up to run for governor to call me about possibly joining his campaign. I met with him at his office in Brunswick, but as an independent with no primary ahead of him, he wasn't ready to fully staff up. So a few weeks later, I told him I had decided to go with Tom Allen, a Portland city councilor who was entering the Democratic Primary for governor. He understood, wished me well, and made a vague suggestion that depending on how the primary worked out, maybe we would talk again later in the year. But there was no pledge or promise or anything like that. It was just him being polite, I thought.

So when the baffled staffer came in to tell me Angus was on the line, I was instantly relieved. That's the thing about political campaigns. You work like hell for many months, twelve- to eighteen-hour days, every day, every weekend, and if you lose, the curtain immediately comes down and staffers are left wandering, dazed with resumes in their hands wondering what's next in their life, or where their next paycheck will come from. I was lucky. I was being thrown a lifeline.

Angus was cordial on the call. "Good luck tomorrow," he said, "I hope it works out. But if it doesn't, let's get together and talk."

So, a few days later, after Tom's second-place showing in the primary, I was once again talking to Angus. He offered me the position of press secretary, and I told him I'd take it. But I had three conditions, at least one of which I thought he'd never accept and would likely be a deal breaker.

First, I told him, I had shared custody of my young daughter, and that meant there would be times when I would have to be with her instead of staying late nights and weekends at the campaign office. He assured me that his campaign was a family operation and that wouldn't be a problem.

Second, I had a plane ticket for a week in Paris in August for a friend's wedding that I really didn't want to miss. Again, he said it would be okay, things are pretty slow in the doldrums of August, he said. I would come back tan and rested for the big push after Labor Day. Of course, Kay Rand, the campaign manager, never let me live it down that I had negotiated a vacation in the middle of the campaign while she and many other staffers were stuck slaving away at the Brunswick campaign office. I felt mildly guilty when I called from a pay phone near the Arc de Triomphe to check in. Did I detect some resentment?

But for some reason, I really didn't think he would go for my third condition, the deal breaker. I was in a rock band, I told him. I tried to assure him that it wouldn't take me away from the campaign very often (I lied) because we didn't practice that much and only played about every other weekend.

There was a pause.

"You're in a band?" he asked. I thought surely, he was reconsidering his offer. "I've always wanted to be in a band," he said. "Of course, I can't sing or play anything."

He asked me all kinds of questions: What kind of music did I play? Where could he come and see me? He actually seemed excited that he was hiring not only a press secretary but a house band to go with him.

A few months later, I learned more about his musical tastes. The Rolling Stones were playing a concert at Foxboro Stadium over Labor Day weekend, the Voodoo Lounge Tour. Through a friend, I managed to get tickets for most of the staff. A few days before the concert, Angus called me on his car phone. He sounded upset.

"Dennis, what's this I hear about you getting Rolling Stones tickets for everyone?" he said.

In a mild panic, I stammered a bunch of excuses to assure him that it wouldn't take a lot of time from the campaign, that the concert was on a Sunday, the day before Labor Day, it would be a good break for the team, etc.

"No—that's not the problem," he said. "The problem is you didn't get a ticket for *me*."

Oh.

He went on to tell me he was a big Stones fan and had seen them on their Steel Wheels tour five years earlier. So, I called my friend back and hustled up two more tickets for the candidate and his wife to join us on our campaign outing to the big show.

That was just the beginning of our musical partnership. During the campaign and after, he would often show up at my gigs and join us onstage to sing and play the cowbell to "Honky Tonk Woman," a performance we repeated at the big inaugural gala in the cavernous Brunswick Naval Air Station. He was wearing a tuxedo coat with tails

THE COURT JESTER

that had "GOV" in big white letters on the back like Governor William J. Le Petomane in *Blazing Saddles*, one of Angus' favorite (and highly politically incorrect) movies. A photo of us onstage was on the front page of the following Monday's Brunswick *Times Record*, and it became the unofficial governor's portrait. He signed dozens of copies of the photo for friends and staff. On mine, he wrote: "Dennis, thanks for helping me to realize a life's ambition. Your friend, Angus."

I never asked him if he meant that his life's ambition was to be a governor or a rock 'n' roll star. I'm thinking it's the latter.

If people didn't realize by then that Angus was a different kind of governor, they would soon. Most politicians are overly programmed, stiff, not very humorous. Angus was different. Curious, engaging, always ready for a chuckle. He was the only candidate I ever met who could completely captivate a boardroom of crusty CEOs, then go out across the street to a seedy biker bar and have the same effect on a gang of beer-swilling Harley riders. It was, and remains, a rare talent.

Once, during the summer when the legislature was out and the Capitol building was ghostly and quiet, a couple of tourists from New York wandered into my office, which was outside the governor's office just off the Hall of Flags. They were touring every state capital and had questions about the building and Maine. I finally said, "Would you like to meet the governor?" They seemed surprised as I led them into the governor's office, where Angus was sitting at his desk. He got up and smiled as I introduced him to the tourists. He asked them questions about their trip, regaled them with a few familiar stories about Maine, and we left.

On the way out, they looked at me and said, "Who was that? That's not the governor." They just couldn't believe that they could walk into the governor's office without an appointment, without going through layers of security, without being somebody important. That wouldn't happen in Albany, they assured me.

I came to believe that my job as press secretary included another very important function: the unofficial Court Jester of the King Administration. It seemed like Angus appreciated my sense of humor, the way I treated the world as my straight man, and he came to rely on me for comic relief as he dealt with the critical issues of the day. I was always good for taking the air out of heavy meetings and bringing everything down to earth.

In one meeting as he was discussing falling student math scores with education officials, he turned to me (as he often did to see if I was awake or paying attention) and asked, "Well Dennis, what do you think?"

"I don't know, governor," I said. "I went to Livermore Falls High School, a really small town. Math in my school was quite simple. It was just 'one, two, shitload.' That was about it."

The room erupted in laughter, and then they all got back to doing serious work.

But it wasn't all fun and games. There was hard, tedious work too.

Just after he came into the office, we were working on a major speech to the legislature. I was going back and forth from my office to his, working on drafts and edits. At one point, Angus called me on my phone and asked me to bring in a copy of a chart about the state's economy that we were working from. I told him that I had left it with him on his desk.

"I don't have it," he snapped, "you have it. You probably can't find it, your desk is such a mess. Bring it in now." He slammed down the phone.

I walked over to his office, and when I entered, he was furiously typing away on his Mac and didn't even look up. I rustled through the papers on *his* (messy) desk, found the chart where I had left it, and handed it to him. He snatched it from my hand, said "Thanks," and went back to typing.

I was pissed.

Furious.

I went home that night and couldn't stop thinking about the way I felt I was treated. I was living with my girlfriend at the time and was inconsolable. "He was an asshole," I told her. I said if this was the way things were going to be, I didn't know if I could work for him. She told me I should talk to him about it.

So, first thing the next morning, I screwed up my courage and walked slowly toward his office to tell the governor of Maine he was an asshole. I was really going to do it. My heart was pounding as I opened the door, but before I could say anything, he looked up. "Hey Dennis," he said, "About yesterday, I'm sorry about that. I was a real asshole. But these things happen, it gets crazy around here, I apologize. You know I love you."

To say I was instantly disarmed is an understatement.

"What are you talking about," I said. "That thing? That was nothing, no big deal, forget about it."

Yeah right, it never crossed my mind.

I remember walking out, thinking to myself that it must have bothered him almost as much as it had bothered me. And I can work for this guy. He has a heart—another thing that makes him different from a lot of politicians.

During my time as communications director, we nearly always held a daily press availability for the State House reporters, what we called "press time," where the reporters could all gather in the governor's office and fire random questions at him. I know that press handlers for governors in other states thought it was crazy to allow unplanned, unscripted access to the governor. But Angus, unlike a lot of the stuffed-shirt, robotic politicians elsewhere, can actually think and talk on his feet.

I would usually go into his office just before press time to let him know what the reporters were likely to ask, and what issues of the day were on their minds. We didn't always get it right.

One day, at the end of press time, a reporter asked a question that blindsided us. A conservative activist had just started circulating a petition to get a question on the ballot to ban what was then called "same-sex marriage." (This was many years before Maine legalized gay marriage in 2012.) The reporter wanted to know if Angus would support it or oppose it.

Unprepared for the question, Angus stumbled a bit, saying basically that he'd have to think about it, that it would ultimately be up to voters, and he wasn't sure if Maine was ready for it, and so forth. As the press filed out, Angus motioned me over to his desk. He was worried about his answer.

"How did that come out," he asked. "Was it okay? I hadn't really thought about that issue."

Once again fulfilling my role as Court Jester, I told him: "What you should have said is, 'I thought same-sex marriage was already legal. I've been married for ten years and get the same sex about every week.'"

I don't think I had ever seen, before or since, Angus laugh as hard as he did that day. I mean, bent over, holding his stomach in a full-body grip of hilarity. There was a group of businesspeople filing into the office for the next meeting who quite naturally wanted to know what was so funny. Angus, once he had recovered, just didn't feel it was appropriate to share.

So I guess that truly, among all my various roles, "Court Jester" still ranks high among my favorites.

STORIES WE DON'T USUALLY TELL
Ethan Strimling and Phil Harriman

Phil Harriman: Mr. Mayor, I know you take politics as seriously as a heart attack, but I was wondering if maybe I could get you to lighten up for just a minute?

Ethan Strimling: Not now, Phil. I am parsing the town-by-town vote patterns of Franco-Americans to see how we can increase the Democratic margin by 2.3 percent in Androscoggin County this fall.

Phil: Did you see *The Shining*? All work and no play makes Ethan a dull boy. Can you please lift your nose off of those crosstabs for a second to lend me your fingertips?

Ethan: Anything for my brother from another mother. What can I do for you?

Phil: We just received a fine request from Chris Potholm, Dennis Bailey, and Dave Emery, three well-known figures of mirth to those on the campaign trails in Maine, asking us to come up with some amusing stories in their new book, *Real Life, Real Funny*.

Ethan: That is a dangerous offer to a couple former State Senators. Let me start. Do you remember Tom Andrews?

Phil: Sure, Maine's former Congressman from southern Maine by way of "The People's Republic of Portland."

Ethan: A true hero to me. He gave me my first paid job on a campaign, and later I worked for him in Washington, DC. He showed me that you could stick to your values and even win. People value those with a true north in politics, as long as you are honest about it.

Phil: Tom's true north was powered by a jet heading west. And by "west," I mean at supersonic speed to the left. No wonder he was your hero.

Ethan: Indeed! Love that man. Anyway, as I mentioned, I got my first paid job in politics working for him in the 1990 Democratic Primary for the First Congressional District. He was a longshot running against a couple of established Democrats, including Libby Mitchell, who would later become the first and only woman in the country to be elected both Speaker of the Maine House and President of the Maine Senate, and Attorney General James Tierney.

Phil: Formidable competition. If this was your first paid political job, I take it you were issued a clipboard to check off on the volunteers who actually showed up for their "essential" duties to shake campaign signs outside television studios before debates?

Ethan: Not even prestigious enough to be issued a clipboard! I was simply the sign guy! My job was to paint, build, and put up wooden signs all over southern Maine. A glorious entry into politics. Which actually gets me to my story. As anyone in politics knows, signs are both the bane of any campaign and an essential piece. But not a necessity in the way you might think.

Phil: I agree with you there. Most volunteers think the candidate with more signs wins. Signs are more psychological to keep your volunteers calm than anything else.

Ethan: Exactly! And for the candidate, especially. Who among us had not had a candidate flip out because their opponent was winning the sign war. Well, this is my story. You see, back around Memorial Day of 1990, literally weeks before the primary, I got a frantic call from our field director, Joe Cowie, one of the best in the business. He told me that Tom was furious because he had driven to an event in Wells, and along Route 1 he had barely seen a single one of our signs. And, of course, he had seen dozens for his opponents.

Phil: Wait a minute. Route 1 at that time of year is almost exclusively used by tourists. No sane Mainer, and certainly few Maine voters, drives that stretch unless they have no choice. I hope he didn't tell you to go plaster the southern half of Route 1 with signs?

STORIES WE DON'T USUALLY TELL

Ethan: He did not, because you are exactly right. As useless as signs are for winning, they are even more useless on a public road mostly driven on by people who don't vote in Maine. However, the reason Joe called is because Tom was going to be driving to an event in Camden the next morning.

Phil: I think I know where this is going.

Ethan: Yup. Joe told me to gather up as many wooden signs as I had in the garage and, leaving at 3 a.m., drive the route Tom would be taking through the Midcoast and plaster the sides of the road with "Andrews for Congress" signs that he would see.

Phil: Candidate therapy session. Classic.

Ethan: That's not the best part. Once Tom finished his event in Camden and was driving home, my instructions were to follow him back, about a half an hour behind, and pull up every one of the signs so we could deploy them somewhere more useful in the final ten days.

Phil: Ha! Keeping your candidate happy is one of the most important parts of a campaign. And did it work?

Ethan: Like a charm. As soon as Tom walked into the campaign office on Congress Street in Portland, he told Joe how impressed he was with all the signs he saw. That it looked like our grassroots campaign was showing results! Little did he know the "grassroots" had taken them all down within a couple hours of being put up. Luckily, he didn't choose to drive that route again.

Phil: Great story. I have one about another renowned Portland liberal, not named Strimling.

Ethan: We Portland liberals come from good stock.

Phil: Before I do, let me remind you that Portland's proudest son and Mayor, Governor Percival Baxter—who cobbled together thousands of acres of land that he then donated to the State of Maine to create Baxter State Park—was a Republican.

Ethan: Ah, for the heady days when Republicans actually cared about the environment!

Phil: The other Portland liberal I'm talking about is Jerry Conley Jr. We served together in the Maine Senate.

Ethan: Great guy. And his father, Jerry Conley Sr., became president of the Maine Senate as another great Portland liberal, with a classic sense of humor and goodwill.

Phil: The Senate was in session. A very busy day of votes on bills coming back to us from committees was ahead. The Chamber is packed with staff, lobbyists, media, commissioners, and more. Jerry comes waltzing into the Senate Chamber stopping to chitchat with lobbyists along the way. Eventually, he sits down and begins working his way through a tall stack of mail and "information" piled on his desk by advocates for or against the bills we were voting on.

Ethan: I remember those days. As the session winds down, there are more papers and more lobbyists. All looking to take just a minute of your time to see if they can change your position on a bill when no one else is looking.

Phil: Well, on this particular day, Senate President Dennis Dutremble was feverishly moving bills along, gavel banging away while Secretary of the Senate Joy O'Brien is reading every bill title out loud, as is her job. She comes to one that would have our biologists determine how many moose could be harvested annually, instead of leaving it to the legislature.

Ethan: "Harvest." You make it sound like innocently picking tomatoes off of a vine, when, of course, you mean shoot and kill! They train them to pull sleighs in Aroostook County.

Phil: Well, Jerry hears this title read and, for the first time all day, quickly pushes the button on his desk to be recognized. He then proceeds to ask President Dutremble whether we are indeed debating the moose harvesting bill? Whether this bill is about where and how many moose can be hunted? The president answers in the affirmative.

Phil: Well, Jerry launches into a rant the way only a Portland liberal named Conley can. He waxes on and on about how the Maine moose is our beloved State Animal. It's on our state seal, which is even stitched into the carpet in the Maine Senate!

Ethan: As I recall, there are a few stuffed ones lingering around the State House on display as our pride and joy.

Phil: Finally, to cap it off, red-veined and venting on why we should not be hunting Maine moose at all, he decries in all seriousness, "Mr. President, the Maine moose is the only game animal in Maine where you can have your picture taken with it *before* you shoot it!" Much to his surprise, everyone in the Senate Chamber roared in laughter and President Dutremble had to bang the gavel and yell, "The Senate will come to order, the Senate *will* come to order!" Jerry realized how accidentally good his close was, took a bow, and sat down.

Ethan: Classic. But did his oratory actually turn any votes?

Phil: Of course not. This was the Senate, also known as the "muffin club" (because House members think all we do is eat muffins in the "upper" chamber), where everything gets decided well before we get to the floor.

Ethan: Okay, I have another one. Okay to make fun of myself this time?

Phil: If you don't, we will. Also, I and the readers are anxious to know which of the thousands of true situations *you* generated will be chosen.

Ethan: When I ran for Congress in 2008, we decided to pull a page from the Paul Wellstone playbook. If you don't know Wellstone, he was a very progressive U.S. Senator from Minnesota. Another hero of mine whom I was lucky enough to spend a weekend with when he was deciding whether to run for President in 2000. He foolishly took my advice.

Phil: Why am I not surprised that all your heroes seem to rise from the Bella Abzug wing of the Democratic Party?

Ethan: Nice reference. We'll let our readers look her up. Anyway, back in 2008, we pulled a page from Senator Wellstone, who, when he first ran for U.S. Senate, bought an old school bus and drove it all over the state spreading the good word about his campaign. In my case, we rented a tour bus that a volunteer had been driving for a local operator and took off for a tour from Kittery to Camden.

Phil: I think John McCain stole that idea before you with his Straight Talk Express.

Ethan: He did indeed. In the end, it worked about as well for him as it did for me. But I digress. My story begins with us renting this Greyhound and decorating it with our campaign materials. We decked it out with all kinds of signs and slogans like "People before profit," "Raise the minimum wage," "End the war in Iraq." You know, some of the greatest hits from the early 2000s.

Phil: Oldies but goodies, as my generation likes to say about ourselves.

Ethan: Once we had the bus all souped up, we traversed the district and met thousands of voters. When the day was done, our volunteer returned the bus to his boss no worse for the wear. Or so we thought . . .

Phil: Did you forget to leave the tank full of gas, I mean recharge the batteries?

Ethan: I wish. My campaign manager, the incomparable Corey Hascall, got a call two days later from the operator saying there was a problem with some of the "decorations" we had put on the bus. It turns out that the markers our volunteers had used on the sides of the bus and the windows were indelible! That is, they were written with permanent markers!

[Editors' Note: For those unfamiliar with Corey, she is very well-known for her campaign management skills and her being the political recipient of the Mother Teresa International Award for her babysitting of young Ethan, and even old Ethan, as he wandered around the political playing fields of Maine often seemingly clueless.]

Phil: We all seek a legacy. Perhaps yours remains on the side of that bus now rusting away in some field alongside Route 1. Here's one from me from the campaign trail.

Ethan: You campaigning? Being a born and raised Yarmouth townie, I would have thought you could just declare your candidacy and wait for Election Day.

Phil: My State Senate district celebrated diversity by having not only Yarmouth but Freeport, Durham, Pownal, and Brunswick.

STORIES WE DON'T USUALLY TELL

Ethan: Not exactly the kind of diversity that most of us are talking about these days when we talk about America being a melting pot but do go on.

Phil: Rest assured, those other towns were not going to rubber stamp a "Yarmouth townie," as you say. I had to be on the move and in touch with the different town priorities and personalities, if I had a chance to get reelected.

Ethan: All politics is local, as someone named Tip once said to a guy named The Gipper.

Phil: With a fistful of brochures and a smile worth a couple bucks, I knocked on a door in Brunswick. A man opens it and, with a screen door between us, I introduce myself and proceed to deliver my elevator message.

Ethan: Been there, done that.

Phil: When I'm finished, he opens the screen door and steps out. At this point I don't know if he's going to shake my hand or strangle me. He puts his hands on his hips and proceeds to deliver a filibuster state of the state address about how we have too much government over regulations, blah, blah.

Ethan: "Blah, blah, blah" is right!

Phil: Finally, he says, "By the way, I do know who you are and I will vote for you. But only if you can make me just one promise."

Ethan: Uh, oh.

Phil: I'm listening, thinking he is going to ask me to vote against all new taxes and spending, which means I'm a shoo-in for his vote.

Ethan: Did he turn out to be a liberal who wanted to tax the rich and fund our schools?

Phil: Nope. The promise he asked for was that I not make any speeches on the floor of the Senate, never propose any new laws, and never, ever, push "Yes" when I vote!

Ethan: Ha! An anarchist who wanted you to go up there and be a couch potato on the government dime! I wish more of you Republicans did that. What did you say?

Phil: I smiled that Yarmouth smile my momma taught me so well, backed down off the porch, and said, "Don't forget to vote!"

Ethan: I have many more awkward moments at the doors than that one. Someday I'll tell you about how I referred to an oak tree as an "acorn tree" when talking to a gardener. Pretty sure I didn't get that vote. But let me give you one more story from the floor of the Senate, literally. In my second term, my two seatmates were Democratic Senator Dennis Damon of Trenton and Democratic Senator Bill Diamond of Windham.

Phil: A distinguished crew.

Ethan: While I have a million stories about Senator Damon and me—including an eventful car ride the two of us took with Stump Merrill, former Yankees skipper, who was said to have quite a command of the words Ralph Waldo Emerson was thinking of when he said, "The language of the street is always strong." For those who don't know Senator Diamond, he's had a very storied career in public service, having served over twenty-five years in the Maine Legislature and as our forty-fifth Secretary of State.

Phil: He actually started serving in the legislature before I did! That goes back a few years.

Ethan: Which brings me to my story. Although Senator Diamond was almost twenty-five years my senior, the guy ran twenty-five miles a week, bench pressed twice his weight on a regular basis and generally kept himself as fit as a fiddle.

Phil: It takes hard work to keep your chest above your drawers.

Ethan: Speak for yourself. Or, as our readers are about to learn, maybe I shouldn't speak so loudly. In the waning hours of another marathon session toward the end of the 122nd legislature, we were all bored stiff waiting for some amendment to be drafted.

Phil: I remember those boring moments well; it was like watching paint dry.

Ethan: So, I decided it might be a good idea to have some fun. I pushed my button to be acknowledged by the president, stood up, and loudly proclaimed (I paraphrase): "Madame President, you may not realize this, but the good senator from Cumberland County, to my right in both geography and ideology (it was not hard at all to be to my right ideologically), has repeatedly claimed that he, having recently entered his sixth decade, could beat me, having not yet even a single gray hair on my head, in a pushup contest! As I hope you understand, I cannot allow this indignity to stand and I request permission that the well of the Senate be cleared for this challenge to be engaged and resolved. That is, of course, if my good seatmate is not scared to put his actions where his words are."

Phil: You asked for a solemn occasion in the august Senate Chamber to do pushups? Never a shy one, that is for sure. What did Senator Diamond say?

Ethan: He immediately stood up and mumbled under his breath, "The first to fifty it shall be," as he marched to the well, discarding his jacket and tie into the lap of Senator John Martin. As I scrambled behind him in a panic, realizing that perhaps I had been a bit too brave, the president gave the countdown to start. I dare say I didn't pump out my thirtieth before the good Senator from Cumberland was done and walking back to his seat. All I can say is, thank God we were not officially in session and none of this was recorded on video. My arms were very sore for a week.

Phil: Too bad. Nowadays you would be going viral on YouTube and picking up sponsors to fund your next grand idea.

Ethan: Except in this case, conservatives would be the ones paying for clicks to watch me get humiliated.

Phil: Well, I think that is enough humiliation for the both of us. Either we made people laugh with these stories, or they are crying that this is what politics is like behind the scenes. Either way, glad you have a sense of humor about it all.

Ethan: You have to. Now, back to my voter crosstabs. After all, someone has to save our democracy around here! Maybe this whole book will get readers to really appreciate the era when politics was fun.

ARREST THE JESUS LADY?
Larry Benoit

NOTHING REALLY PREPARED ME FOR THE MOST INTERESTING JOB I EVER had, except that coming from Maine, our culture here prizes "getting things done" and "where there's a will, there's a way." In 1994, I was nominated by the Majority Leader, Senator George Mitchell, and elected Sergeant at Arms and Doorkeeper of the Senate by unanimous consent. I was deeply grateful for Senator Mitchell's trust and confidence in me to take on this important position in the U.S. Senate.

The title is actually quite antiquated, because the historical security and law enforcement responsibilities of the Sergeant at Arms are only a small part of their contemporary responsibilities. These include an amazing number of items: computer systems, telecommunications, printing and copy shop, beauty shop, barber shop, Senate Page School, photography and television studios, and many other duties. The current budget is approximately $200 million with approximately nine hundred civilian employees, plus approximately half of the U.S. Capitol Police force on the payroll.

The post produced a number of humorous and challenging tasks for me. For example, not long after I was sworn in, a report appeared in a local newspaper that I was threatening to evict Jesus Christ from the grounds of the U.S. Capitol.

"Wait, what?" I thought. "This seems pretty strange."

I didn't know anything about the matter, let alone my role in it, so I quickly buzzed my deputy, Bob Bean, who had been working for the Office of Sergeant at Arms for more than twenty years and knew all about the history of Jesus on Capitol Hill. Incidentally, Bob also knew many secrets of the Senate, which will never be told, as sadly he died tragically at age forty-three of a heart attack.

I quickly learned that Rita Warren, a Christian faith activist, for many years had hauled a life-size mannequin of Jesus to the Capitol grounds. Many visitors and tourists were attracted to her Jesus, some taking photographs and listening to Rita—the "Jesus Lady"—share her message of faith. In the meantime, she had been engaged in a recurring dispute with the U.S. Capitol Police over where and when she could display Jesus.

Just what I needed my first weeks on the job, taking on a devoted Christian lady and her followers.

In my capacity as Senate Sergeant at Arms, I was ultimately responsible for security of the Senate wing of the Capitol and also served with House Sergeant at Arms Werner Brandt and Capitol Architect George White on the U.S. Capitol Police Board, which oversaw the Capitol Police and all security matters.

Unbeknownst to me at the time, the Capitol Police had asked Rita to relocate Jesus from the steps of the U.S. House of Representatives to another location on the campus for security reasons. If she didn't comply, Jesus would not be allowed on the campus. But Rita was upset, because in her mind, the new location was not a prime spot to attract the attention of tourists and visitors to see Jesus and learn about her crusade. Apparently, she had mistakenly assumed that the *brand-new and inexperienced* Senate Sergeant at Arms was somehow behind this dastardly order.

Of course, the last thing I wanted was a dispute with Jesus and the "Jesus Lady," and she probably realized that as well so I quickly encouraged the Capitol Police to work out a solution that balanced Rita's First Amendment right to free speech with the security needs of Congress.

The Jesus Lady remains a good introduction to my job as Sergeant at Arms for the U.S. Senate. Rita Warren continued to bring Jesus to the Capitol for more than two decades until passing away at age ninety-two in 2020. And I continued to meet some very interesting—and challenging—people throughout my career.

Among the ceremonial duties, the Senate Sergeant at Arms is responsible for receiving and escorting visiting heads of state into the Capitol. During my tenure, they included president of South Africa Nelson Mandela, King Hussein of Jordan, Prime Minister of Israel Yitzak Rabin, and President of Russia Boris Yeltsin. While merely ceremonial in most aspects, my interaction with these leaders was a fascinating and rewarding experience.

President Yeltsin was one of the most interesting and provided his own set of challenges. He was scheduled to meet with key members of the Senate leadership on September 28, 1994. While awaiting his arrival, we received a message from our liaison with the Secret Service that he was delayed. He was reportedly hung over from a late night of drinking at Blair House and was behind schedule; otherwise the details were scant.

Unfortunately, Yeltsin was addicted to alcohol, which not only hampered Russia's transition from a failed communist empire to an aspiring but struggling democratic state, but also caused a number of us severe heartburn. When he finally arrived, I welcomed him at the Carriage Entrance and shook his large and meaty hand. He was just as he appeared on television—a bear of a man, who had confronted and routed communist "*pustchists*" atop a tank outside Russia's parliament. I escorted him to Senator Mitchell's office, where he met with Senate leadership, held a brief news conference, and departed immediately thereafter.

Nearly fifteen years later, we learned that during his visit to Washington in the wee hours of the morning the "Secret Service agents had discovered Yeltsin alone on Pennsylvania Avenue, dead-drunk, clad in his underwear, yelling for a taxi," according to Taylor Branch in his book *The Clinton Tapes*. That could perhaps explain his demeanor and the glazed look in his eyes.

King Hussein and Prime Minister Rabin visited the Capitol on July 26, 1994, to meet with Congressional leadership and address a joint session of Congress. The occasion was set to mark a peace agreement between Israel and Jordan and help advance a comprehensive framework for peace in the region through the Oslo Accords.

I greeted both leaders when they arrived at the Senate and escorted them along with many members to the House of Representatives. While gathering in the Speaker's office before their speeches, I had an opportunity to chat with both leaders.

King Hussein was incredibly warm and engaging, which matched his legendary reputation. Nearly twenty years later, I became a licensed amateur radio operator and incidentally learned that the king was an avid amateur radio operator, who matter-of-factly communicated with hundreds of hams worldwide as "Hussein" with call sign JY1. Many hams did not realize that they were chatting with the king of Jordan. By the time I was active in amateur radio, the king had passed away at age sixty-three in 1999.

For his part, Prime Minister Rabin was fidgety. A well-known chain-smoker, he always managed to find a moment for a brief cigarette. A courageous man and true hero, he was taking great personal and political risks in pursuit of a perilous path to peace in the Middle East. Tragically, he was assassinated in 1995 by an Israeli extremist who opposed the Oslo Accords. In retrospect, his death may have doomed the last good prospect for a two-state solution with a durable peace among Israelis and Palestinians. Today, nothing seems more distant—almost impossible to imagine.

It's difficult to articulate my emotions upon meeting Nelson Mandela, president of South Africa. I welcomed him at the Senate Carriage Entrance and subsequently escorted him to the House of Representatives for a speech before a joint session of Congress. We chatted while he was waiting in the Speaker's office to give his address. I told him that I was in awe of his courage, sacrifice, and persistence in his decades-long struggle to free native Africans from the chains of Apartheid. He carried a quiet strength and kindness, speaking in a soft and deliberate manner.

I felt in the presence of imperfect greatness, but is there really any other kind? Imprisoned for twenty-seven years and freed by President DeKlerk in his mission to end Apartheid, Mandela negotiated with DeKlerk to guide South Africa through an occasionally violent transition to become a constitutional democracy with universal suffrage. While he was not another Gandhi, having been a communist, trained in guerilla warfare, and sometimes blind to corruption and violent crime within the African National Congress leadership, Mandela was nevertheless a great man and a formulative leader of his people.

Perhaps most surprising of all, one of my remits dealt with arresting severely disabled protesters, for another of my numerous responsibilities was the security of the Senate wing of the Capitol. The Senate was about to take up amendments to the Americans with Disabilities Act (ADA), which brought on a challenge that I never expected—arresting severely disabled people! Why would the chief law enforcement official of the Senate do such a cruel thing?

I was working in my office on the third floor when I was notified that an illegal demonstration was underway outside the office of Senator Robert Dole, Republican Leader, while another group of protestors were outside the north entrance of the Capitol and were trying to force their way through secured doors.

Just what I needed, a situation calling for the arrest of severely disabled people in the Capitol.

Senator Dole was a key player in the effort to strengthen the ADA, but some disability rights groups were nevertheless disappointed that the amendments did not go far enough to expand the rights of people with disabilities. Disability rights advocates clandestinely organized a demonstration by bringing small groups of activists into the Capitol ostensibly for sightseeing and other business.

What irony to embarrass their champion—in politics, sometimes your friends are your worst enemies.

At a predetermined time, they all converged into the "closed" hallway outside Senator Dole's office and commenced a very loud demonstration with percussive instruments and screaming chants.

After being notified of the demonstration, I went to observe the situation and consulted with a Capitol Police captain on how they were handling the situation. The noise was utterly deafening, echoing off the stone surfaces and arched ceiling. After consulting with Dole's staff, we decided the demonstration would be allowed to continue for a few minutes, provided there was no violence or vandalism.

Several of the protesters were in wheelchairs and two were on four-wheeled stretchers. In due course, the Capitol Police announced that demonstrators would be arrested if they didn't disperse. Fortunately, most left, but some wanted to be arrested as their personal expression of civil disobedience in support of the needs and rights of Americans with disabilities. I spoke with three or four of them and confirmed that they *really* wanted to be arrested. One man, lying on a four-wheeled stretcher, had a portable respirator to assist with breathing and insisted that he be arrested. Again, I told them they were free to go, but several remained to be arrested.

I was very concerned about the safety and welfare of the disabled protesters. They were ushered into a nearby elevator, and I followed along with the arresting officers to a processing area in the basement of the Capitol. The Police handled the matter well, and all protesters were safely and respectfully processed and released without incident. I was very relieved and enjoyed more than my share of some oaky chardonnay that evening.

A final memory to share occurred when I was responsible for coordinating with the U.S. Air Force the transportation of the Senate delegation that attended Nixon's funeral at the Nixon Library, in Yorba Linda, California. I flew out with the delegation on LBJ's Boeing 707 Air Force One, which was surprisingly still in service.

The Nixon funeral was one of grand contradictions. A former president, disgraced by one of the worst political scandals in American history, was lauded for his major achievements in domestic and foreign affairs. It was attended by five presidents, former and present, representatives from eighty-five countries, and at least three felons convicted for their role in the Watergate scandal. It was sometimes surreal.

For a Maine native, serving as a multitasking Senate Sergeant at Arms, it was a very memorable experience. And not without a few anxious moments as well. Parenthetically, considering his progressive legislative record and foreign policy, Richard Nixon would qualify as a conservative Democrat today!

FINDING LEG ROOM ON THE CAMPAIGN TRAIL

Spiros Droggitis

IN 1973 AT THE END OF MY JUNIOR YEAR AT BOWDOIN, MY CLASSMATE Jed Lyons convinced me to stay on campus the week between graduation and reunion weekend. Many unlikely events followed that invitation—including the reelection of Senator Ed Muskie. One night we were attending a reunion party at one of the fraternity houses and Jed asked me if I knew Charlie Micoleau. I did not, and Jed introduced me to him. Little did I know at the time that introduction would be a career- and life-changing moment. Charlie was in the Bowdoin Class of 1963 and was back for his tenth-year reunion. Turns out, Charlie was Senator Ed Muskie's executive assistant. I told Charlie that I was a government major and would love to have an opportunity to work in Washington, DC.

I probably told him that I had attended Boys State in Orono my junior year of high school and that I had an interest in the workings of government and the legislative process. The Senate Watergate hearings had just begun. It seemed like an interesting time to be in Washington. After reunion weekend, I returned to Biddeford to continue my summer job working in the law office of former Biddeford Mayor Ted Gaulin, principally searching titles at the York County Courthouse in Alfred and not thinking much of my interaction with Charlie.

I returned to Bowdoin for my senior year, living in a house owned by the college with Jed and several other of our classmates. The house, which Jed named the Kinsey House in honor of a distinguished Bowdoin

FINDING LEG ROOM ON THE CAMPAIGN TRAIL

alumnus, was located in between the Dean's house and the Psi Upsilon frat house on Maine Street in Brunswick. My plan after graduation was to return to Biddeford, work in the family restaurant, the WonderBar Steak House, and apply to law school.

That was, until I got a call in the spring of 1974 from Washington, DC. It was Charlie Micoleau from his office asking if I was still interested in coming to Washington. I told him I was. He said I would be under Senator Muskie's patronage as a doorkeeper working for the Sargent-at-Arms of the U.S. Senate and that when the Senate was not in session, I would work in the Senator's office doing casework and other duties as assigned.

Now, I should mention that my cousin Lexi was married to Senator Muskie's son Steve. While I don't recall this family connection ever coming into play, it probably didn't hurt. I also recall Charlie saying that I would not be paid very much, probably ten thousand to twelve thousand dollars a year. I was shocked! At the time, I never dreamed that I would be making that kind of money.

I started in the U.S. Senate in July 1974. Doorkeepers enforce the Senate adopted rules of protocol in the Senate gallery. No talking, no photos, no writing, no standing, no protests. In other words, sit and listen to the Senate proceedings.

After a year or so, I was moved to a far more exciting position. I was a doorkeeper off the Senate floor in an area called the President's Room. This was a small, ornately decorated ceremonial room where, back in the day, presidents could come to sign legislation. It was rarely used for that purpose but became the area where national and local press would request to speak with Senators. When journalists like Roger Mudd, Connie Chung, and Sam Donaldson wanted to speak to a Senator, they would come to the President's Room and ask me or another of my colleagues to ask if the Senator was available to come off the Senate floor to speak to them.

On occasion, Don Larrabee, who covered Washington for Maine newspapers, would stop by seeking to speak with Senator Muskie or Senator Hathaway. It was always a pleasure seeing Mr. Larrabee. He was a true gentleman and was always genuinely interested to know how things were going in DC and back home in Biddeford.

As I mentioned, it was a very exciting time to be in Washington. It was on August 8, 1974, when as a result of the Watergate scandal, President Richard M. Nixon announced his intention to resign after revelations uncovered by the Senate hearings and other investigations. I remember that day vividly as I was housesitting in Charlie Micoleau's house in DC while the Micoleaus were on vacation in Maine. I watched President Nixon's announcement in the Micoleaus' den. Gerald R. Ford became president and he chose Nelson Rockefeller of New York to become his vice president. Senator Muskie gave the Democrat response to President Ford's State of the Union address in January 1976.

I recall one on my "duties as assigned" was to be a runner between the speechwriter Richard Goodwin and the typist who was typing the speech into a teleprompter. Mr. Goodwin had been a speechwriter for Presidents John F. Kennedy and Lyndon B. Johnson and was married to Presidential Historian Doris Kearns Goodwin. He was in the cafeteria in the basement of the Dirksen Senate Office Building handwriting on long yellow legal pads of paper and I would grab three or four pages at a time and run them up to the Russell Senate Office Building where they were being typed into the teleprompter.

It was all very chaotic and unorganized and, of course, it was well before modern information transmission capabilities, but it somehow seemed to all come together. One thing I recall is that Mr. Goodwin had the habit of chewing on the ends of plastic BIC pens. There must have been ten to fifteen pens on the tabletop with the tops chewed off.

In 1976, Senator Muskie was up for reelection. I don't recall the circumstances, but I was in Biddeford visiting family during the August recess and, since it was an election year, Congress may have been out of session for the conventions and for campaigning. One day someone from Senator Muskie's staff, most likely Gayle Cory, contacted me to see if I could drive Senator Muskie to Bath Iron Works for a ship dedication and launch. I don't recall Gayle's title, but she was the "fixer" in Senator Muskie's office. Gayle was from Bath, Maine, and knew everybody in

FINDING LEG ROOM ON THE CAMPAIGN TRAIL

Maine and in DC. Every good Congressional office has (or should have) a Gayle Cory. I said, sure I would drive the Senator.

Gayle said the only glitch was they didn't have a car so I had to use my own car, which I didn't own, so I had to use my father's. I was a little nervous since I had not had any real one-on-one interaction with the Senator. On the night before I was to pick him up, I got a call from my father at the WonderBar saying that there were Muskie people at the restaurant and that I should come down. When I arrived, Charlie Micoleau, the Senator's administrative assistant Maynard Toll, and I believe press secretary Bob Rose were sitting in a booth on the bar side of the restaurant.

I joined them for a beer. I told them since this was going to be my first interaction with the Senator, what should I do or say? After all, here was a man who was on a national ticket to be vice president of the United States and had run for president. They told me that the Senator was not one for small talk. But they did say that the Senator was a fan of the Washington Redskins, who were playing a pre-season game that evening against the Los Angeles Rams on the West Coast. They suggested that I watch the game so I would have something to chat about. So that evening I stayed up to watch the whole pre-season game which started at 9:00 p.m. and ended around midnight.

The next morning, I drove to Kennebunk Beach to pick up the Senator. Now, my father had an early '70s vintage Oldsmobile with bench seats. My father and I were about the same height, close to five foot seven, whereas Senator Muskie stood around six foot four. When he got into the front seat and swung his legs around, they bumped up against the dashboard. He looked at me and said, "Damn it, they always get me short drivers!" I hastily moved the seat back, extended my leg to be able to reach the gas pedal and we were on our way to Bath.

As we traveled north on the Maine Turnpike, the Senator said he knew nothing about the ship that was being launched and asked if I had any information. I responded that I did not. He reached into his coat pocket and pulled out an envelope and began jotting down notes. Now during his campaigns for national office, the Senator had been referred to as "Lincolnesque" for his tall stature and intellectual presence. The thought did cross my mind, could this be the next Gettysburg Address?

As we proceeded to Bath, I asked the Senator if he had watched the Washington football game. He responded that he didn't because he didn't think they were going to be good that year and wasn't following them anymore. So that was it for small talk.

We arrived at Bath Iron Works with no issues. The BIW security pointed out the VIP parking area, and I escorted the Senator to where he was supposed to be. The ship that was being christened and launched was the *Oliver Hazard Perry*, a new guided missile frigate. The ceremony started with various elected officials saying a few words. As I recall, U.S. Representative Dave Emery got up and spoke about Maine's seafaring heritage. Maine Governor James Longley got up and spoke about Maine's seafaring heritage. Senator Muskie got up and spoke about Maine's seafaring heritage. My hopes of being present at the creation of remarks of major national significance were dashed, although they were important to Maine. I thought I already knew enough about Maine's seafaring heritage, but obviously all three of the speakers thought I should know more.

Things did not go smoothly thereafter.

First, Commodore Perry's great-granddaughter tried twice and failed to break the champaign bottle on the bow of the ship.

Second, Secretary of Defense Donald Rumsfeld's wife, Joyce, succeeded in breaking the bottle on the ship. However, the ship did not move.

After a momentary delay and a little confusion, the actor John Wayne, who was also in attendance, slowly sauntered up to the ship, placed his hand on the bow, pushed. Sure enough, the ship began to move and was launched to the cheers and laughter of the crowd. It was quite a moment. He lived up to his reputation of being a real hero in times of crisis, at least in the movies. John Wayne saved the day and made BIW look good!

After the ceremony ended, my next task was to drive the Senator to Lewiston, where his daughter Martha would be attending Bates. We met Mrs. Muskie, who had a car full of Martha's belongings. This was most likely the reason why I had to use my Dad's car that day. What I

FINDING LEG ROOM ON THE CAMPAIGN TRAIL

specifically remember was helping the Senator maneuver a large trunk up a narrow stairway to Martha's dorm room. Once again, I thought, here is a man who ran for president and vice president of the United States, and here I am helping him move his daughter into her college dorm room. After moving everything to the room, no further services were required of me so I headed back to Biddeford.

Upon further reflection, my guess is this was my audition to be the Senator's driver for the campaign. Very soon after that day, I was asked if I wanted to stay in Maine to work on his reelection and to be his driver. I responded positively, and I was no longer an employee of the U.S. Senate and now on the campaign staff.

It was a wonderful experience for a young man. We crisscrossed the state, making many campaign stops where the Senator would give his stump speech. We showed up at factory and mill gates at the shift changes to shake hands with workers. I even got to meet former Georgia Governor Jimmy Carter at former Maine Governor Ken Curtis's house in Cape Elizabeth after a campaign rally. I also learned that campaigning can be exhausting, and although he may not be one for small talk, the Senator used the travel time between stops to recharge and maybe get in a little nap.

And remember I said Gayle Cory was a fixer? She got me a car from Shep Lee's car dealership in Lewiston with bucket seats!

From then on, Senator Muskie did not have to complain about leg room as he could now adjust his own seat to his own liking.

I was the talk of the WonderBar for weeks afterward.

I think.

Oh by the way, Muskie won his reelection, 60 percent to 40 percent.

Probably it was all that smooth driving that pushed him over the top.

GOOD CLEAN FUN AT THE MAINE STATE HOUSE
Maria Fuentes

When I first set foot in the State House after getting a new job at Maine Better Transportation Association, I questioned why I had been hired as I soon realized I didn't know the legislative process or the players. As the session moved on, I did feel more comfortable in the Transportation Committee room. Since I represented transportation interests, things made more sense since members discussed and worked through legislation that impacted our members. But the goings on in the House and Senate chambers on the third floor of the Maine State Capitol seemed like a mystery.

Soon it came time to follow a piece of legislation that affected my members, so I knew I would need to spend more time up there. Back then, long before the internet, you subscribed to a document service where you picked up stacks of documents to see what bills had been printed, when public hearings and work sessions were taking place, and other business of the legislative branch of government. While poring through the day's catch, a friendly man with a big smile came over and said: "Young lady, I have seen you in the Transportation Committee, and you have impressed me. You are doing an excellent job." He sat down and we began chatting.

He was short and energetic, with a friendly smile and a husky voice as he asked me about myself and my family and then began regaling me with stories about some of the characters in the Maine State Legislature.

GOOD CLEAN FUN AT THE MAINE STATE HOUSE

He wanted to warn me about some of them and let me know who I could trust, and he assured me I could trust him and said he was someone who liked "good clean fun." God knows what that would mean today!

As elected officials walked by, he gave me a running commentary on them:

"Watch out for this guy: he is phonier than a three-dollar bill."

"That one is number than a pounded thumb," or

"Holy ship, Maria! They didn't know until she was five years old whether she would walk or fly."

His name was Tony Tammaro, and he represented Baileyville in Washington County, where the Woodland Pulp mill—a place he had worked at for some forty years—stood. Tony ran for office because his good friend Edmund DelMonaco had encouraged him to go to Augusta and "tell those politicians to stop ignoring Washington County." Tony's priority was rebuilding Route 9—the Airline Road—and that is what led him to the Transportation Committee.

The more I got to know him, the more I learned about his two loves: his family and sports. After playing baseball at Woodland High, he joined a semi-pro team until he served in World War II. In the Army, he was a Gold Glove welterweight boxer, and while stationed in Alabama, he played and umpired and became friends with Tommy Lasorda. When he came home, he started numerous leagues, including a Border League with both Canadian and American players, and two Native American teams. When I asked if he stayed in touch with Lasorda, he said, "No, but he was a good guy! It was time to move on and come home."

Tony was equally well-known in basketball circles as an incredibly popular high school and college referee. In addition to his love for sports, he would talk about his children, and mostly spoke of his wife Marge, or "Mum." When session was done for the week, he would beat feet to his car and drive home—no time or desire for socializing. He would report back the following week that he and "Mum" had gone dancing, and he spoke with such pride about what a great dancer she was.

In the 1990s, legislators socialized in groups more than today. Tony wasn't interested in fraternizing but would make an exception if sports or dancing were involved. His stories about the legislative dances were fun as well. Sighing, he would say: "Boys, Maria. I make sure I dance with everyone—I don't want to leave anyone out—but dancing with her was like pushing a rope up a hill!"

Tony didn't suffer fools gladly and couldn't tolerate phony people. He dubbed a member of the other legislative body "Sir Lunch-a-Lot," because of his grandstanding, and as someone crossed our path, he would shake his head, "He's such a looney tune, you can't believe a word he says."

And you knew the people he really liked. When Governor Joe Brennan nominated Dana Connors as Commissioner of Transportation, Tony and his Route 9 Committee comrades were the first group Dana met with—even before his confirmation hearing. He would later say, "Dana and I are best friends. He was quite a ball player—scored 42 points in a quarter-final game—he almost broke the tournament record!" Then he would imitate him shooting up a basket. "He was short and quick, like me . . . a great guard. And you know, Maria, the ladies really liked him—he sure does know how to dance."

Tony was a staunch defender of his friends. One time he thought a legislator had said something disrespectful to me. He went over and looked up at the guy, nearly twice his size, wagged his finger at him and quietly excoriated him, saying, "You better show some respect to this young lady." The larger guy looked nonplussed. Tony then shuffled toward him—as if he were in the ring—and put his fists out as if he were getting ready for a match. The other guy quickly moved on. Tony turned to me and said: "He won't bother you again." I didn't think the legislator had stepped over a line, but it warmed my heart that Tony had my back.

There are people that you come across during your journey that you never forget. For me, Tony was one of those people, and that he was a legislator is what brought us together, along with his love for "good clean fun." When Tony finished his final term, he said he wouldn't be coming back to the State House, but he would stay in touch. And he was true to his word. He never returned to the Capitol, even when colleagues asked him to return for welcome back days. He'd had a job to do, he got it done, and it was time to move on.

But he did stay in touch, and I got to meet "Mum," who I felt that I already knew quite well. He even talked about fixing me up with his son.

GOOD CLEAN FUN AT THE MAINE STATE HOUSE

When I called him to tell him I was getting married, I said, "You will like him. He's Italian, and he likes sports."

Tony said, "Well that is all well and good. But, Maria, can he dance?"

Tony was still dancing, umpiring, and refereeing until his sudden death in 2002 at age eight-five. His service was in a huge, packed church in Calais. His family asked his best friend Dana Connors to eulogize him. What a run he had.

A year after he died, the legislature passed a bill to dedicate the eastern part of Route 9 the "Tony Tammaro Memorial Highway" in recognition of his tireless work to fix the Airline Road.

I will always remember his kindness, his boundless energy, and the everlasting twinkle in his eye. When you were with him, you felt like the most important person in the world.

Tony sure was, indeed "good, clean fun" and his judgments of people in the world of the legislature were always spot on.

EVERYBODY NEEDS HELP ON THE CAMPAIGN TRAIL
Janet Mills

CAMPAIGNING FOR PUBLIC OFFICE MEANS GETTING OUT OF YOUR COMfort zone, going to where the people are, and listening to folks directly. Social media and TV ads and debates alone really don't cut it. There's simply no better way to find out what's on people's minds, and no better way to earn the vote than to go to their doors—which includes going to barber shops, church suppers, beauty parlors, corner stores, and grange dinners.

Campaigning for the House of Representatives four times, I went to every door in my district at least once, and I left palm cards with handwritten notes on them if no one answered the door. Campaigning for Attorney General in Maine also meant doing doors in communities all across the state, as I worked with Democratic candidates for the House and Senate, building relationships with them and, in turn, earning their support for the nomination for that constitutional office in the joint caucus of House and Senate Democrats that follows the general election.

Thousands of doors in hundreds of communities with dozens of candidates taught me a few basics that I have shared with others. Those tips include how to deal with dogs that try to block your passage to a door, mapping out a neighborhood to prevent getting lost, and clinching the vote once you've made your pitch.

These things I learned from experience—bad experience. One time I was helping a House candidate in Washington County. When she took a shortcut to the next house by jumping the hedge, I yelled, "Watch out for the big black dog!" as I reached for the tennis ball and dog biscuits in my pocket that I used for dog decoys. Those tricks usually worked.

Not in time! Just as she got to the doorstep, the dog lurched at her and took a bite out of her backside. Fortunately for us, the lady of the house was apologetic and offered skin cleanser and Band-Aids. However, despite my limited medical training, it was I who had to apply the medicinal accoutrements while the resident told us a heartfelt tale about losing her job and having a hard time paying taxes. We gave her advice on property tax relief and employment opportunities. My candidate got the homeowner's vote, and I got the candidate's support.

My first time campaigning for the House of Representatives occurred after I had had hip replacement surgery that had required several weeks of convalescence and several months on crutches. Back then we did not have the benefit of computerized walk lists but relied instead on cross-referencing the municipal tax lists and the voter lists. Mistakes were made. At the end of one long day, as I was trying to make up for lost time, I hopped out of my sidekick's pickup truck hoping to clinch another vote.

I was hobbling toward the door, with a gaggle of farm animals, goats, dogs, and geese, gathering around me when a man yelled from the porch, "Watch out for the one with the bump on his beak," pointing to the goose closest to me with a large open beak.

I turned on the dirt driveway to get back to the truck as quickly as I could. Unstable on my feet and unable to run, it was a close call as I grabbed the door handle and hoisted myself up into the passenger seat along with a loose set of crutches, as the big angry goose attacked my foot. Once safely inside the vehicle, I double checked my printed lists. That's when I noticed that the house was listed to a Massachusetts resident, that the car in the driveway had out-of-state plates, and that the address was nowhere in the voter lists. "Measure twice, cut once," I reminded myself. Or, in other words, "Haste makes waste."

I perhaps also got the sympathy vote, if nothing else, which no doubt helped me as the first election was pretty close. My mother was my biggest supporter and a great help during those House campaigns. She had taught English at the high school for decades. People knew her better than they knew me and, fortunately, she was popular with her former students for training them to conjugate verbs while doing calisthenics during afternoon classes. She would stand with me at the polls for long hours in the pouring rain on those chilly November days and greet voters with a steady smile. A lot of them probably voted for her!

Campaigning on crutches made me realize just how many steps and stairs there were in my town. There were no elevators in the apartment buildings, and in the old neighborhoods, every house had steps. Often I would hobble up long flights of rough stone steps to get to the front door of a house only to find nobody home or nobody answering the door. On one occasion, one homeowner who didn't recognize me called my mother to complain. Her message was, "Kay, tell Janet she shouldn't be using that poor crippled girl to campaign for her!"

Although my physical challenges were only temporary, I felt long-lasting empathy for those who deal with physical challenges every day of their lives. I realized why Congress enacted the Americans with Disabilities Act.

Today consultants and social media and mail experts dominate campaigns at every level. But doing doors, meeting people where they're at, is still the best way for a candidate to get to know voters. Shaking a hand and asking for the vote is still the key to campaign success.

POLITICS 101
Ruth Foster

It was 1981, and the 110th Legislative Session was about to begin. The three branches of state government had assembled in the Capitol. The executive branch—I recognized Governor Brennan—tall and well-dressed. Members of his cabinet were scattered throughout the hall and in the balcony. The judicial branch—the Justices (*Supremes*) were all men and recognizable only by the fact they were disguised in long black robes, somber and intimidating. The legislative branch, House and Senate members, consisted of 184 members: 137 men and 47 women. Pretty hefty odds. I must admit, I was surprised at how few women were there.

Glancing around the Chamber at the array of styles, I noticed the women in dresses, skirts, and jackets (very colorful), and a few in pantsuits (ahead of their time)—each a standout in their own way. But the men wore suits and ties, whether from Brooks Brothers or off the rack from an outlet store, all looking alike. Not a fashion plate among them, that's for sure. But wait! The president of the Senate and the Speaker of the House bedecked in morning coats, a black jacket with tails, white shirts, and striped pants, were standouts, resembling "Emperor Penguins." And I soon learned that they were.

All of these characters, never to be called by their first names again, but addressed as The Honorable, Your Honor, Senator, or Representative, gathered together to now become lawmakers and interpreters of the laws, beaming, and very proud of themselves, smiling for the television cameras and news media.

I wondered, *Who are these people? What do they do in* real *life? Where do they live?*

I was about to find out.

The session ended and we were off to our committee rooms—mine the Labor Committee—the hearing room located in the bowels of the State House. The committee consisted of thirteen members—eight Democrats and five Republicans. I had reached for my House Register to check on my fellow members to learn about them before the meeting—archaeologist, lawyer, emergency medical technician (handy, though I hoped we wouldn't need one), teacher, real estate brokers, businessmen, cleaning person, mill worker, theater education, homemaker, and a retiree.

Since there were no photos of this cast of characters, it took me some time to put names to faces. In addition, there was an ad hoc committee consisting of a lawyer representing labor, another lawyer representing businesses, a union leader, and a self-appointed lobbyist for the business sector. Though one of the Labor Committee members might miss a meeting, none of this special interest committee of four ever did.

The hearing was contentious, trying, and unpleasant, and upon ending, the committee went into executive session. Mount Vesuvius erupted, "You, G%d D$!ned A$$holes, F#?king B#stards, Sons of B&tches, Stupid Jacka$$es, and p#ssheads, we have work to do!" A whole litany of language new to me, flowed like lava from the volcano.

What had I gotten myself into? I wondered.

Whereupon two other members of the committee began swiftly speaking what I thought was French and was actually French *Canadian*, their arms waving, gesturing, and eyes flashing, then to be joined by another speaking French *Acadian*, gentle, slow and soothing. I did not enter the conversation, since my French was "tourist French" learned from a Berlitz French course, which consisted of being able to order from a menu and find the bathroom.

The opera ended and the dark clouds and bolts of lightning passed, just as if nothing had happened—replaced with smiling faces, glad hands, and hugs.

Time to get on with the business of the day, and the cause of this conflict—Worker's Compensation Legislation.

That night, I called my daughter, Jennifer. I was so anxious to share with her the new words that I had heard, since she had attended a preppy girls boarding school in Massachusetts, and on her first visit home, almost sent her father into cardiac arrest with words that came out of her mouth. I told my tale of the day. A long silence prevailed, and finally she answered, "Mother, come home."

But how could I? I had too much to learn and so much to do!

A few months later, I received an invitation from Governor Joseph Brennan to attend a dinner at Blaine House. A small group of House and Senate members had also been invited. The governor greeted us in the Blaine House parlor—a luxurious room with a glowing fireplace, comfortable chairs, floral arrangements, wine, and hors d'oeuvres. We moved to the dining room and the brilliance of a chandelier, elegant china, sparkling crystal goblets, maid service, and gourmet cuisine. It was a welcome change from the lounge room and cafeteria at the State House.

The dinner ended and I could hardly wait to go back to the parlor for what I thought would be great conversation and a chance to meet my fellow legislators. But that was not to be.

The governor had his own idea of a fun evening—a pool party . . . not a swimming pool but billiards. He had his own pool room located off the dining room. Exit the governor—enter Joe, pool shark extraordinaire. Let the games begin! They did and lasted for what I thought was forever. The few women who were there just sat and watched, as the men began their challenge. They were having so much fun, but I was bored out of my gourd. The games ended, and so did the party.

When it was time to go, we were escorted to the front door and the maid came running up to me. "Representative Foster, you left your sweater." After a very dull and boring evening, I thought I would lend a little humor (of the Irish wit variety!) to make this event memorable. In a very seductive voice and coy manner, sporting a smile, I responded, "And what about my slippers?"

Dead silence.

I walked out into the cold night air, which felt warmer than the House I'd just left.

The governor and I had many encounters over the next ten years. Some good, some bad. And although we were of different political persuasions, we were both Irish and became part of the "Fighting Irish" and the "Feisty French," who had quietly invaded the world of politics in Maine and undercut the "Powerful Yankees."

This leavening of the body politic was a good thing!

By 1993 I was the Senator from Hancock County when a subject that I had not dealt with in my previous years in Augusta came to the floor of the Senate—*An Act to Increase the Number of Moose Permits and Make Other Changes in the Moose Hunting Laws.*

The first speaker had heard that moose are a danger: They use our roads, thus causing accidents.

What?, I thought. *This is moose country, and many stretches of roads winding through their habitat have moose signs and pictures warning drivers to slow down—ignored, putting moose and driver at peril!*

But the speaker said moose are a nuisance. He told of a man who had encountered a moose that had wandered into his swimming pool and the great cost of removing his uninvited guest.

Maine law states swimming pools must be fenced in.

"So, who's to be blamed for this incident?" he asked.

The moose, of course.

The solution to this horrible threat to one and all—more permits . . . fewer moose.

Another speaker jumped to his feet, yelling, "No way!" He realized that moose are a big tourist attraction. However, he wanted to remind us, the moose kill around Greenville has been tremendous every season, and tourists line up at the tag station to have their photos taken. It draws them like flies.

Hours went by, and I'd listened to these stories, and finally I'd had enough, I was on my feet and was recognized by the president of the Senate.

"Thank you, Mr. President, Ladies and Gentlemen of the Senate . . . this is just not the good old boys today, because I am going to say something. Many years ago, there was a man in the Senate by the name of Frank Whitehouse Anderson, and he asked, 'Ruth, when you get down to

Augusta, would you make sure to look after the moose? If they take one, they will take two and they will take a hundred, and a thousand and two thousand.' Well, this bill takes thousands. So here's one for you, Frank! I move Indefinite Postponement of this Bill and all of its Accompanying Papers and ask for a roll call. Thank you."

"Is the Senate ready for the pending motion? The doorkeepers will secure the Chamber. The secretary will call the roll."

Six Senators voted in the affirmative to postpone the bill and twenty-nine voted in the negative.

What a disaster!

The motion failed, and the moose lottery continues to this day. But it remains the State Animal and is still pictured on the State Seal and the State Flag, so I guess that is at least a small victory.

You can't win them all, as they say, but during my tenure in Augusta, I discovered you can weigh in on a lot of them!

A BULL, A BUSH, AND SOME FRIED DOUGH
Rob Caldwell

IN THE FALL OF 1984 I WAS ASSIGNED THE FIRST OF MANY POLITICAL profiles I would do as a reporter in Maine. My subject was the Democratic nominee in the Second Congressional District, a candidate with a name that cut through the noise: Chip Bull. (He preferred Chip over his given name of Chipman.)

Like many longshot candidates, Chip marched to the beat of a drum only he could hear. He had worked as an administrator in various Maine agricultural agencies before landing a job with the U.S. Department of Agriculture in Washington, DC. His responsibilities in that post kept shrinking and his salary kept growing until he found himself making almost as much money as a member of Congress but with so little to do that he took to reading novels in the office.

Fed up with the job (or maybe just tired of reading), he eventually quit and returned to Maine, where he announced that he would challenge Republican incumbent Olympia Snowe. To boost his name recognition, he handed out wooden nickels bearing the slogan "It's Bull!"

Chip never really had a chance. Snowe, popular and well-known after three terms in the House, would have been a formidable candidate on her own, but with the added help of Ronald Reagan's coattails—he would win forty-nine states in November—she was all but invincible. Chip didn't help his cause when he talked about his experience reading novels

A BULL, A BUSH, AND SOME FRIED DOUGH

on the clock, arguing that his inside view of how tax dollars were wasted left him well suited to reform the system. Voters didn't buy it.

When I caught up with the candidate one day as he was shaking hands in downtown Bangor, the outcome of the race was a foregone conclusion. His campaign was badly underfunded, and most of the people he tried to talk with had no idea who he was. The situation left him, understandably, a touch cranky.

After interviewing him, I stepped back about fifteen feet to watch him try to win over voters. Before long, a man came walking down the sidewalk, and Chip reached out to shake hands and deliver his standard pitch.

"Hi, I'm Chip Bull and I'm running for Congress—"

The guy never broke stride, never so much as looked at Chip, and in a moment was five feet past him.

"—and you obviously don't give a shit," Bull said as he watched the man walk away.

In November, Olympia crushed Chip 77 percent to 22 percent. He never ran for political office again, later working as a chef at a country club in Florida before returning to Washington and a job in the U.S. Senate Post Office, where he may have had more time for more pleasure reading.

That moment on the sidewalk stayed with me, though. For one thing, it was funny. Yet it also revealed a side of politics rarely seen by the public or reporters—a frustrated candidate, unburdened by consultants, liberated from any expectations of victory, who had no use for the usual platitudes. And it taught me a valuable lesson: The best sound bites usually come from politicians with nothing to lose.

I wish the serious, competitive ones were as candid.

That point was driven home again twenty years later in a setting that couldn't have been more different. On a glorious autumn morning, I was sitting on the lawn of Walker's Point in Kennebunkport, having scored an interview with George H. W. Bush.

For a reporter, the prospect of getting to talk with a former president at his own home is, of course, terrific . . . until it's time to come up with questions, fresh questions, questions that haven't been asked a thousand times before and wouldn't prompt him to cut the conversation short and take his speedboat out for a spin. I decided to go with word association and ask what first came to mind when I mentioned some world leaders and political heavyweights he'd known and worked with.

First up, Bill Clinton, the man who in 1992 denied Bush the second term in the White House he so badly wanted and believed he deserved.

"Great politician. Great political leader," Bush said of him. "And a Houdini when it comes to getting out of trouble."

Up next, Ross Perot, the Texas billionaire who as an independent presidential candidate in 1992 had won a stunning 19 percent of the popular vote.

"No comment," Bush said, before offering a tart comment. "You know, you never want to blame people. But I think Ross cost me the election. Used to be friends. He used to come right in here and stay with Barbara and me. I don't like to say bad stuff, so I won't. But I don't have much good to say about the man."

There was another name I had been saving, that of Michael Moore, the director of the documentary "Fahrenheit 9/11," a cinematic missile fired at President George W. Bush over his handling of the war in Iraq.

The film, released about three months earlier, had generated intense controversy for its scathing criticism of Bush and his administration's policies. Moore—reviled by conservatives, embraced by liberals—was a gifted polemicist and provocateur, and his movie became the highest-grossing documentary ever made up to that time. I didn't know if it was an ace, but it was the best card up my sleeve.

So I said two words to President Bush: "Michael Moore."

He answered without hesitation. "Total ass. Slimeball. And outrageous in his lies about my family."

This was gold. I knew it the moment the words left his mouth.

As soon as we aired the interview, the Associated Press, *New York Times*, *Washington Post*, and other news outlets picked up the story, and it rapidly went viral. We'd made news. It was, for me, immensely rewarding.

But as we packed up our gear at Walker's Point and prepared to return to the newsroom, it was only late morning and there was no time for self-congratulatory musing. When anchoring and reporting for a

A BULL, A BUSH, AND SOME FRIED DOUGH

news magazine program with limited resources that airs five nights a week, one doesn't work for four hours and then call it a day.

I had another assignment fifty miles away that evening—anchoring our broadcast live from the Fryeburg Fair, the biggest and best of Maine's celebrated agricultural fairs, an entertaining pageant featuring everything from prize-winning pies to some of the best people-watching in the state.

Later that night, tired but happy as I drove home after the broadcast, I marveled at what I'd experienced. That morning I had been talking with the former leader of the free world. That evening I was broadcasting from—I am not making this up—a fried-dough stand plunked down in the middle of barns and amusements and farm animals.

That's how things work in Maine, a place that has a way of keeping reporters humble.

MAINE AND MITCHELL, GUNS AND PIGS

Corey Hascall

MAINE POLITICS IS PERSONAL AND FULL OF SURPRISES. WHETHER you're managing a hundred-dollars-a-week campaign in Portland or one of the biggest U.S. House challenger races in the country, meeting a former U.S. Senate Majority Leader in a hotel room or discussing wind power while a handgun rests casually on a kitchen table, you quickly learn that no two days—and no two people—are ever the same. Over fifteen years on the campaign trail, I met legends, locals, my husband, and a few characters in between.

In 2003, I found myself in the middle of my very first political campaign as the part-time manager for Ethan Strimling's first State Senate primary race in Portland. By *part-time*, I mean I was juggling this gig during nights and weekends, and since Ethan was a Clean Elections' candidate I was pulling in a whopping hundred dollars a week. My day job was processing disability claims at Unum—a job I took because it didn't involve waiting tables.

It was my first "big girl" job and included paid vacations, health insurance, and weekends off. And yet, Ethan's campaign quickly took over my life—a theme that lasted for more than just one cycle as we walked down a long multi-campaign trail together.

Everyone knows that the Democratic Primary in the People's Republic of Portland is the real contest when it comes to races for the Maine Legislature, and this race was no different. Ethan was a fantastic candidate—smart and articulate, attractive but humble, a natural mentor with good values, a relentless door knocker (and he's got the burned-out sneakers to prove it), and the kind of guy who asks a lot from the people around him.

I was constantly overwhelmed with the intensity and newness of campaign life, the endless work to juggle and the people to engage. I had never worked on any campaign before in my life, let alone *run* one, so Ethan spent a lot of time teaching me what to do and managing my feelings. I was green, but he knew I was a hustler and that was just what he needed in his first race.

I hated the impostor syndrome that I felt because I didn't yet understand how campaigns worked. Who did I think I was anyway, taking on this campaign when I had a new "real" job and no clue what I was doing? I asked myself daily: Do I really want all of this stress and pressure? I already have a job; why do I need this hassle?

On no fewer than three occasions, I tried to quit the campaign. I mean, I didn't just try. I said, "I quit!" The problem was that Ethan didn't take no for an answer, and he talked me down each time. On my fourth attempt, I was serious. I sat Ethan down, looked him in the eye and said, "I am done with this crazy, ridiculous life!"

But then Ethan switched tactics. He knew my weaknesses. Wine and an inspirational speech (the guy literally went to Julliard!).

He sat me down, handed me a glass of very good red wine and told me that it was completely okay if I wanted to stop. He assured me that the campaign would indeed survive. I said great, finished that glass of wine, and asked for another. He handed me a second and then continued, "But I'm worried about you and how you'll feel about yourself if you quit. I don't want you to look back on this moment and regret that you gave up on something that I know you can do, and that you're really good at."

I wasn't sure if he meant drinking red wine or being a campaign manager, but something in his words resonated with me. I didn't have a lot of people in my life at that time telling me they believed in me or that they saw a talent in me I didn't recognize. But Ethan understood what I needed to hear—and maybe what I was hoping he would say in response to my quitting.

Or maybe I just really liked that bottle of red wine.

Either way, I agreed to stay on, and I didn't ever try to quit again. We won that campaign, and many after it. We lost some too. But I never looked back—and I never worked for a hundred dollars a week again. Although, I do still expect a nice glass of red wine for when the going gets tough.

Fast forward a year to the fall of 2004. I have no idea how I was tapped for this special mission, but one morning a Maine Democratic Party leader called me with an unusual request: Senator George Mitchell needed to record 151 State House endorsement messages in two hours that afternoon, and they needed someone to bring recording equipment to his hotel room right away.

Wait, what? To George Mitchell's hotel room? Me, in my twenties. Him, in his seventies. I wasn't so sure about this.

But, hey, you only live once, and I would be bringing recording equipment with me if he tried anything! So, I said, "Sure, I can do that."

Speaking of that, did I have any professional recording gear? Absolutely not. Would I have known how to use it if I did? Also no. But did I have Headlight Audio-Visual's phone number? You bet.

Armed with rented equipment, crib notes from the AV tech, sheer determination, and lots of trepidation, I knocked on the door of Senator Mitchell's room at the DoubleTree by Hilton in South Portland. The door opened and I saw the legend himself while trying not to hyperventilate in the presence of the man who brokered peace in Northern Ireland (and also spoke at my 1993 South Portland high school graduation). As is usual for him, he was fully outfitted in a suit and tie ("Does he sleep in that thing?" I thought) and could not have been more friendly, immediately saying my name and welcoming me into his modest room. I noticed Tim Feeley, a fellow minion, was there too.

Thank God, because even if nothing shady was about to happen, a twenty-something female campaign staffer alone in a seventy-something politician's hotel room looked too many shades of bad to be ignored by a GOP operative who was looking to make a name for himself.

At this point, my job was simple: Explain to Tim how to operate the equipment so Senator Mitchell could crank out those robocalls and get on a plane to New York City. I barely said a word to the senator other than, "Here's the name of the next candidate."

What I would have given for one of those glasses of red wine.

It was over in half an hour. I left, exhaled, and reflected on how remarkably normal it all seemed. George Mitchell was as nice a person as I had ever met, and he always remembered me when I saw him over my years working in politics (I think our next encounter was at Simones' Hot Dog Stand in Lewiston). But mostly, I was just very thankful no one took pictures of me entering and leaving that hotel room.

As a side note to the whole episode, one of his endorsement recordings that day was for a first-time candidate named John Brautigam. Spoiler alert: I married that guy eight years later. Here's that story.

The year 2004 wasn't just the year I met George Mitchell. It was also the year I met John Brautigam. Initially, I wasn't interested in managing his State House campaign. I didn't know the guy or his values. Plus, he lived in hoity-toity Falmouth. As a gritty SoPo girl who went to the University of Southern Maine, I didn't need to help some Stanford-educated lawyer convince other rich people to vote for him so he could just go and vote for things rich people wanted.

But Tobey McGrath, then working for Speaker Glenn Cummings, convinced me otherwise. He said John was a great guy with progressive values, he needed my help, and it would be a good experience for me. *Good experience?* I was basically George Mitchell's closest confidant at this point.

Anyway, long story longer, I relented. I figured this would be a short gig. I could make a little money, help secure the Democratic Majority in the State House, and then get out of Falmouth as quickly as I got in.

Twenty years later, and I'm still in Falmouth.

The problem was that far from being some rich elitist lawyer who just wants to help other rich people pay lower taxes, it turns out that John is a brilliant lawyer, a kind person, and a dedicated father to two boys—a real down-to-earth family man who cared deeply about other people, injustice, and making the world a better place. He'd also spent much of his life at a family camp just south of Seboomook on the quiet northwest corner of Moosehead Lake. How bad could he be?

He quickly became one of my favorite candidates and people. Maybe a little too *favorite*.

When I stopped by Dale Rand Printing in Portland (it was the only union print shop in the First Congressional District), I'd joke to Dale that "I'm here to pick up my future husband's lawn signs." We joked about this every time I went in the shop even though I had barely met the guy and John was also married at the time.

At one point during the campaign, I introduced John at a big event and I could feel myself going overboard in expressing my admiration. Why couldn't I stop gushing? I mean, I know that is what a campaign manager is supposed to do, right? So, "Let me introduce you to the greatest candidate I have ever worked for who will be the next John F. Kennedy!" But this time I was actually feeling a little flushed when I said it. A little tingly, let's just say. And I hoped that no one noticed.

As it turned out, Lesley MacVane from Community TV Network recorded the event that day, and she definitely noticed. Years later she told me that she still had a copy of the event if I ever wanted to see my introduction and John's speech. She said she thought it was sweet, but I was mortified. No! I absolutely did not want to see that video!

Apparently, it was crystal clear to her, and to everyone else, just how much I thought of John.

Thankfully, John won that first House race, although by just twelve votes (I guess Tobey was right about John needing my help!). He was, as expected, a standout legislator, and by his 2006 reelection, he crushed it.

Fast forward a few more years, a few more election cycles, a few interim boyfriends that I would rather forget, and John ended up divorced (and I had nothing to do with it!). But roundabout 2008, John and I started dating, and in 2012, we tied the knot.

I've always said we need more love in politics. I guess I am just practicing what I preach.

And because campaign families are truly some of the best families, Dale Rand Printing generously printed and gifted us our wedding invitations, and Lesley MacVane's daughter-in-law made our gorgeous Maine blueberries wedding cake. And Ethan brought red wine.

MAINE AND MITCHELL, GUNS AND PIGS

My work as a campaign consultant eventually took me to all corners of Maine, including to Frankfort on the Penobscot River estuary. In 2010, I made my first visit there and spent many days advocating for a wind power project being considered in an upcoming town vote.

One of the things I picked up on right away was that Frankfort was one of the most conservative places I'd ever been to in Maine and was certainly not the kind of place that I'd ever organized in. After all, my hometown of South Portland is practically Boston as far as some Mainers are concerned.

My first stakeholder meeting was located at the home of a longtime resident, a real old-timer who had lived there all his life. He resided at the end of a long dirt road—the kind that wasn't made for my bougie Volkswagen Jetta.

When I arrived and walked into the living room of his trailer, I noticed right away that he had two long guns on full display: one rifle on the couch (where he invited me to sit) and another that looked like a machine gun on a stand pointed out the back window. To say it was a culture shock for a city girl like me to see two guns in someone's house right out in the open would be an understatement.

That said, I honestly wasn't sure if the guns were there to intimidate me into backing off the wind project or whether this was some kind of northern Maine art installation.

Thankfully, he moved the rifle on the couch when he saw my hesitation (such a gentleman!) but then asked if I'd like to see what he was up to in the backyard. I figured going outside might be safer with all these guns lying around, and certainly the air would be fresher.

It was perhaps safer, but the air was definitely not fresher. He'd strung up a dead pig to lure and then shoot coyotes.

Now I understood why the gun in the living room was pointing out the back window!

Later that day, after I had calmed my nerves and aired the rotting pig smell out of my clothes, I met with another town leader—a planning board member—to talk about the wind power project. Once again, I was invited to sit and have a chat about wind power (and he also wanted to tell me how much Barack Obama and the federal government were going after the common folks). Low and behold, just lying there on the kitchen table, was a handgun.

I am honestly not sure I can recall a single thing we talked about, as I kept looking at that thing out of the corner of my eye wondering if, somehow, he was sending a not-so-subtle signal that, "No wind power is going in my backyard!"

I have been to big cities all over the country (and the world) and, honest to God, I am pretty sure I hadn't seen three guns in my entire life, let alone in one day. It turns out that neither of them opposed the project. They just liked their guns. And now, with a whole lot of hunter's breakfasts under my belt, I came to understand Maine's hunting traditions a lot better. That doesn't mean I don't support sane gun control laws, but those first encounters in Frankfort were certainly a baptism by gunpowder of a religion I didn't know or understand.

Emily Cain was a Maine political prodigy. She was first elected to office at twenty-four years old (meanwhile at twenty-four, I was mastering the art of upselling antipasto salads at Ricetta's Pizzeria in SoPo). Over five terms in the Maine Legislature, Emily shattered glass ceilings like it was her side hustle: Chair of Appropriations, youngest woman House Minority Leader in state history, and one of the funniest people to ever grace the halls of Augusta.

By 2015, Emily and I hadn't crossed paths much. She was "way up north" in Orono; I was in Falmouth. I knew of her, of course. Who didn't? Ambitious, confident, sassy, and extremely smart. Also, a great singer! But Appropriations Chair? Really? Wasn't she, like, twelve when she got the job?

Then one day, Emily asked me to run her second Congressional campaign against Bruce Poliquin, the Republican incumbent who beat her two years earlier. This wasn't just any race—it was set to be one of the biggest, most expensive challenger races in the country that cycle. And she wanted me to pack up my life, leave my husband and young step-kids, and move to Bangor for fifteen months.

When I learned that I could score campaign housing with a family in Brewer with five adorable pugs, obviously, I said yes. Emily and I sealed the deal at the Irving station diner in Newport over home fries (and, let's be honest, home fries are a close second to red wine when it comes to winning me over). Emily held my hands like we were swearing a sacred oath in a Taylor Swift song. And just like that, we were a team.

The campaign offices were in Bangor and Lewiston, and we spent most of our days in a blur of fundraising calls, spreadsheets, and strategy meetings. But when the opportunity came to hit the road and meet voters, we grabbed it like we were sneaking out of high school detention. We called these adventures "off-roading with Emily," and they were everything.

Off-roading with Emily meant sunrise handshakes at Bath Iron Works. It meant eating three hunter's breakfasts in Old Town, then in Lincoln, and finally in Medway—all before most people had even poured their first cup of coffee. It meant marching in the Potato Blossom Festival parade in Fort Fairfield, sitting in on bingo games after the Common Ground Fair, and watching Emily sing the national anthem at MMA fights in Lewiston before heading north to stuff our faces with *ployes* (yes, that is a food!) at the Acadian Festival in Madawaska.

We met firefighters, farmers, and lobstermen (oh my). We dodged wildlife in the road, grumbled about dead cell zones, and waved at GOP trackers trying to catch Emily saying something scandalous (spoiler: she didn't). We also had our fair share of car trouble—I still had a VW Jetta and it felt like it was held together with duct tape and dreams by this point.

My personal favorite off-roading memory? The International Association of Firefighters. These guys were the ultimate campaign wingmen. They canvassed for us, filmed TV ads, and even took us target shooting in a back field (because nothing says bipartisan appeal like learning to handle a firearm safely). They also created these blazing yellow "Firefighters for Cain" tee shirts that you could practically see from space.

I wanted one. Badly. Except I didn't want it to say "Cain." I wanted it to say "Firefighters for Corey," because my Corey-confession is that I've always really loved firefighters. Like, in the firefighters calendar kind of way. But getting my own named shirt would've required me to run for office—and I'd sooner chew glass.

Here's the thing about off-roading with Emily: It's easy to underestimate her. She's bubbly and relentlessly positive, like the human embodiment of a rainbow. But don't let that fool you. Beneath all that sunshine is a political powerhouse who builds relationships like a mason builds walls—strong, sturdy, and meant to last. She raises big money like a boss. You want fiscal responsibility? Let Emily Cain slay that budget for you! She's the badass next door, and off-roading with her wasn't just fun—it was inspiring.

And, for the record, Bruce Poliquin definitely does not own a "Firefighters for Bruce" tee-shirt.

So, what did I learn from fifteen years on the political trail?

First, campaigns have a way of turning hundred-dollar jobs into lifelong careers—and sometimes into lifetime partners. Second, George Mitchell is as impressive in person as he is on C-SPAN and meeting him might just set you up for meeting your future spouse. Third, a glass of red wine can fix just about anything, from quitting campaigns to shaking off awkward moments with armed Mainers.

Finally, I learned that politics in Maine isn't just about winning elections—it's about the people you meet, the stories you collect, and the unexpected ways they shape your life. Along the way, I got a husband, a network of unforgettable friends, and enough material for a lifetime of dinner party stories. And if there's one thing I know for sure: no campaign, no meeting, and no challenge is complete without a good glass of wine.

Cheers to that.

A WALK, A RIDE, AND A POSSIBLE RETIREMENT HOME

Chris Potholm

It was the summer of 1972. As Bill Cohen's campaign manager, I had promised him that I would join him on his historic Walk the first day, the last day, and one in between. I had fulfilled the first two, and now he was heading for the finish of his 650-mile walk across Maine.

Originally he was expected to stop at Houlton after walking all the way from Gilead on the New Hampshire border, but the reception he got along the way was so positive and so transformative that he decided to continue up through Aroostook County and down the St. John Valley all the way to Fort Kent.

As Cohen neared the finish line, Professor Richard Morgan and I joined up with the Walk crew led by Jed Lyons. We spent the night before the end of the Walk at the home of State Senator Don Collins, father of the then twenty-year-old Susan Collins. Bill stayed with the Collins family in their home, while Jed, Dick, and I stayed at their camp on a lake. I've blocked the name of the lake—no doubt because I foolishly drank some of the camp water and became quite ill.

All night long.

Jed and Dick Morgan slept like proverbial babies, due perhaps to their ingestion of copious amounts of fifteen-year-old McCallum scotch, which must have had marvelous medicinal properties as they were unaffected by the beaver-fouled water I had foolishly drunk.

But it was the last day so I had no choice but to suck it up and walk with the party the next day, albeit with a terrible, terrible taste haunting my mouth. I remember being amazed at the crowds that lined the roads and the positive reception Bill was receiving from the overwhelmingly Democratic electorate in the Valley. I got more and more excited as the Walk continued to cheers and clapping.

More manic too, perhaps.

Bill seemed to be the only major Republican candidate to have ever walked the Valley, and the people seemed very impressed. So naturally I got a bit carried away telling the people along the way how much Bill liked the Valley. At one point, one of the crowd said how much they appreciated his fondness for the Valley and its people but wondered if this was just a campaign stunt.

"Stunt? Stunt? Are you kidding? He wants to retire here he loves it so much," I blurted out with seemingly heartfelt fervor. "Yes," I added for emphasis, "he definitely wants to retire here."

The person smiled gleefully. "That's great. I'm a realtor. I'll show him some properties."

Uh-oh.

Thinking this conversation would be the end of things, I answered "That's nice, I'm sure he'd love to." I even accepted his card and made a big show of putting it in my wallet.

And forgot all about it as we walked another three or four miles.

As we approached Fort Kent, there was quite a crowd at the finish line cheering as Bill came into view. For some reason, I got it in my head that it would be better if Bill arrived alone and not with a cluster of local politicians who had joined the march, and I began to try to distract them. Even to the point of obstructing their access to the candidate.

"Get out of the way" said one, a state senator, shoving me aside as he rushed to get level with Bill as he entered Fort Kent proper.

Flushed with success and relieved that the Walk was over, Bill was in a fabulous mood. His joy was palpable. So too was his confusion when a man appeared with a large sheaf of papers, each one depicting a fine property for sale in the Valley, some from Saint Agatha, some from Madawaska, and some from other lovely locales.

A WALK, A RIDE, AND A POSSIBLE RETIREMENT HOME

Bill looked baffled, even when the man added, "For your retirement. For your retirement."

Ever quick on the uptake, Bill smiled and took the papers and thanked the man, but rolling his eyes at me after he left.

Later after the crowd had dispersed, he asked me "What was that all about?"

"Oh, I guess they want you to come here when it's time to retire. Let me take those, we can look at them later."

So the Walk concluded and the people disbursed. Bill was whisked away to return to campaigning in the south.

Professor Morgan and I got into the campaign car, a none-too-healthy Vega, and headed south, relieved that it had all gone so well, the many property sheets safely out of sight in the trunk. Jed Lyons wisely stayed with the candidate, who he knew would get fast, good service on the way home.

As we headed south we were in a happy mood: mission accomplished, Walk over, candidate basking in glow of successful foray down the Valley, retirement decisions awaiting another day.

Too soon the relief faded.

The campaign car, the Vega with too many hard miles on it, died.

Just north of Patten, Maine.

I mean it really died with a totally seized-up engine block.

Herr Morgan and campaign manager Chris were stuck by the side of the road.

The tow truck that eventually arrived was piloted by a man with a huge beard and a big, big smile when he announced. "It's finished. I'll tow it to my station for the parts."

Great.

Two professors with about twenty bucks between them stranded.

Before cell phones. Before the internet.

The tow truck driver gave us a ride to Patten. After a long time, we found a working pay phone.

What to do?

Four or five frantic calls later, we located Bill's media consultant, Mike Harkins of The Agency fame. Luckily, it turned out he was in

Augusta editing film from the Walk for our next round of commercials. A fine coincidence, surely!

Harkins was pulled off that assignment forthwith. Otherwise we might still be stranded in the Great North Woods north of Patten.

An hour later, he arrived and graciously drove us back to Harpswell, at least somewhat interested in our accounts of the end of the Walk.

We made sure he was well fed and thanked profusely as we toasted the demise of the up-until-then faithful Vega.

So all ended well, except that I, of course, always wondered what happened to the properties for sale sheets that went with the Vega to the great car cemetery in the sky.

As of this writing, Bill Cohen has still not retired, so despite the lure of Morocco or Kuwait, perhaps there is still a possibility of a Valley abode in his future.

Madawaska perhaps?

PART II
LIVING AND LAUGHING IN THE PINE TREE STATE

MAINE IS A SPECIAL PLACE WITH A UNIQUE HISTORY, A RICH AND vibrant culture, and people to match. The stories in this section acknowledge the diversity of experiences and the challenges that Maine's many facets of life present to individuals and groups.

Growing up in the Pine Tree State offers a mother lode of tales, some of which we have captured here. Our stories originate from the coast, mill towns, and cities, as well as from inland farms. Some recount special toys, unique situations, or athletic events, celebrating childhood, adolescence, and adulthood. Some vignettes describe significant—even extraordinary—people in Maine. Others tell stories coming of age, the challenges of first jobs, finding true love, and the other vicissitudes of life.

We also get a sense of the gritty self-reliance of the Maine spirit and the God-given ability to laugh at oneself, like nearly naked blue fishing, a former Congressman's literal gut-wrenching tales of leaving his gastric mark throughout Maine, and a father's badly misunderstood instructions about the birds and the bees. Read on for the highs and lows, ins and outs, and everything in between.

LAND OF THE DISAPPOINTING TOYS
Dennis Bailey

As a kid, I had an active imagination. Maybe overactive. Yes, of course, overactive. Still do, as a matter of fact. I suppose an active imagination is a desirable trait for a kid growing up in a rural, low-income household in Maine. You had to rely on your imagination for enjoyment when more pricy forms of entertainment—a movie, a new bike, a Red Sox game—were way out of reach.

But my active imagination also made me easy prey for all the commercials and advertisements aimed at kids' toys. This was the late '50s and early '60s before strict Federal Trade Commission rules and other regulations clamped down on misleading or fake advertisements.

One example: A favorite show at the time was "Supercar." This was a futuristic adventure series with marionettes, and the star was Supercar, a flying craft that could do anything—rocket into space, dive into the ocean, or soar through the clouds. Amazing! The show was quite popular, and soon, there was a toy Supercar that was shown in the ads doing all those things that a Supercar does. I had to have it.

So, I begged my parents to get me one for Christmas, and they dutifully obliged. I'm not sure if they saw the shock and disappointment on my face when I realized the toy Supercar was not so Super. It didn't fly. It didn't rocket into outer space. It was more like a little windup toy that slowly crawled around the living room floor. *That's it?* I thought. Yes that *was* it.

LAND OF THE DISAPPOINTING TOYS

Supercar is one of a long list of disappointing toys of my youth. Many of them came from the old Johnson Smith Company catalog, a black-and-white mail-order digest with hundreds of pages of novelty items, magic tricks, and gag gifts. It was like something from a different era, the '20s and '30s, and provided hours of entertainment for me and my brothers, who would thumb through the catalog over and over, imagining what a hit we would be at school if we could just afford everything in it.

There was the Ventrilo, a tiny device you put in your mouth to "throw your voice" like a professional ventriloquist (though it didn't work.) There were the "X-Ray Specs," glasses that allowed you to see through walls (they didn't, but it didn't prevent us from pretending they did). There was the "smoke from your fingertips" trick, a Vaseline-like paste that you spread on your fingertips, and when you rubbed them together, it created these hairy wisps of glue that kind of looked like smoke but didn't fool anybody.

There was the exploding cigarette gag, tiny loads you stuck inside a cigarette that snapped and blew up the cigarette when it was lit. We stuck one into a cigarette that my mom lit while she was driving; that was the first time I ever heard her use the F word. I also remember itching powder, sneezing powder, smoke bombs, and toxic substances that worked but are no doubt banned today.

There was fake vomit, fake dog poo, fake blood, whoopee cushions, invisible ink, and a "dribble glass" that had a tiny slit in the frosted decorative flowers adorning the glass that made a drinker slobber every time they took a sip (to the delight of everyone in on the gag). Chemistry sets, ant farms, the Atomic Energy Mineralogy Kit with "actual samples of atomic bomb ores" (35 cents). Spy cameras, walkie-talkies, a live chameleon! I had one; it lived for about two days.

We wanted it all and sent away for many of the items. But as I said, only a few lived up to the hype. Like Sea Monkeys. The ad promised delivery of special eggs that you put in water and within days hatch to become a family of beautiful, human-like sea creatures. The ads showed them smiling, swimming, some in tux and tails. "A bowl full of happiness," the ad said, "instant pets! Just add water."

Sure. Who doesn't like pets? I put two dollars (cash from my paper route) into an envelope and sent it away, and a few days after I put the eggs into a tank of water, there was . . . nothing. Nothing I could see, anyway, until I looked more closely. Yes, something had come to life and was wiggling around in there. But they sure weren't monkeys or human-like. They were more like Sea Mites, or microscopic Sea Dust. Nothing like the happy family I was promised. It turned out they were just brine shrimp. Not at all entertaining. I'd been had.

But that didn't stop me from searching for the perfect toy. I was a space nut, too, and one ad showed this big desktop domed contraption that allowed you to view the stars and planets. That's what I wanted for Christmas, I told my parents. They tried desperately to talk me out of it but saw the tears well up in my eyes whenever they suggested I should ask for something else. They gave in, as they often did, and on Christmas morning, I opened a giant box with my big plastic space observatory (assembly required).

But somehow, I had gotten the idea, probably from the ad, that this wasn't an observatory but some sort of space portal transmitting a live view of outer space. Maybe I'd see a comet go by, a meteor hitting the moon, or better, a UFO! My Dad patiently worked with me for hours putting the thing together, and when we got to installing the light bulb that would project the stars onto the dome, another light went off in my head. A disappointing one. Ooops. This was no space portal; this was an educational planetarium for eggheads. I felt stupid, and my observatory sat on a table in my room for years gathering dust. None of my friends were interested in it either.

I guess there's a fine line between an active imagination and naivete. Or being a sucker. Looking back, it seems like I was easily conned and failed to learn my lesson. Like the time I saw an ad in one of my (many) comic books for "Three solid-fuel aluminum rockets" for $5. The ad promised that the rockets would reach tremendous heights, thrilling friends and neighbors alike.

Okay, I bit and off went another $5.

I kept an eye out for what I imagined would be a flatbed truck arriving any day to unload the huge aluminum rockets onto our front lawn. Would we need a crane to hoist them up, or a gantry? Would their powerful thrust destroy our lawn or disturb the neighbors? My mind ran wild with anticipation.

Finally, the day came. The rockets arrived . . . in a regular letter-sized envelope. Inside were three wooden matches with their tips wrapped in aluminum foil. We followed the instructions and heated the tinfoil with another match, and the "rocket" went "phhttt," about twenty feet in the air. Yup, just as advertised, solid-fueled aluminum rockets. Hard to argue with that.

Oh well. Lesson learned.

Imagination is a far greater gift than any toy.

Some say life and politics in Maine require it because a lot of this stuff you cannot make up.

CHARLIE'S BULL
Keith Brown

I GREW UP IN THE EARLY 1940S WHEN WAR WAS FOUGHT IN BOTH Europe and the Pacific. Most of the able-bodied young men were drafted into military service to serve their country. We lived in a coastal community where older men and women and children were left to try and survive by raising victory gardens, having cows for milk, and eating beef or chickens only for Sunday dinners. Government food rationing stamps were issued to each man, woman, and child to allow them to purchase limited quantities of food at the stores. We had to do a lot on our own.

As you drive through many of those communities in Maine today, you see old farmhouses built in the 1890s and 1900s with attached barns to house the animals. Animals were a key part of daily life for many Maine people, especially those living in rural areas, and many people's lives revolved totally around those of their livestock—feeding them, watering them, and seeing to their needs.

Charlie was a middle-aged man in our community who lived on his farm with his wife and assorted in-laws. He always looked like he stepped out of a Grant Wood painting, not a Norman Rockwell one. He was five foot five with a scruffy beard and spoke in gruff, short sentences. I guess you'd say he was *taciturn*, but in those days, we didn't know that word; we just knew he was *grumpy*.

He did not have a job outside of his farm but did other things to make money. For example, he would slaughter animals for the local farmers. You would take a live critter to Charlie and pick it up a couple of days later, cut into neatly quartered pieces and covered with old sheets of newspaper to keep the flies away. Instead of paying Charlie money, many people who used his services would give him some cuts of meat in trade for his cutting-up work so he could have meat on days other than Sunday!

Charlie also owned a big black bull that looked very ferocious at times. Charlie and his bull provided breeding services to local cow owners for a fee, which was another way he augmented his income. You could bring your heifer to Charlie's and they would release the bull and have him in the barnyard to impregnate the female. Sometimes, the bull would sniff around a bit, and other times he would get to work fast and get the job done right away.

Charlie charged five dollars for the bull's services, with satisfaction guaranteed or your money back. No dickering about it; it was obvious that the bull either did the job or he didn't.

My Dad had bought an old, dilapidated farmhouse; the roof leaked, the sheds were falling apart, and none of the structures had electricity or running water. We would milk our cows and keep the milk in a metal can and then lower it into our dug well to keep it cold. Dad paid two thousand dollars for the farmhouse and barn, which was located on eight acres of land. He put down one thousand dollars and then added installment payments of twenty dollars per week for one year.

We grew up with no TV or no cell phones and led a very sedentary existence. We heated exclusively with wood and were constantly cutting wood and carting it to our wood shed and then into the house. We probably touched each piece of wood four or five times before we burned it. We were poor but didn't know it, or at least we weren't allowed to think about it for too long. Pretty much everybody was in the same boat.

My friend Scotty and I played around the farm after school and all during school and summer vacations. Those were glorious days, and the summer stretched on forever when we got out of school, but then time flew by.

We wore no shoes in summer to save on shoe leather and could run down the gravel road like the wild wind.

Once we toughened up our feet that is!

Scotty and I explored many old paths into the forest in the surrounding communities. We felt like explorers in a strange land and imagined ourselves back in time. We'd climb trees and wash our feet in cold water brooks. Scotty and I liked to bring our sandwiches out into the woods and eat them there, far away from everybody.

One day, we heard that Charlie's bull was missing, but we did not pay much attention to it because it did not affect our family. On this warm summer day, however, we ventured down a path leading to the shore and thought we heard some strange noises down by a stream.

Being two curious youngsters, we decided to explore where the sound came from, and a short time later, we came on this big black bull. There he was: Charlie's bull. Our first thought was that there must be a reward for such an outstanding bull on the loose.

We wanted that reward in the worst way.

But first, we had to capture the big bull.

We went to my father's barn and got a ten-quart bucket of cattle grain and fifty feet of good, strong rope. We returned to where we last saw the bull, and he was still there. We sprinkled some grain on the ground leading to the base of a large tree and laid the rope around the bucket. It didn't take long for Mr. Bull to get curious and stick his nose into the bucket; a flip of the rope and the noose was firmly tightened around the bull's neck.

He tried to resist, but when he realized that the rope was tied firmly to the tree, he gave up. Now off we went to see if we could get a reward for our gallant undertaking.

But we thought if we just led the bull back to Charlie, he might just thank us and not give us anything.

We approached Charlie's farmhouse to find Charlie out feeding his chickens. "Charlie, we heard you lost your bull," we said. His reply was a grunt, which we guessed was an affirmative response.

I said, "Does your bull have a big white spot between his eyes running down to his nose?"

This question caught Charlie's attention, and he said, "Do you boys know where my bull is?"

CHARLIE'S BULL

We said we might know where he could be and might be able to catch him if you was paying a reward for it.

He grunted some more and allowed as how it would be worth a dollar if we found the bull and detained it.

We laughed, pointing out that his bull must be worth more than a dollar for him because you would get five dollars for one heifer service.

We were only eight and nine years old, but good negotiators all the same. We kept at it, and after a lot of bickering back and forth, Charlie agreed to a five dollar reward.

Off we went, pretending we had to search far and wide for the bull. We took our time sauntering around this way and that way and laughing at how clever we were.

Finally, after about an hour, we went back to Charlie's and said, "Okay, Charlie, come with us; we think we have your Mr. Bull."

We led Charlie down a long path one mile from his farm and then went way off into the woods. Charlie never would have known to look where we had it tied. Once Charlie saw his big bull tied firmly to a tree, he turned to us and said, "That's my bull, alright. You boys did some good." Charlie even smiled a big smile, one we'd never seen before.

"Now help me get this bull back to my farm, and I will pay you boys the five dollar reward." Charlie then took his nice long stick with a hook on it and placed it in the nose ring. As soon as he did that, the bull calmed down, and we all headed to Charlie's place. With the bull firmly secured and locked in his stall, Charlie's bull was back in business. Charlie then just took out his old, worn wallet and counted out five $1 bills.

As Scotty and I walked away, we hollered over our shoulders, "It's nice doing business with you Charlie, see you next time your bull gets loose."

We then headed to the local store to get a nickel root beer and some penny candy, marveling at our good fortune.

Everyone was happy.

Charlie got his bull back.

Scotty and I had a lot more money than when the day started.

And Mr. Bull . . . well, Mr. Bull had a smile on his face when he saw the new heifer Charlie had lined up for his service.

Those were the days, my friend.

We thought they would never end.

But they did, of course.

I still smile to myself, though, when I think of the day the bull walked into our lives and left five dollars behind.

THE TALE OF THE BAT BOY AND THE PRESIDENT
Juliana L'Heureux

How did a Biddeford batboy get a shoutout in the presidential library of President H. W. Bush?

Here's how!

Any roving reporter who spends time in York County, Maine, will come across someone who tells a friendly story about Kennebunkport's famous Bush family. I know the experiences my family enjoyed when President Bush and his wife Barbara attended two family weddings.

In fact, the Bush family's legendary interactions with the local community are woven into the area's history. A remarkable and unforgettable skydiving feat on June 12, 2014, celebrated President Bush's ninetieth birthday in Kennebunkport. He marked the occasion by leaping from a helicopter at six thousand feet, harnessed to Sergeant First Class Mike Elliott, a retired member of the Golden Knights, the Army's parachute team.

The family's Walker's Point summer home in oceanside Kennebunkport was purchased in the late nineteenth century by David Davis Walker, who was President George Herbert Walker Bush's great-grandfather. Walker's Point juts out into the ocean in York County's coastal community of Kennebunkport, located approximately midway between Portland, Maine, and Portsmouth, New Hampshire. The property was previously known as Point Vesuvius.

One particular story about our forty-first president is documented in the *Biddeford Journal Tribune* about when he was a young man playing baseball in the York County leagues. This story was told to me by Norman Faucher, who was a well-known resident of Biddeford, a businessman who was active with the Chamber of Commerce, served on several nonprofit boards, and dedicated volunteer time to his Catholic parish. Throughout his life, he was a sports enthusiast, and baseball was his favorite game. He played for the Portland Twilight League for two years when he was contacted by pro-league scouts and was coached by former Boston Red Sox shortstop and Sanford native Freddie Parent. He also played at St. Michaels College in Vermont for four years.

Like many young Franco-American boys during the late 1940s, Faucher couldn't wait to play baseball. He was only fourteen years old on September 7, 1947, when he came face to face with the young George H. W. Bush, who played first base for the summer Collegians team in Maine's York County Twilight League after making the Yale varsity team.

Faucher was actually the team's batboy and should not have been playing, but he took to the field anyway as a first baseman. When the young Bush made a base hit, he had the chance to take a close look at Faucher.

"He told me I was pretty young to play baseball," Faucher recalled. "I was. I never dreamed he'd become president of the United States."

Newspaper accounts of the game between Faucher's Biddeford St. Andre's Apostles and the Kennebunkport Collegians report a 21-3 rout, with the Apostles winning. The Biddeford team's runaway score is likely the reason Faucher was able to make himself a first baseman and get in the game.

Faucher's baseball story is woven into his family's Franco-American oral history.

Local newspaper accounts in the *Biddeford Journal* listed the lineup of the September 7, 1947 Twilight League game, and the documentation put Faucher's name into Maine's Baseball Hall of Fame. Future President Bush had a good game night, with three hits in three times at bat.

Foucher's Maine Hall of Fame induction in 2003 puts him in sports history and in partnership with his youthful opponent, George H. W. Bush. In fact, President Bush was also inducted into Maine's Baseball

THE TALE OF THE BAT BOY AND THE PRESIDENT

Hall of Fame in 1994—nine years before Faucher. The president's Maine Hall of Fame recognition was not just about the game he played in 1947 but because of his experience playing in the summer leagues during his college years at Yale University while spending summers with his family at Walker's Point.

And wait, there's more!

After my interview, Faucher clipped the stats from that game and kept the original in his family's archives. The story he told was published and accepted by the George H. W. Bush Presidential Library as part of their trivia collection. Archivist Buffe Hollis wrote, "We appreciate your generosity in providing this item to the George Bush Presidential Library."

The bat boy who turned first baseman is now in a presidential library. Quite an honor!

Regrettably, I was not offered a finder's fee for this fine addition of true and even magnificent trivia to the Bush Presidential Library, nor was Faucher ever asked to speak there—which would have made this story even more impactful. But the original newspaper article is still available as proof that in America, you never know who you're going to encounter and where they—and you—will end up in life.

Experiences with politicians running for statewide office will always find York County to be a challenging place to campaign. Although the area looks small when compared to the rest of Maine on the map, many people leap to the conclusion that York County is a small and rich tourist destination. Actually, a good chunk of York County is rural in areas west of the industrial communities of Sanford and Biddeford. Small towns like Parsonsfield, Shapleigh, Newfield, Waterboro, and Cornish, to name just a few, are off the tourist map and hardly ever make the news.

This diversity between the wealthy coastal areas, the industrial communities, and the rural towns creates confusion among political advisers who have little knowledge about the area. When I lived in Sanford, I found the population to be closely aligned with New Hampshire, while Mainers who live north of York County nicknamed it "North Massachusetts."

In 1994, when Angus King was seeking his first term as Maine's governor, his campaign called to ask if I could help connect him to York County's Franco-Americans. We set up a meeting with his driver for breakfast in Sanford at Jerry Arsenault's Diner, on the corner of Maine and Lebanon Streets. My advice was to somehow connect with workers at the Portsmouth Naval Shipyard in Kittery, because the area employed thousands of people who lived throughout York County, many of them Franco-Americans.

Of course, the problem was that "civilian" Angus King had no authorization to enter the base. So I created an opportunity. I had a military identification card and a "base sticker" authorizing my entry because my husband is retired Navy.

Many people know very little about the Portsmouth Naval Shipyard in Kittery, but the location is historic. The base archives contain data dating back to American colonial times, and a museum on the site contains this information. I felt it would be possible to get Angus an appointment to visit the curator because, as a gubernatorial candidate, it made sense for him to know what was in the museum. Nevertheless, he would not be allowed to visit with workers.

But I had a plan for that, too. I knew many employees at the Shipyard because of my years working on the Federal Employee Campaigns for the United Way. So, I called a few and told them about the visit I scheduled for Angus to the museum. They agreed to have their union colleagues stand outside the work buildings to greet him as we drove to the museum. It worked like magic! Hard hats tipped their heads as we drove by.

But the rest of the story is even more significant. Unbeknownst to me or Angus, the museum curator was anxious to show us a colonial-era original deed signed by the King of England confirming that the land in Kittery was part of Massachusetts.

Therefore, in 1820, when Maine became a state, this property was included in the newly designated state's territory. Taadaaa! There was the proof! In spite of decades of controversy about whether or not the Portsmouth Naval Shipyard was located in Maine or New Hampshire, even though it is on the border of the two states, the King of England's document clarified that the property was never part of New Hampshire. Certainly, it was important information for the future governor of Maine to know about.

We all had a few chuckles about the way history is made and how history is recorded.

THE CURSE OF A WEAK STOMACH
Dave Emery

Let's face it . . . some folks can handle things that are gross, and others . . . not so much. With me, it's complicated; lobster bait, even *old* lobster bait, doesn't bother me in the least. Neither do worms, maggots, or any of the multi-legged creepy-crawlies that you might find under a log in the Maine woods. Moreover, I'm an avid hunter and fisherman, so blood and guts don't gross me out (as long as they're not my own).

But what gets to me are certain bad smells or combinations of smells, particularly when accompanied by motion I can't control. Certain textures and tastes affect me immediately, particularly greasy ones. Rocking and pitching motions are particularly devastating to my system, often affecting me in strange ways. Flying doesn't bother me at all, nor do automobiles, but rocking boats get me every time; I can get seasick looking at an aquarium. Once, I even got nauseous on a treadmill!

That is where it gets complicated.

When I was a kid, I always looked forward to the Rockland Lobster Festival, particularly because I liked the carnival rides. I would watch the carneys set up the rides, and later, I would try to build them with my Erector Set. When it came to riding, the Ferris wheel was too calm for me; it had to be the octopus or the tilt-a-whirl. I couldn't get enough of them. My stomach handled all of them just fine.

So when my son was old enough to be introduced to this magical machinery, I was anxious to take him to the Festival, and I was excited to relive a part of my own youth.

Big mistake!

About the second revolution of the tilt-a-whirl seat, I could feel the two chili dogs I had just eaten begin to rebel . . . they wanted no part of this adventure. And my head was spinning in a vain effort to find stability, somehow, someway. Fortunately, we managed to disembark without incident, but as soon as I was on terra firma, I found that my head was still somewhere spinning around on that accursed contraption, much to the amusement of my son . . .

YACK . . . most of it landed in a nearby garbage can!

And I was done for the rest of the day.

Another time, my family and I were in Leesburg, Virginia, and went to breakfast at a popular local restaurant. It was typical fare . . . bacon and eggs, orange juice, toast, and a few home fries. The restaurant was quite busy, and several people were approaching the entrance as we left . . . which was exactly when my system decided to reject the greasy bacon and home fries . . .

RALPH . . . right in front of the entrance. I heard someone cry, "OH my GOD!" and at least six dissuaded patrons hurried away, probably for good. "Let's not eat here, Emma," I think one of them said. Neither Fodor nor Michelin have ever come up with such a convincing or effective rating system!

Another time, I was in Winslow campaigning for reelection back in '78, as I recall, when I was scheduled to tour a poultry processing factory. The plant manager was an enthusiastic supporter, eager for me to *see* and *appreciate* every aspect of the process. And so it went, from doomed chickens being efficiently dispatched by what he referred to as "the killer" to the de-feathering, evisceration, cleaning, packaging, and shipping.

He was careful to explain that "the broiler you buy at the grocery store isn't necessarily packed with his own giblets . . . why, a worker just takes one of each from the tray, plus a neck, and places them in a small bag, then into the cavity."

I knew this to be true because, many years ago, while preparing the Thanksgiving turkey, my grandmother suddenly exclaimed, "Look at this . . . our turkey had *two hearts*!" She had evidently never considered the

THE CURSE OF A WEAK STOMACH

necessary shortcuts of the commercial process; she had only been familiar with the way it had always been done on the *farm*.

Anyway, a poultry processing factory is not a pleasant place for a tour (or for work, if we're honest), especially on a hot July afternoon. The smells are dreadful! It is likely even worse if you have to spend days and weeks on end working on the production line.

BLAAAH... right into the hedge along the walkway to the parking area. No KFC that night!

Yet another episode occurred in Quebec City. We had gone to Quebec as tourists with another family and were staying in a comfortable hotel conveniently located near *La Citadelle de Québec* and *Les Plaines d'Abraham*. As we got onto the elevator to our rooms, I was bothered by a strange and unidentifiable odor, not necessarily biological in origin but quite pungent and decidedly unpleasant.

WOOF... fortunately, all of our party left the elevator before I did. Later, we took the stairs.

But the most notorious incident of all occurred on a fishing boat somewhere in the Gulf of Maine. I grew up in Rockland, which, at the time, was one of the most important fishing ports in New England. Although I did not come from a fishing family, some of my ancestors were seamen and even masters of vessels. So, while I can get seasick just by looking at a glass of water, *somewhere* buried in my genes is an affinity for the sea and for those who go down to the sea in ships.

When I was in the State Legislature and later as a U.S. Congressman, Maine fishermen and their many issues were at the top of my priority list. I served on the Merchant Marine and Fisheries Committee in Congress and spent many hours meeting with representatives from all sectors of the Maine fishing industry.

Our committee was considering the two hundred-mile limit bill, which would establish an exclusive fishing zone for American fishermen up to two hundred miles from the mainland. So, naturally, when I was invited to spend a day aboard a trawler and see how it was done, I jumped at the chance.

I met Captain Stan Bayley at the wharf in Portland at about 3 a.m. and off we went. But I forgot my sea legs... and after a couple of hours, the rocking and pitching began to get to me. The diesel fumes didn't help either. So I left the pilothouse for some fresh air, but it didn't help much. A couple of rolls and pitches later ...

B O O T ... I suppose that would be *das Boot* in German. I grabbed the rail and heaved until I thought I would turn inside out. Stan and his crew were undoubtedly amused, but I was too sick to find any humor in it. The worst part was that they had work to do, and I certainly couldn't expect them to give up a day's pay just to make their Congressman more comfortable.

Of course, that story was broadcast up and down the coast from fishing boat to fishing boat ... truly too good of a story not to share. So, months later, at the annual Fisherman's Forum, more than one person asked if I was the guy who puked all over Stan Bayley's fishing boat.

I guess it's nice to be known for *something* distinctive!

I also take comfort in knowing that I'm not the only public figure to have had to deal with this sort of thing. In January 1992, President George H. W. Bush was on a diplomatic visit to Japan when he fell ill at a banquet given in his honor by Prime Minister Kiichi Miyazawa. Not only did he vomit, he also managed to toss his cookies all over the astonished Prime Minister.

Apologies were made and all was forgiven, and President Bush was able to complete his visit with no further illness. A month or so later, after returning to his duties at home, Bush came under some criticism for not having been tough enough with the Japanese in the ongoing trade negotiations.

"Whaddya mean?" quipped Bush. "I puked all over them, didn't I?"

It may be embarrassing and messy, but at least it's not dishonorable!

THE BIRDS AND THE BEES AND THE SONNY NEWCOMB WORD
Dennis Bailey

I grew up in Livermore Falls, a small mill town on Maine's mighty Androscoggin River. Today, it looks nothing like the town of my youth. Once, it was a vibrant community filled with locally owned shops, drugstores, restaurants, and gas stations. My father owned a furniture store (the town had two of them, almost side by side), which was started by his father and prospered for many years.

But by the late sixties, cheap gas, good roads, and the shopping malls of nearby Lewiston-Auburn sucked business away from the downtown. Because of lower prices and a wider selection, driving thirty miles just to buy groceries didn't seem that crazy anymore. And when the big paper mills, the town's lifeblood for decades, began to shrink, its fate was sealed. At its peak, the International Paper Company mill in nearby Jay employed fifteen hundred people, but in 2006, it was sold to Verso Holdings LLC, and by then, only seven hundred workers were employed there. The workforce was down to five hundred when it was sold again to Pixelle Specialty Solutions, and finally, the mill closed for good in 2023.

Seeing the empty buildings and boarded-up storefronts today makes it hard to imagine that my memories of the town are more like something out of a Thornton Wilder novel. Perhaps it was inevitable, but it's sad nonetheless.

Most of the kids I went to school with had shallow horizons: Get a high school diploma (or not) and go to work in the mill, like their father before them. That was the primary goal. Really, for most, their only goal. The paper mills of Chisholm and Jay dominated the towns and, when the wind was just right, enveloped the communities in a sulfurous, rotten-egg stench. We often joked about which town smelled worse, Rumford or Livermore Falls/Jay. But for most of the inhabitants who relied on the mills for their hefty paychecks, it smelled like money.

It was a tough town, full of hardworking, blue-collar mostly Franco-American Catholics. (We were Methodists, or as the saying went, "Baptists who can read.") In grade school, there were plenty of swaggering bullies—ruffians, hooligans, juvenile delinquents, whatever you want to call them—terrorizing the hallways and the school playground. It's only a slight exaggeration to say that when the English teacher asked, "Class, what comes after every sentence?" most kids raised their hands and said, "An appeal."

One such bully was Sonny Newcomb, a loudmouth braggart who was best to avoid. Sonny was older than me (I was only eight or nine at the time) and he scared the hell out of me. He also had a favorite word that I was unfamiliar with—the F word. He used it constantly, every third or fourth word, it seemed.

I later thought the English teachers missed an opportunity by not using the F word for those boring lessons on diagramming a sentence, which I never really grasped. It would have made a lot more sense using the F word because it's so versatile. It can be a noun ("I don't give a f***"), a verb ("Go f*** yourself"), an adjective ("I have so much f***ing homework!"), as an adverb enhancing an adjective ("Mary is so f***ing gorgeous!"), and so on. It also, depending on the tone with which it was delivered, had positive ("You are so f****** beautiful") or negative ("You're such a f****** jerk") connotations. Diagramming a sentence would have been so easy, and we would have all graduated with advanced English degrees.

Anyway, Sonny Newcomb gave the F word a daily workout, in all its iterations. But at my tender age, I had no idea what it meant. I didn't even know it was a swear word. He used it with such authority and such emphasis; it just seemed like a powerful word to enhance his threatening demeanor.

THE BIRDS AND THE BEES AND THE SONNY NEWCOMB WORD

One night at supper (we called it supper, not dinner, which was probably a verbal class marker), my older brother Kevin used the F word in a sentence. I don't remember exactly what he said, but it was probably something like, "I don't want any more f***ing peas," or "Why the f*** are we having fish again?"

Both my parents gasped, horrified.

"Kevin," Mom scolded, "where did you hear that word?"

We all agreed: It came from Sonny Newcomb, and forever after, the F word became the "Sonny Newcomb Word," as in, "Mom, Doug said the Sonny Newcomb Word again!"

Judging from my parents' alarmed reaction, we knew it was a bad word you can't use at the supper table, or anywhere else. But why was it such a naughty word? We pleaded with our parents. What does it mean?

"Your father will explain it to you after supper," Mom said.

So, after the dishes were cleared, we gathered in the bedroom. Dad sprawled out on the lower bunk bed, my twin brother Doug sat next to him, Kevin was on the left, and I clung to the ladder leading to the upper bunk.

This was the moment that my Dad was to deliver his first lecture on the birds and the bees, enlightening his children on the facts of life, the miracle of creation—the full Monty, as momentous an occasion as a bar mitzvah.

He began:

"So, you guys have been to your Uncle Elmer's farm, right?"

We nodded, yes, of course. Uncle Elmer, my mom's brother, had a farm just a few miles from us. We often rode our bikes there to help with the chores or play with my cousins.

"And you've seen all the cows in the pasture and his barn, right?"

Again, we nodded. Of course, Uncle Elmer had a good-sized herd, it was a working dairy farm, after all.

"And you've seen one cow get on top of another cow."

Hold it. Wait. What?

My brothers both nodded, like of course, they've seen it many times. Not to be embarrassed, I probably nodded too, though I had never seen such a thing. I was confused. In my mind, I had a picture of a cow standing on top of another cow. How did that work? Was a ladder involved, a step stool? Did Uncle Elmer give the cow a boost? And what did this have to do with the Sonny Newcomb Word?

I don't remember what Dad said after that. My head was spinning. I don't know if he imparted great knowledge of procreation to my brothers that I somehow missed; we never spoke of it again.

But the next time I was at Uncle Elmer's, I kept an eye out. I wanted to see this. A cow on top of another cow. That would be something. But I never saw it.

It would be many years before I came to a full comprehension of the Sonny Newcomb Word, and I learned most of it where all the sex education was imparted in those days (and probably still is on all the really important dimensions of it)—that is, on the school playground.

But thanks for trying, Dad.

COVID CAPERS
Will Davis

It was another slow day in a summer full of them in Harpswell. Cloudy, foggy, with off-and-on drizzle. By the afternoon, the drizzle had turned to a raging downpour and steady winds, the strongest the summer of 2023 had seen. The summer so far had been a doozy. I was preparing myself for the start of high school while trying my best not to think about classes starting up again in September. At age fourteen, that's just what you do.

One of the main highlights of the summer is the annual trip my cousins make to Maine from Virginia in August. Unfortunately, my grandfather, Bobby, contracted COVID right before their arrival. Even today, I still find it very ironic that my grandfather got COVID. He was the most COVID-averse person I know, wearing a mask everywhere and avoiding contact with all humans and their pets whenever possible. You know that person you see in the car driving alone with a mask and gloves on? Well, that was him.

So I was really surprised when Grandpa got COVID and had to stay indoors. He is very demanding when sick. Deep down I think my Grandma, Dee, was wishing she could just leave him by himself and limit contact herself. Nonetheless she was doing everything in her power to prepare for our other family members' arrival while also being the doctor, nurse, and cook of the household. Granted, seeing the messes her husband often leaves behind after his meals, serving him herself might have been more helpful for her.

One thing she couldn't necessarily help with was his boat. The main problem with the boat turned out to be the inadequate bilge pump that had broken down sometime over the course of the summer. This fact would become significant as the storm worsened. We learned afterward that Grandpa went out into the storm trying to start a second pump, but that didn't work either. So, in a panic and feeling soaked and chilled, he returned to the house, picked up the phone, and called us. He needed help, and he needed it fast.

My father and I had just settled on the sofa after a long day, cozying up inside away from the rain. We heard the phone ring and waited a bit. Seeing that nobody was going to answer it, as typical guys do, we looked to my mom. Annoyed, she sighed and walked to the phone. With the phone to her ear, she announced to us in a hesitant voice, "It's my Dad. He sounds very worried."

After putting the phone on speaker, we heard the serious concern in his voice as he described his sinking boat. Dad and I jumped off the couch, slipped on whatever shoes we could grab the fastest, and headed out to the truck.

The rain poured down, increasing heavily as we pulled into my grandparents' place. Through the glass door, I saw Grandpa standing next to Grandma with a mask on. I couldn't help but crack a smile at his image. His hair was plastered to his skull but spiked off in multiple directions like Albert Einstein on a bad hair day, and his glasses were crooked. He looked dazed and just barely able to give us his signature salute with all of the layers of clothing he had on. Keeping our distance—since we, who have taken few if any precautions, had not gotten COVID and didn't want to—we only opened the door a bit.

Grandpa looked wet and very distressed. Despite his condition, he had been out in the pouring rain trying to save his boat. The bilge pump had totally died, and the waves were coming over the transom. He was afraid the boat would sink and he'd been out in the elements trying to hook up another pump.

"I hope you guys can help," he says, pointing to his now sinking Whaler getting lower in the ocean with each passing minute. Dad walked confidently down to the dock, seemingly unfazed by the task, despite the conditions. He is a seventh generation "Bailey Island boy," so I had confidence he could solve the problem. As a young man, he once worked on a commercial fishing boat, the "Walter Leeman," going for swords on the Grand Banks when Linda Greenlaw (immortalized in the movie *The Perfect Storm*) was the ship's cook. People are impressed when they hear all that! I know I am.

After we appraised the situation for a few minutes, I looked back at the house and saw Grandma standing by the window next to her wild-haired husband, joyfully waving down at me. Eventually, Dad had an idea about how we could redirect the boat's position. The plan was to swing the boat around so the waves crashed against the higher, elevated bow instead of the low-lying stern.

As Dad grabbed the bowline, ready to command the prow to the front of the dock, he directed me to untie the stern line. I did, but then I dropped it after I noticed him struggling with the bowline. Before I could get there to help, he pulled hard on the rope until suddenly, the line that we thought was attached to the bow flung itself onto the dock and out of Dad's grasp.

Stunned, Dad looked into his empty hands. What a mess! We had come to solve the problem and now it looked like we *were* the problem! One of Grandpa's most prized possessions was now totally detached from his dock and blowing away into the open ocean. We both did a double take. Dad's mouth was hanging open and his eyes were as wide as a bug's.

You didn't have to be a lip reader to guess that my father is cussing. "What the F***?"

I can only imagine my grandparents' reaction watching through the window: "Is the boat floating away?"

"Well, it sure does appear that way, doesn't it?"

Dad slipped off his shoes, and I watched him get into his first sprinter's stance since high school football conditioning. He barreled down the dock, half-committing to the jump but not quite making it to the boat. His clothes, wallet, and everything else didn't.

Kaploom!

Did I mention my Dad had a very bad right hip and was getting a hip replacement in a couple of weeks? *We may have to push up that schedule,* I thought.

Not a good scene.

Dad, fully clothed, neck-deep in the ocean, and entering the darkness, swam toward the boat while it continued to float away into the fog. In a panic, I asked, "Should I jump in too?" Before he could answer, I checked my pockets for my phone and dropped it onto the dock, slipped my shoes off and took the leap of faith before plunging into the frigid water.

Splash! Big splash. Water very cold.

And to think we came to help Grandpa. Now he may have to help us. Lots of luck with that—not sure how much a COVID patient could do at this point. My grandparents watched as the intense current ripped us out from the bubble of light surrounding the dock. I swam up for air as I looked forward, seeing Dad bobbing out of the water, doing his best attempt at a breaststroke. Meanwhile, back on land, unbeknownst to Grandpa, Grandma had made a beeline out into the rain and raging wind with nothing but her white nightgown and a flashlight.

Now Grandpa didn't have just two of his closest family members missing but also his beloved wife.

The water was clear enough to at least see Dad swimming with just one leg as I caught up to him now in a doggy paddle, a three-legged dog at that. At this point, the boat started to outpace him, so I was glad I had made the decision to jump in with him. Now that we were next to each other, I asked rhetorically, "What were you thinking?"

Before I could ask him what we should do next, I realized there was a dangerous threat fast approaching the boat. The neighbor's dock seemed to be growing larger and larger, appearing out of the darkness. *Oh great,* I thought, *not only would the boat be destroyed, but we were also going to destroy someone else's dock!*

I picked up the pace and took a few more strokes until I was an arm's length away from the bow. I reached out, grasping the boat's siding, and held on just long enough to grip the railing next, somewhat slowing down the boat's trajectory by using my other arm as a paddle to move us toward shore and away from the neighbor's dock, thinking at least if I let it go, it might go under the ramp instead.

There's only so much a 140-some-odd-pound kid could do, though. Looking back, I could see I just had to hold on a little longer before Dad would be able to come in for reinforcements. I was able to swing the stern out just enough so he could grab onto the back and gain some leverage and give his hip a rest for a moment. We may have both latched onto the boat. However, it was still completely controlling us, and the question in my mind was, how are we going to get on this thing with no ground to stand on as we were hanging off the side?

The job was far from over.

Tension was building both on land and at sea.

Taking a deep breath, I caught a glimpse of a flashing light coming from the woods.

"Will!" the light shouted. Nope, not the light itself, just Grandma. By now, she had worked her way all the way down just above the steep cliff that dropped off to the shore in the dense forest between her house and her neighbor's.

"We're here!" I shouted back. Of course, through all the rain and wind and ruckus, she was unable to hear me, and she continued shouting in our direction.

With my last bit of energy, I used the railing to pull myself far enough up to where I could swing my leg out of the water and over the railing. This was another reason why I was glad I jumped in after Dad. It's hard for me to imagine him pulling off that move. I sent myself tumbling into the boat right beside a rusty treble hook lure. If I didn't end up drowning, tetanus would surely do the trick.

I pulled myself to my feet, and finally, Dad spoke up. "Grab the oar!" he shouted. Now, it is common knowledge that every vessel should be properly equipped with an oar, and I don't think it would take a genius to figure out why. However, even as smart as Grandpa is, I cannot give him credit for having an oar in his boat in the case of this emergency. I searched the boat from stem to stern, splishing and splashing in the shin-high water, unable to find one anywhere. And to be truthful, there are not many places an oar could be hiding.

While searching I heard another voice, "Sandy! Sandy! Where are you?"

Now, my ill grandfather was outside roaming the woods and combating the weather as he searched for his wife, who was still frantically shining the light across the strait, surveying the water for us everywhere.

Unable to find the oar, I replied, "I don't see it."

"You don't see it?!" This was a shock to Dad, who was raised never to leave the dock without an oar in your boat.

"I don't know what to tell you."

Dad scoffed, "What about the keys?" This was a stupid question. If I couldn't find the oar, good luck with me finding the much smaller keys that weren't in the boat's ignition. I once again started to search, but before long, the boat began moving weirdly. When I snapped my head back around, I did not expect to see Dad wrestling the boat toward the shore, panting and groaning with all his might.

As he pulled the boat further toward shore, still floating down the narrows, I asked, "You touching?"

"Ye—"

He couldn't finish his response before his head disappeared beneath the waves as he fell off the rock that he had thought was the muddy seafloor. He stuck his head back up after a couple of seconds, coming to the realization that, huffing and puffing, he was still far from the bottom.

Above us, I could tell my grandparents were getting close to each other as the yells of "Will!" from Grandma had turned to "Chris!" To us, it was obvious they were close, but often they'd yell at the same time, saying something sounding like "Sanrisy!" *If one of them just shut up for a few seconds, maybe they'd be able to find each other*, I thought to myself under my breath.

Finally, I can tell my Dad is standing—on one leg.

"Thought I lost you there for a second," I said.

He laughed, which made me feel a little better and lightened the mood slightly.

"Gimme a hand."

I reached down to the side of the boat, pulling his arm as hard as I could as he pushed off the flats with his good foot, lifting the bad leg over the gunwale. He tumbled into the swaying boat, floundering into the water that accumulated in the stern of the boat. Our mood suddenly sunk again (pun intended!) after noticing that we were drifting once again with nothing stopping us, especially with the mysterious disappearance of the key.

Dad barely made it to his feet, pushing me to the side with his dripping wet hand. He shuffled his other hand back and forth on the dash, checking all the compartments until he stuck his hand into the console right above the ignition, only to find the keys immediately.

"How hard did you look, buddy?" he asked.

"Rumdumdumdum." The boat spit, then "Ruuuuuoooooooom" as it kicked into gear just in time as we are about to go under the neighbor's ramp and sideswipe their boat. Dad threw it into reverse and then throttled us forward.

Safety beckoned. We now had hope.

Just as my grandparents found each other, they heard the boat motor start, a reminder of how far you'll go for love. I looked up in their direction as the light turned toward the driveway, which made me feel a lot better that they weren't still searching for each other, or for someone they think could be dead, or for somebody who is no longer out there.

"We're going to beach this thing in the cove," Dad said. "I'm not dealing with it anymore on the dock tonight."

In my head, I thought, *Well, I'd hope so*. But this only produced in my mind the image of the boat flying into something like a ledge or a rock in the pitch-black while trying to gain speed to make it up on shore. *Oh, brother*, I thought, *Titanic 2.0*.

"All righty," I responded, holding my breath now and secretly crossing my fingers behind my leg as the boat motors around the point, battling the whitecaps. The boat accelerated as we approached the cove. I closed my eyes, braced for impact, and held my seat with a death grip.

Thud!

I opened my eyes to the boat sloshed in mud and eelgrass but safely up on land. Dad turned off the engine. We used the nearby trees to tie a non-frayed rope to secure the boat once and for all this time—or at least all night.

As Dad finished tying the last knot, we heard my grandparents clapping from the house as a thank-you and goodbye. They did not want to get either of us sick but acknowledged our efforts even though they both had to be freezing cold. I think that was the best send-off they could have given us. Dad waddled over to me, all weathered and teary-eyed, looked me dead in the eye, and we both broke into hysterics.

Somehow the trauma of the adventure when we thought we were going to die turned into a laughable moment.

"What just happened?" I said, laughing.

"This is a night we'll never forget," Dad replied.

"Wait until Mom hears about this," I cackled.

Dad smiled as he went in for a drenched bear hug and gave me a pat on the back. Just for a moment, it seemed as if the rain stopped and the wind halted and it was just Dad and I sharing a connection we had never felt before.

If there was one thing that night taught me, it is that for starters, I have a really great family. But also just to enjoy any adventure that comes to you. If something doesn't go your way, sometimes that is half of the fun.

As I write this, I remind myself to give my grandfather a new bilge pump—or even a used one—for Christmas and make sure it gets installed on his boat before the next disaster.

THE BROTHERS STRIKE BACK
Bob Whelan

When I matriculated from Bowdoin in 1958, it was a far different college than it is today. There were no restrictions on alcohol, for example, but sex was discouraged. Drugs were virtually unknown. There were even some students expelled for taking a date to the second floor of a fraternity house or dorm. As I now understand it, social life at Bowdoin is the reverse of this situation: All kinds of sex is okay, but alcohol is dangerous and is discouraged, though I doubt that anyone is expelled for taking a bottle of scotch to the second floor of a dormitory or frat house.

In our day, alcohol was central to our party weekends. A rather odious tradition developed when I was a member. On Sunday mornings, there was the "milk punch" free to one and all. The fraternity had big old-fashioned metal milk cans that could hold gallons of milk. The brothers would carefully gather up all the alcohol left over from the night before—wine, gin, vodka, rye whiskey, and bourbon, to say nothing of rum and various odious liquors. This wretched mess was mixed with milk "to soothe the stomach."

Weird behavior often followed its ingestion. Sometimes, the brothers would don choir robes and climb onto the pointed roof of the house to greet the churchgoers below as they walked to or returned from the First Parish Congregational Church, which was just down the road from the frat house. I've always wondered what the churchgoers thought about the huge, noisy bats that serenaded the passersby. Perhaps it evoked images of Heaven. Perhaps not.

Today, no fraternities are allowed at Bowdoin, and there were never sororities during my time, as it was an all-male school. However, fraternities were a significant presence at Bowdoin in the past. Almost everyone belonged to a fraternity, as the college relied on them to feed students due to the absence of a central dining facility. The Moulton Union was not equipped to serve the approximately eight hundred students under the Bowdoin Pines.

The first week for freshmen at Bowdoin was devoted to rushing fraternities. By the end of the week, over 99 percent of students had pledged to one fraternity or another. The remaining less than 1 percent were independents who ate at Moulton Union. I pledged a fraternity and began freshmen orientation, a somewhat sanitized version of hazing. There was no physical abuse, but the emotional pressure could be disconcerting. Most of us received pledge names, some of which stuck. Mine was "Evil." At mealtimes, pledges were required to recite various bits of knowledge that the brothers deemed crucial to being a good Bowdoin boy and brother. For example, we had to sing the many Bowdoin songs we had memorized, including *Bowdoin Beata*. Nowadays, most Bowdoin students can barely sing even one unaided.

We also had to recite fraternity lore, which covered the chapter roll; that is, the list of chapters at other colleges and universities. These recitations were often done standing on a chair with all the pledges and brothers listening, and the brothers screaming negative feedback at the reciter: "You are a sad specimen of humanity, pledge. Why can't you learn even simple things? Stupid, stupid, stupid!!" Imagine students taking that kind of verbal abuse today. No, sir! There are now at least a couple of deans available to stamp that out.

As you see, mistakes were met with aggressive derisions of intelligence and character. The brothers' focus on humiliation was orchestrated by a "Hazing Master" who led the verbal assaults. Ironically, perhaps, or maybe even understandably, the pledge who received the most abuse as a freshman returned as the next Hazing Master to carry the tradition forward. We also had to wear beanies; to be caught without one brought on exponential verbal assaults again on character and intelligence.

THE BROTHERS STRIKE BACK

Some of us pledges could keep things in perspective, but others took it all too seriously and could be brought to tears. Of course, after a few weeks of this kind of slow torture came Hell Week, which culminated in THE TRIAL!!! Pledges were brought together in a holding area, waiting their turn to go to the cellar and face THE TRIAL!!! Then, each of us was brought down alone to a pitch-dark cellar and led maybe blindfolded (I can't remember) to a chair facing blinding lights. Behind the lights were the brothers, and we were asked a question: "If you saw a fraternity brother commit a murder, would you turn him in?"

Obviously, there was no right answer—saying yes to the pledge would be verbally assaulted as not being fit to be a brother because no brotherly loyalty was displayed; saying no, again, the pledge would be verbally assaulted as not being a good citizen by letting a murderer go free. Pledges simply couldn't win. I guess that was the whole point of the exercise. Can you imagine today's students putting up with this kind of bull?

At the end of Hell Week, when we were all made full-fledged brothers, we still had to put on a talent show and keep the brothers in beer. Two of us put on a comedy routine that drew good rounds of laughter from the brothers. The favorite routines were singing, from serious classical pieces to doo-wop, and then there were renditions of the songs of popular music stars, Chuck Berry, Paul Anka, and Neil Sedaka, which were popular in 1962. There were also new brothers who tried dancing, which was met with much derision.

One of us had the great idea to spike their beer with Ex-Lax to get even for the verbal hazing. And it was done. Payback is a bitch, so they say. Toilets were in short supply that night, so substitutes needed to be found. Some brothers headed to the dorms, which, unlike today, were unlocked, and others headed to nearby fraternity houses to ask for permission to use the bathrooms.

An ironic footnote: It was customary for the newly minted brothers to "kidnap" the Hazing Master for his actions during the pledge period, bring him to a remote location, and drop him off, sometimes without pants.

In my senior year, the Hazing Master was brought to the Allagash region in the Maine North Woods and dropped off. Ironically, he got back to the fraternity house before the kidnappers; hitchhiking on a dirt road, he was picked up by a hunter who was speeding back to Massachusetts and was brought by him to the front door of the frat house long before the evil brothers' return.

Other brothers sought revenge in unusual ways. One thought the entire initiation ritual, featuring a stuffed owl and a real human skull, was too ridiculous. These "sacred objects" were kept in a locked inner sanctum of the chapter house. However, on major party weekends, dates were permitted to stay there—while the brothers were actually banned—and female chaperones were stationed at the door all night long.

In exchange for a great deal of "making out," that brother tipped his date off about where the sacred objects were located. She then chose to put the skull in her suitcase and walk off with it. Obviously stimulated by this larceny, she went well beyond "making out" as a reward for the brother.

Weeks later, when the sacred skull was discovered missing before the next chapter meeting, all hell broke loose. A wild search followed, and accusations flew hither and yon. The president and his chief minions "investigated," quizzing the brothers and promising "justice." What could be the outcome?

But the perpetrator was never uncovered. Some of us always wondered what the date eventually did with the sacred skull, as she never returned to the campus, and her date never visited her at Wellesley or searched her room to see if it ended up on her desk as a trophy.

Still, it was quite humorous all around.

Thinking back, though, it was probably also a sign of the times that none of the brothers bothered to ask where the skull had come from in the first place. The best guess would have been that it did not involve grave robbing or an archaeological dig, as those would have been too intense and, frankly, too much work for the majority of the brothers. Rather, most likely, it had been a prop used in one of Professor Quimby's drama productions such as *Hamlet*. Poor Yorick's skull ending in a Wellesley dorm as a trophy? Who knew? Just imagine if a human skull were to be found in a dorm room today! Especially if it were found to be a Native American skull like those in various museums today.

THE BROTHERS STRIKE BACK

Bowdoin from 1958 to 1962 was much different than the Bowdoin of today. Our culture had remnants of earlier years—same-gender schools, fraternities unregulated by the school administration, big party weekends, with bands like Duke Ellington, sexist pranks, lack of racial diversity, and so forth. But it was heading to the full-blown revolutionary days of the late '60's—sex, drugs and rock 'n' roll. There is humor in each generation of student life, but the subjects of humor are different.

These stories are examples of what made us laugh in those days.

MISTAKEN IDENTITY
Dana Connors

I NEVER THOUGHT I WOULD HAVE SUCH A LONG AND VARIED CAREER. OR be mistaken for a genuine movie star—however briefly and inadvertently. I majored in public management at the University of Maine and worked as Assistant City Manager for approximately six months before I was promoted to the position of City Manager in Presque Isle.

My second position came when then-Governor Brennan asked me to be the Commissioner of the Maine Department of Transportation. After a brief, volunteer-based stint helping Governor Angus King transition into the Blaine House, I took the position with the Chamber in 1994, working with sixty local chambers of commerce.

I loved each opportunity, and I loved the people.

There were many stressful times, however, and I remember one of those with great fondness—at least afterward. One year, after a grueling referendum, I desperately needed some downtime and a break from the public stage.

We had finally prevailed at the ballot box and I needed to recharge my battery, so to speak. While our side won, it had been a stressful several months, and taking time to relax on the beaches of Aruba was just what the doctor ordered (so at least my imaginary doctor did at the time).

And so, off I flew to that blessed isle.

Before I go further with my moment in Aruba, however, it will be helpful to know that in my early years, the color of my hair was a mixture of blonde and light brown, depending on the time of year and the amount of sunlight I'd gathered. That all changed by the time I reached my nineteenth birthday, as white was beginning to gain prominence, and by the time I reached the age of thirty, my hair was all white.

Now, back to my time in Aruba.

It was just what I needed: a beautiful hotel right on the beach, with sun, sand, and crystal-clear ocean water. Life was good! It was the third day, and I was missing my book that I had brought along to help escape the worries of the world. I left the beach, heading to my room. To gain access to the hotel, it was necessary to traverse an expansive patio with a restaurant on one side and a pool on the other side.

The pool was very popular, especially for the twenty-somethings. As I passed by the pool, I overheard female voices saying: "It's him, hurry, we need to get his autograph," and "Maybe he'll join us." I quickly looked around to see who they were referring to. When I saw no one that I recognized, I knew for sure that it wasn't me, so I accessed the hotel to retrieve my book.

Fifteen minutes later with my book in hand, I was on my way to the beach for some serious reading. As I passed the pool, those same girls were there waiting in anticipation. For whom, I still wasn't sure. Their comments were similar to those expressed earlier. Like "I told you it was him." And "If you don't ask for his autograph, I will." I looked around for someone, anyone that might have celebrity status. Again, I saw no one even semi-famous; just then, the three girls approached me, asking for my autograph. They seemed very excited, talking over each other, wanting to know what my next movie was titled, and asking if I'd join them and others at the pool.

Whoa Nellie!

Needless to say, it was clearly a case of mistaken identity. However, at that moment, I chose to ignore that very important point. I thought, *I could be the man.* It's fair to say I loved the attention, or better said, I let my ego get the best of me. I quickly came to my senses and asked the right question: "Who do you think I am?"

They looked at each other in total confusion, turned to me and asked: "You're Leslie Nielsen aren't you? The actor starring in the movies *Airplane* and *Naked Gun?*"

I hesitated.

What if I said yes?

Ah, the mystic cords of memory.

I was living in the moment and enjoying the limelight, however briefly, but I quickly replied, "No, I'm not Leslie Nielsen. Do I look like him?" I asked.

"Yes, a lot, but it's your white hair that convinced us."

Awe shucks.

Yes, it was the white hair we both possessed with similar hairstyles that were responsible for the mistaken identity and my resultant experience.

More's the pity!

Alas, here is where this experience and my moment came to a close with words of appreciation to the three of them for making me feel special. With tongue in cheek, I said that I'd see them in the movies. They headed back to the pool, and I to the sand and waters of Aruba . . . they I'm sure disappointed, me a little embarrassed but flattered.

I've reflected many times since that time so long ago, and even today, as I recall that moment in time, I ask myself if it is a moment to remember or not.

Hell yes it was.

And it remains so.

Editor's Note: It is the mark of a memorable writer that his or her words are evocative enough to stimulate the reader to recall similar events and thoughts. For his part, editor Dennis Bailey notes that long known for his skillful leadership of the Maine business community as head of the Maine Chamber of Commerce, Dana was also revered for his very stylish clothes and very cool nickname "The Silver Fox." Dennis also points out that being taken for Leslie Nielson was not the first case of mistaken identity for Dana. When he accompanied Angus King to his first meeting of the National Governor's Association after the election, many people came up directly to shake Dana's hand, saying "Congratulations Governor," guessing that Dana's white hair and tailored suit made him look more like a governor than Angus, who, while adequately dressed for a trip to L.L.Bean with his black-and-red woods shirt, never looked like he had just stepped out of *GQ* magazine. And unlike most

MISTAKEN IDENTITY

governors, Angus had a mustache, rode motorcycles, and seemed to have spent far less time color-coordinating his attire.

And another of our editors, Dave Emery, stimulated by all these examples of mistaken identity, adds his own mini-vignette:

> A few years after I had returned from DC after serving in Congress and following my stint at the U.S. Arms Control and Disarmament Agency, my wife, Carol, and I were out to dinner somewhere in the Augusta area. Shortly after being seated, it became obvious that the middle-aged waitress recognized me and was acting rather nervously and a bit star-struck, it appeared.
>
> Let me digress for a moment. I am well aware that I am not the movie star type. I have never had that certain *je ne sais quoi* that gives actors and actresses the sparkle, infectious personality, and dramatic flair that makes them, well, stars. I've always had to work hard at it, but that's okay; I never wanted to be a movie star anyway!
>
> When I was in Congress, I served with several colleagues who were blessed with those qualities, two of whom—Olympia Snowe and Bill Cohen—were in our own delegation. They always looked great, dressed well, and carried themselves with confidence and style.
>
> I remember campaigning with Bill in 1978 when he was running for the U.S. Senate. It was a hot summer day in York County, and we were walking together along Route 1 to meet voters. After a couple of hours, I was hot and sweaty. My shirt was soaked with perspiration, my face and neck were red from the heat, my hair was hot and unruly (I actually had some hair then), and I probably was getting *a bit ripe* as well. Cohen, however, was fresh as a daisy. Not a hair out of place. No wrinkles to be seen on either his pants or his shirt. Hair coiffed perfectly as if he was about to be interviewed on TV. Dry and cool! Looked like he had just stepped out of the cover of *Esquire* magazine. That qualified as je ne sais quoi if I ever saw it!

So, back to the restaurant. The food was good, and the star-struck waitress had been especially attentive, so I gave her a nice tip.

"Oh! Thank you, Senator Cohen!" she gushed.

I wonder if Bill—or Dana or Angus for that matter—have ever been greeted with "Oh! Thank you, Congressman Emery!"

Probably not.

Finally, in a final, desperate attempt to arrest this parade of mistaken identity tales, editor Chris Potholm is moved to declare, "Perhaps Maine needs some more readily identifiable political leaders as we go forward."

DEAH PAHTS
Scott Hood

Noah was a Labrador "retriever" in name only. A lumbering, yellow, 110-pounder, he lived to eat and had little interest in moving too far from his bed in the kitchen. Outside, he had at his disposal nine acres of woods and lawn fronting the Androscoggin River in Topsham. But, despite the tendency of his breed to explore, he showed little interest in stealing a swim or straying uninvited into the neighbors' lands.

And *retrieving*? If you tossed a stick, he'd give you a withering look that said, "*You* threw it. *You* get it." He had a thing for crows, but even a murder of them on the lawn drew nothing more than a raised head and a halfhearted "Grrrrufff." He was a dog who honestly could not be bothered.

Except for that one time.

Because he wasn't apt to wander, Noah was a dog you could just let out. Like most dogs, for him, the outdoors was for doing his business, and you could just open the door, and out he'd go. When he wanted to come in—which, as I've explained, would be almost right away—he hurled himself noisily at the kitchen door.

One Saturday, he crashed into the door, and I opened it without a thought. Noah burst in, animated and gleeful in a way he normally wasn't, something big hanging from his mouth. Something bloody and—was that fur?

It *was* fur. It was a full, disembodied deer leg.

I pushed him back out the door, shrieking for my wife, Alison (I'm from Connecticut; she is not). Noah hopped around on the deck, the deer leg swinging wildly. Alison grabbed it away from him, I shoved Noah inside the house, and we set off to figure out where this sickening prize had come from (obviously nearby). Within a few minutes, we found a dead deer in the woods just up the hill off the driveway.

Since it wasn't hunting season, we theorized that the deer had been hit by a car and limped into our woods to die. The poor thing was mostly intact, but Noah clearly wasn't the first animal to have discovered it—a few bits were strewn around in the leaves.

Now what to do? Noah wasn't going to forget about it, so we couldn't just leave it there. I figured the local police would help.

Nope.

Not their jurisdiction unless I was the one who hit it and needed a damage report for insurance. They suggested I try the animal control officer.

No luck there either. "Don't know what to tell you," was the suspiciously dismissive reply (clearly, a dead deer in the yard is not an emergency around here). "Try the game warden."

A bit of research revealed that the Maine Warden Service is responsible for law enforcement, investigation, search and rescue, and data collection. Nothing about deer collection. It took a few phone calls. Eventually, a game warden called me back.

As I explained what had happened, he was not so much suspiciously dismissive as outright dismissive. I said, "I can't just leave it there, my dog has already found it and brought a leg to the. . . ." Now I had his attention. Now he was talking. Only he wasn't telling me what to do with the deer, he was telling me *what to do with my dog.* "You can't let your dog just wander around," he scolded. "Once a dog gets a taste of 'deah pahts' you can never stop him. You've got to shoot him!"

I hung up, horrified. Noah had his failings, but no way was he going to become a deer hunter, chasing prey all over Topsham. He was not, as I've explained, in any way energetic. But I was freaking out: *Was the game warden going to come over and shoot my dog? Did he expect me to shoot my dog?!*

Completely out of options, I called the town clerk pleading with her to help me. She sighed and said, "I know someone who might be interested. I'll give him a call."

Interested?

Pretty soon, two guys in a pickup pull into my driveway, and I show them where the deer is.

"Nah, it's been too long," says one of them, and they turn to head back to their truck. It took all of twenty seconds for them to decide.

I don't remember what I said, but I must have looked pathetic, standing there helpless and still horrified. They glanced at each other, and one of them said, "Oh, let's just take it for him."

They clomp over, and one of them just grabs the deer by its front legs and heaves it up on his back. I was both impressed and thoroughly grossed out. The other one gathers up the various parts lying around, and they start to walk away.

I see a glistening lump on the ground and yell to them, "What about that?"

One says, "That's the paunch! Just bury it." Then they were off.

The paunch? Not knowing a thing about deer anatomy, even I grasped the need to get rid of *that*. So, I grab a shovel and start digging, which isn't easy in a pine grove with roots at every turn. Eventually, there's a hole large enough to contain this very full deer organ. I tip it into the hole with the shovel, top it with a bunch of dirt, and add a large stone on top for good measure. *Thank goodness*, I think, heading inside to wash my hands with the hottest water I can stand. That's that.

A couple of hours later, it's time for Noah to go out again. Same deal—out for about five minutes, and he hurls himself at the door. I open it. This time it's something new in his mouth that he wants to bring inside—the rock on top of that hastily dug hole that was clearly not going to prevent this canine joy. Pushing him and his prized paunch back out onto the deck, now I really want to gag.

"Alison!"

Alison appears, holding a garbage bag. When fully contained, the paunch was completely foul, but now it was punctured, leaking, and covered in dirt and leaves. With her bare hands, Alison grabbed it from Noah, dropped it into the bag, tied it up, walked it over to the garbage can, and dropped it in.

Did I tell you she's from Maine?

God bless her.

INVESTOR BLUES
Chris Potholm

It had been a long day. I had gotten up about 5 a.m. and flew out of Augusta for a meeting in Williamstown, Massachusetts. In those days, when I went anywhere in New England for political or general consulting, I flew by private plane—whenever possible at the client's expense. Two pilots, too, just to be on the safe side. Once I got the hang of it, I'd add matter-of-factly to the prospective client, "It'll save you a lot of money if I don't have to stay over." So, I had some flexibility to ensure I wasn't too far from the Maine coast for too long in the summer.

This day, the blue fish were running wild, chasing pogies all over the southern Maine coast, and I thought wistfully all day that they were in Casco Bay peeling paint off shorefront houses (the stench of pogies dying en masse in a small cove is beyond imagination) and here I was stuck in western Massachusetts. By the time I finally got back to my house that night, it was about 7 p.m. I got into my hot tub and was relaxing, happy that the next day would be free. My good friend George Smith, the head of the Sportsman's Alliance of Maine (SAM) was coming down, and I'd promised to take him out blue fishing.

But just as I was sitting there contentedly, my beloved wife made what could be considered a tactical, if not strategic, error by saying, "There's a big school of bluefish right off our dock." Without hesitation, I leaped out of the hot tub, grabbed a large towel, and wrapped it around my still-dripping body. I raced to the window, and sure enough, the blues were right there. I didn't want to waste any time, so while saying, "Don't worry, I'll just catch one," I dashed out the door, barefoot and with only the bath towel wrapped around my waist. *Maybe from the float,* I thought.

Well, time, tide, and bluefish chasing pogies wait for no woman and no man, so by the time I got to the float, I needed a boat to chase them. There were about three or four inches of water in my boat, but I couldn't wait to bail it first. I jumped into the wooden skiff and followed the churning mass of bluefish and pogies with the squealing terns overhead. I quickly caught up to the school and cast a big blue atom popper. Crash, bang, strike. I'd rather eat striped bass any day, but I'd rather catch a blue fish, at least in this way. The fish fought hard, thrashing around this way and that, the reel screaming.

The fury, the excitement, the violence.

What fun!

I happily reeled it in and chucked it in the bottom of the boat.

Fleetingly then—and I mean very fleetingly—I thought of my vow to catch only one. "Naw," I said to myself instantly, "I can't stop now; I'll just catch another one." To pay for my foolishness, one, then another bluefish, hit the plug, and the line snapped. By the time I got rerigged, the school had moved farther up the bay, so I started the motor and followed.

I went back to fishing.

There was no way I was going to pull off that flurry with only one blue. I drifted with the current and the school up the bay. The towel was none too securely fastened so I had to keep having to stop and pull it up to retie it every other cast, but I hooked two more blues and managed to boat one of them. He slashed and bit like crazy, and he caught me good in the finger as I was trying to unhook him, and my finger began to bleed a lot. I yelled out loud—really out loud, my cries echoing up and down the bay—and hopped around on the seat. My neighbor said he heard it a half mile away. But I finally ripped the blue off the treble hook and threw him in the bottom of the boat. Then I hit him with an oar. That quieted him down a bit.

My heart was still pounding, and I was struggling to hold up the towel and cast, but soon I was in the school again and latched on to another blue. This one didn't give up for quite a while, and since the skiff leaked, by the time I got him into the boat, there was a good bit of water in the hull, and he fell off into it—splashing around in the bottom of the boat as if he were going to find a way out. Since I was still foolishly barefoot, I climbed up onto the middle seat and danced around as he thrashed hither and yon. He was splashing around in bilge water, flapping like crazy, seemingly angry to be inside the boat rather than outside it.

I went back to fishing.

I was just thinking I was the best fisherman around with four or five blues in the boat and the water boiling all around me, but then I heard my neighbor Bob Hunt telling his daughter Kelly to quit fooling around and reel in the fish on her line. Hearing my agonized scream and seeing the swirl of birds earlier, they had come up from the south and were at the edge of the school. Like any good fisherman, I was about to go over and tell them how to catch these blues. After all, I was hauling them in like I knew what I was doing, but just then, Kelly said, "But Daddy, I have two on, it's hard to reel them in."

Then I watched her boat the two at once. *Must be beginner's luck*, I thought. But luckily, I did let go of the idea of coaching her.

I kept fishing.

As the moon rose, my arms were aching, and I was being bitten all over by swarms of mosquitoes, still having nothing on but that towel, a towel that was now wet and limp. All my dancing around on the seat didn't drive away the bugs. It was then I got the bright idea of splashing the bloody oily water from the bilge as an insect repellant. I took the bailing scoop from the bottom of the boat and poured the blood, saltwater, and general bilge gunk over my head. I doused myself several times. Remarkably, it worked, and apparently nauseated, the mosquitoes at least paused their assault.

Now, I was covered with a greasy, fishy, smelly film, and the towel was soaking wet. I was bug-bitten and cold, and my arms and shoulders ached like crazy.

I was having the time of my life.

I went back to fishing

Then on the next cast, my rod broke. It just snapped as two blues hit the same big blue and white Rebel popper and struggled to pull it every which way. I got down on my hands and knees and slowly pulled in the line, grabbing the wire leader at last and horsing the two blues into the boat. This time, I didn't bother to try to unhook them; I took the broken rod as a sign from the gods of the outdoors that it was time to go home.

However, then I discovered that standing on the middle seat, I could barely reach the cord on the motor, and when I gave it a good, if awkward, yank, the motor didn't turn over. Then I gave it another. Then another. Nothing. The motor would not turn over as I couldn't get enough purchase on the cord. So, I sat down and took stock of the situation. I said to myself, *This hunt has blown up, I should row for home.*

Still, the waters all around the boat were continuing to churn with blues, and of course, there were now six or seven blues *in* the boat, some of whom were still swimming around gnashing their teeth. *What the hell,* I thought. *I can still jig for them by hand.*

So, I cut off the lure with the two blues on it, rigged another wire leader, and put it on the line with a new lure. As soon as I threw that over the side, I hooked another bluefish. By the time I got that one in the boat, it was dark, and the mosquitoes were out in full force.

I went back to fishing

That's when my neighbor Bob, perhaps foolishly, stopped by to say goodbye. It was getting dark, and they had gotten their fill of horsing in the blues.

That's when I asked him for his rod. He looked at me like I was nuts, but he kindly gave it over, carefully laying it on the gunwale so I wouldn't have to drop the towel. He looked like he'd never see his rod again. A good guess, perhaps.

I went back to fishing.

Finally, much later, with a dozen blues in the boat and the bloody water level rising, I decided enough was finally enough.

That's when I tried to start the boat.

That's when the motor really wouldn't start.

I then began to row. It was very slow going down the bay against the tide, with water and fish sloshing around the bottom of the boat. The adrenaline was wearing off, and I was really very tired. It took quite a while, and I remember the moon coming up.

That's when I heard it first, a lobster boat chugging along in the moonlight. It was very quiet and tranquil with no wind so I could hear and then see it quite well.

I realized I must have presented a truly bizarre sight to the two bay men after a hard day of hauling. I could hear them popping their beer cans as they came down the bay. I was standing on the seat, paddling like a Venetian gondolier, covered in blood, muddy water, and a soaking wet towel.

I could even hear them chattering on the lobster boat. Their voices carrying clearly across the bay as they caught sight of the nearly naked apparition dancing on a seat in the gloom.

"Who the hell is that?" asked the sternman, "He looks like a crazy person."

"I don't know, his name," replied the captain, "but he's some kind of investah."

The sternman paused and laughed, "Investor? . . . well he should invest in some pants."

Hard to argue with that.

ODE TO BROTHER GEORGE
Edie Smith

WHEN GEORGE SMITH PASSED AWAY ON FEBRUARY 12, 2021, AT THE age of seventy-two after a valiant battle with ALS, or Lou Gehrig's disease, his death was announced on the front page of every major newspaper in Maine. Every television station in Maine ran stories about George's life. Maine Governor Janet T. Mills issued a press release stating, "George loved Maine and Maine loved George."

Downe East magazine featured an article about George, while *Maine* magazine hailed him as one of Maine's most influential people. Sister Edie states, "George would have been tickled pink by all the attention ... not because he had a big ego (which he didn't), but because he would have been humbled that Mainers of all stripes were agreeing on something!"

George started out as a Republican political operative. He worked for Bangor Mayor Bill Cohen in his campaign for the U.S. House in 1972, crisscrossing the Second Congressional District as Bill's driver and personal aide. George loved telling the story of how he almost fell asleep at the wheel once after a particularly long day, so Bill insisted on driving; Bill drove the car while George took a nap in the back seat.

(Editor's Note: In another vignette in this work, reporter Don Carrigan shares another time Bill Cohen needed a ride to his mother's house, no less.)

In 1974, George worked for a young Republican upstart, Dave Emery from Rockland, living out of an orange Volkswagen van while Dave campaigned for Congress against four-term incumbent, Peter Kyros, beating him and becoming the youngest Republican member of the U.S. House of

Representatives. George became Dave's Chief of Staff at the tender age of twenty-six. Dave and George had no money when they first arrived in DC in that orange van. So they rented a house with little furniture, and they put in a pool table that also served as their dining room table.

George's management of several referendum campaigns greatly impacted the state. While he may be best remembered for saving Maine's bear hunt in 2004, not many people know that it's thanks to George that they can shop on Sundays and holidays in pretty much every retail store in Maine.

By 1990, all New England states except Maine had eliminated their blue laws prohibiting small retailers (those with less than five thousand square feet) to be open on Sundays and holidays. George managed the successful petition signature-gathering stage of putting a question on the 1990 ballot that would give all retail stores the option to stay open. He then managed the campaign to convince Maine voters to say yes. And they did. The initiative won at the ballot box 52.48 percent to 47.52 percent. Next time you shop there on a Sunday, thank George!

The story that George loved to tell about that campaign was not how he helped increase retail sales in Maine but how he became friends with Maine retail icon Bob Reny. Bob was vehemently opposed to the referendum. He did not support his stores being open on Sundays, so he featured Reny stores in television ads, lambasting the referendum question. It was George vs. Bob, but it was a battle of respectful opponents. They agreed to disagree, and after fierce public debates, they would shake hands, hug, and talk about the importance of small businesses to Maine's economy.

With both George and Bob having a love of all things Maine as well as wicked Maine accents, they enjoyed their bantering and knew that no matter what the outcome of the referendum, they would be fast friends forever. And they were—a lesson that sadly has not been carried through to modern-day politics.

From 2002 to 2016, George co-hosted *Wildfire,* a community-access cable TV show with well-known outdoorsman Harry Vanderweide. The show was widely viewed and eventually streamed on social media. The running joke about it was that George and Harry were such talkers that the guests they would host on each show could never get a word in.

ODE TO BROTHER GEORGE

The most telling example of George's listening abilities and his openness to embrace opposing views was the development of what was initially proposed as a large national park in the Katahdin area, on land purchased by Roxanne Quimby of Burt's Bees fame.

Straight out of the gate, George was one of the first opponents of the plan. He wrote about what a terrible land grab this would be and spent time printing "Ban Roxanne" bumper stickers and placing them on as many vehicles as he could.

The tide, however, began to turn when Roxanne started hosting monthly meetings with a small group of opponents, including George. She also stepped back from being the public face of the effort and brought in her son, Lucas St. Clair, who is a master negotiator. Lucas went to people's homes, spread maps on their kitchen tables, and asked, "Okay, what can we do to get you to support this effort?"

George listened. George learned. George negotiated. George helped change the maps. And an alternative plan was developed that eventually, through Congressional legislation, became Katahdin Woods and Waters National Monument.

George cherished the friendship he formed with Roxanne and Lucas. They continued to work together on improvements to the Monument, emphasizing that fishing, hunting, snowmobiling, and other traditional uses of land would not only be allowed but promoted. George went from the plan's number one opponent to its number one proponent, and Maine is better for it.

Other tidbits about George:

He harped to his conservative friends the dangers of climate change even before "global warming" became a thing.

He was instrumental in creating the Maine Outdoor Heritage Fund and Land for Maine's Future Program. George's love of the outdoors, hunting, fishing, and our heritage industries kept him on his path of advocacy for all things Maine.

He was known for his love of the drink Moxie, which his sister Edie calls "rancid root beer." George drank it by the gallon, and pictures of him often show him wearing his Moxie T-shirt.

George was always having a lot of fun, and his doings were legendary. As Dave Emery tells the story:

There is a *universe* full of George funny tales. One of them relates to the madhouse DC morning rush hour composed of Capitol Hill and Pentagon employees challenged on a daily basis to get to work on time in traffic that is unimaginable to Mainers, who might only ever be confronted occasionally by summer traffic, or in some places, by the odd cow in the road. As I recall, this particular incident occurred in late fall or winter, so George, naturally, was wearing his blaze-orange hunting jacket and matching blaze-orange hat.

We were commuting to the office from the previously described Alexandria house in his blaze-orange Volkswagen camper. All we needed was a .30-06 in the rear window and maybe a deer carcass on the roof rack, and we would not have drawn so much as a sideways glance in Columbia, Maine . . . but in the District of Columbia . . . a different story altogether!

In any event, there was some kind of a slowdown that morning, probably caused by a fender bender somewhere in the mass of traffic, and we finally came to a halt in the right-hand lane. It was getting late, so George said, "To heck with this," and steered his orange monstrosity into the breakdown lane. A few minutes and about two miles later, a motorcycle with flashing blue lights appeared behind us.

"License and registration," the officer demanded.

"What's the problem, officer?" George asked meekly. "I couldn't have been speeding."

"I'm going to give you a citation for driving in the breakdown lane."

"What's a breakdown lane?" George asked. Dave and I were trying not to burst out laughing.

"What do you mean, 'what's a breakdown lane'?" the officer asked incredulously. "You're driving in the breakdown lane, and it's only for emergency vehicles."

"Gosh," says George, "Up home in Maine, we can drive on *anything* that's tarred."

At that point, I was sure we were all going to jail. But the officer's radio crackled to life, and a minute or so later, the officer let us go. He apparently had a more urgent matter to attend to.

ODE TO BROTHER GEORGE

So if you are ever stranded in DC rush hour traffic and decide to use the breakdown lane ... better think twice about it *unless* you have Maine plates and are decked out in blaze-orange from head to toe!

While George, through his company Mainely Marketing, was well-known for his management of many referendum campaigns, it was his eighteen years as executive director of the Sportsman's Alliance of Maine that defines his legacy. George turned his love of Maine's outdoors into fierce advocacy in the halls of the State Legislature and beyond. When George took the helm at SAM, the organization had about two thousand members. When he retired from SAM in 2010, the membership had ballooned to fourteen thousand. Thanks to George, SAM became a lobbying and advocacy powerhouse.

George's most poignant battle was his last. He was diagnosed with ALS in 2017. It was an unimaginable and cruel blow to George, his family, and his friends. But true to form, George used his experience with this crippling disease to advocate for others with ALS. He wrote about his challenges with the goal of bringing much-needed attention—and money—to the cause of fighting ALS and, along the way, finding a way to live with the disease. George became a lead fundraiser for ALS research. The annual "Walk to Defeat ALS" in both Bangor and Portland became a showcase of "George-ness." He was a fundraising machine, and dozens of friends and family walked and raised money in record amounts. Among the walkers, you would find Governor Janet Mills, U.S. Senator Angus King, U.S. Congressman Jared Golden, many state legislators, environmental advocates, and George's high school and college friends alongside his family.

It was a sea of green t-shirts with the team motto: "GIVE IT THE G.A.S.—for George Arthur Smith."

Poignant to the story, the route of the ALS Walk in Bangor took the crowd past Stephen King's House on West Broadway in Bangor. George and Stephen were classmates at the University of Maine at Orono. George loved to tell audiences that he used to sit next to Stephen King in English class at UMO, and together they went on to write and sell millions of books, although Stephen's sales were a bit more robust than

George's. George thought that fact was hilarious, as did his audience. They still do.

George loved to write. His newspaper columns, articles in *The Maine Sportsman*, and his books tell a love story of George and all that Maine has to offer. His books include *A Life Lived Outdoors: Reflections of a Maine Sportsman, Maine Sporting Camps, A Lifetime of Hunting and Fishing: The Ones That Got Away and the Ones That Didn't*, and, co-written with his wife Linda, *Take It from ME: Insider's Guide to Where to Stay and Eat in Maine*.

George was steadfast in his beliefs but not so much so that he was too close-minded to compromise or change his mind. He was not afraid to say he was wrong, even if the words came with a grimace.

During his battle with ALS, once again bringing humor and a touch of humility to his words, George said, "I was born a Republican but am going to die a Democrat." George's political views shifted due to his life experiences. He liked to say that if you had to classify him in a certain category, he was a "Compassionate Republican," although he added, again with a grimace, that many people would consider that an oxymoron. He maintained lifelong friendships with Republicans, Democrats, Independents, Greens, and anyone else who enjoyed discussing politics. However, he admitted later in life that his views softened, his compassion grew, and his children convinced him that he could evolve.

A very important part of George that many didn't realize was his strong faith. All the Smith kids grew up singing in the junior and senior choirs at Winthrop Methodist Church, where their beloved mom, Ada, was the organist and choir director. In adult life, George was a faithful member of the Readfield Methodist Church, where he sang in the choir, swaying to the music with a big smile on his face and a strong tenor voice. It was inspirational just to watch him sing.

George always carried a small, smooth rock in his pocket—a treasure from West Quoddy Head Lighthouse in Lubec, where Ada grew up. George didn't wear his religion on his sleeve, but the way he conducted himself, his respect for all people, and his devotion to his community were testaments to his deep faith. He *lived* his faith, and we are all better for it.

JIMMY
Bobby Reynolds

THE FIRST TIME I SAW JIMMY FOX WAS DURING DRILL SCHOOL. IT WAS one of those dull late-afternoon sessions that seemed to drag on forever. Suddenly, Jimmy walked into the classroom. Ronnie, one of my classmates who had been on the job for six months, blurted out, "Hey, Mongo-man, what's up?" The remark caught me off guard. I wasn't sure if it was Ronnie's sharp humor or the fact that it was the first time I had met someone with Down syndrome that made me uncomfortable. Either way, that initial unease quickly disappeared.

I had heard about Jimmy from some of the guys at the station. He had a range of nicknames—some endearing, like "The Fox" or "Foxy," and others less kind, such as "Mongo-man" or worse. Jimmy had been part of Bramhall Station's life long before I arrived. The story went that, back in the late sixties, the firefighters of Bramhall found him handcuffed to a telephone pole while returning from a call.

A group of local kids had convinced Jimmy to hug the pole, then locked the cuffs on him as a cruel joke, leaving him terrified and humiliated. The jakes of Ladder 6 cut him free, and from that day on, Jimmy loved the firemen—and the feeling was mutual. The Bramhall crews became his second family.

For years, Jimmy lived behind the station with his mother and stopped by every afternoon on his way home from his job at Goodwill. After supper, he'd come back for the night shift, staying until the 9 p.m. bell. On weekends, Jimmy would arrive around 10 a.m. and spend the whole day with us, leaving just before the evening meal.

His father, who had passed away years earlier, had been a well-respected physician in the Portland area. His mother, Mrs. Fox, was a woman of grace and strength. She was also a person of great patience—not just for Jimmy's challenges but for the antics we pulled with Jimmy. She was heard to say on more than one occasion that it felt as if she had forty teenage sons living right behind her place in the West End, because she knew that, although firemen (yes, during my time, it was all *men*) looked fully grown, more often than not we acted as if we were still fifteen.

During the decade and a half I worked at that firehouse, Jimmy's life slowly began to change. As time went on, his brother Jack would occasionally pick him up. After Mrs. Fox passed away, Jack regularly came by, and Jimmy then lived with him across the river in South Portland.

I could write a book about the pranks we pulled on Jimmy and how much he loved being in on the jokes. Because we worked four shifts, Jimmy had four birthday parties every year. Even though he was born on December 12, he would start reminding us about his birthday as early as Labor Day. He knew we'd give him a frosted balloon in place of a real cake before eventually surprising him with the real thing, and he knew the annual threat that Christmas or Easter had been canceled was just a tease.

But he always played along, never missing a beat. Fact is, Jimmy was a step ahead of us on the many gags we'd cook up, making sure to do his part in goofing on us rather than the other way around. And he wasn't there just for the laughs. I still remember attending a funeral for a fireman from Ladder 1 up on Munjoy Hill who had succumbed to injuries he suffered at a fire. Jimmy was there for us. You've witnessed true humanity when you see Jimmy—all of five feet tall—comforting a hulking six foot, 215-pound Portland firefighter who is heartbroken at the loss of a brother.

Every fireman who worked at Bramhall during those years had their own bond with Jimmy. He had a knack for giving people nicknames: "Neeny-weeney" for Al, "Jay" for the guy we called the Twin D, "Goat Breath" for a certain deputy chief, "Peteinamore" for Peter Finamore, and "Wayna" for his absolute favorite fireman, Dana.

JIMMY

Like many with Down syndrome, Jimmy's life was too short. Eventually, Jack could no longer provide the full-time care Jimmy needed, a decision I'm sure broke Jack's heart. Jimmy moved into the Barron Center City Hospital on Brighton Avenue. Even after that, the Portland fire companies continued visiting him until the end.

When Jimmy passed away, the Bramhall jakes gave him the sendoff he deserved. During the calling hours, Portland firefighters stood in uniformed honor by his casket. His funeral procession passed by Bramhall, where the crews of Engine 4, Engine 6, and Ladder 6 stood at attention on the ramp. As the hearse passed, honors were rendered with a hand salute and dipping the American flag to half-mast for our friend and brother Jimmy Fox.

Although my career as a fireman in Portland feels like another lifetime, I still remember the men I served with and my time as a professional firefighter. I also think of Jimmy often.

One memory stands out vividly. Jimmy would stop by for a cup of coffee every weekday after his shift at Goodwill. If I was working, I'd pour him a cup from the old pot under the Bunn coffee machine—hours old and black as coal—and add a few spoons of sugar and a healthy shot of milk. I'd slide it across the counter, and Jimmy would grab it with both hands, take a big sip, and say the same thing every time: "Hey, not bad."

That was Jimmy Fox—and that was the lesson he had for all of us. Some of us are simply more fortunate than others, and it would have been easy for Mrs. Fox, Jimmy's brother Jack, or Jimmy himself—all of blessed memory—to lament certain limitations. But they did not. They gobbled up life and lived it to the fullest.

To this day, if you run into a retired Portland firefighter and ask if they knew Jimmy Fox, they're likely to count him among their friends.

I loved him then and I still do now.

GERRY, GERRY
Bill Nimitz

I GOT CALLED A LOT OF NAMES OVER FORTY-SEVEN YEARS AS A MAINE journalist. But the one I remember most was Gerry.

It was May 1998 and I was three years into my tenure as a columnist for the *Portland Press Herald/Maine Sunday Telegram* when my editor approached me with a dream assignment: Go to Belfast, Northern Ireland, and, from a Maine perspective, write about the upcoming referendum on the Good Friday Agreement.

The hook was obvious. Without the steady hand of former Maine Senator George Mitchell, who, as President Clinton's special envoy, patiently guided the United Kingdom, Northern Ireland, and the Republic of Ireland through two years of hard-fought negotiations, there would have been nothing to vote on. Now, for the first time in more than a quarter century of sectarian strife between Ireland's Catholics and Protestants, a peace deal appeared to be at hand.

I packed my bags and headed for Belfast along with photographer John Ewing, oblivious to one complicating factor. Back in those days, I apparently bore a strong resemblance to Gerry Adams, longtime leader of the Irish Republican Party, Sinn Fein.

It's not like I hadn't been forewarned. Three years earlier, I'd devoted one of my first columns to a visit Adams made to Portland—the first stop on a thirteen-city U.S. fundraising mission for Sinn Fein. As a small, enthusiastic throng of local Hibernians awaited his arrival at the Portland International Jetport, more than a few told me I was a dead ringer for the man of the moment. Maybe it was the brown hair and beard, the wire-rimmed glasses, whatever. But the more they talked about it, the more self-conscious I felt.

Moments later, I briefly interviewed Adams, and as we parted, I mentioned that folks here thought we looked alike. We paused, each taking in the other, and then laughed it off with a simultaneous "Nah."

Sure we didn't. That evening, more than four hundred Mainers gathered to honor Adams at the Holiday Inn by the Bay in Portland. I went to the reception, hoping to pick up more color for the column, and found a piece of wall space by the main ballroom entrance precisely when the master of ceremonies boomed, "Ladies and gentlemen, please welcome the beloved son of Ireland, Gerry Adams!"

Or not. Gerry must still have been walking into the hotel lobby. A ballroom spotlight darted around frantically searching for him and, alas, finally settled on me. Squinting into the glare, just able to make out all those people applauding and smiling straight in my direction, I panicked. "Oh my God," I thought, "they think I'm him."

I looked to one side, then the other—finally spotting a buffet to my left. Without further ado, I grabbed a small plate and headed for the cheese platter. There I stood, frozen in place with my back to the crowd, munching on a piece of cheddar until the spotlight gave up on me and the real Gerry mercifully arrived.

Back to Belfast.

It didn't take long to realize that the likeness between myself and Himself—a man worshipped by Catholics and reviled by Protestants throughout his native Belfast—would dog me throughout our one-week visit.

On our first afternoon, pursuing one of the countless cultural, social, and family connections between Belfast and Maine, John and I walked up a long driveway to a Catholic rectory on Crumlin Road in West Belfast. As he readied his camera equipment and I knocked on the door, a gaggle of kids walked by the end of the driveway on their way home from the nearby grammar school. Spotting me in the distance, they stopped dead in their tracks.

"Sinn Fein! Sinn Fein!" they began hollering. "IRA! Hey Gerry Adams! IRA!"

The back of my brain reminded me that Gerry Adams had long denied any direct ties to the Irish Republic Army, and the front of my brain told me to run. Thank God, the door opened, and a kindly housekeeper offered us sanctuary from the growing hubbub outside.

The next morning, I woke early and sauntered to a nearby smoke shop to pick up the daily papers. While I perused the blaring headlines, all focused on the looming referendum, a little leprechaun of a man in a tweed flat cap sidled up next to me and mumbled something in a brogue so thick it bounced right off me.

"Pardon me?" I asked politely.

He leaned in even closer. "D'ya know ya look like Gerry Adams?" he repeated.

I chuckled. "I've heard that," I replied. "Actually, I'm a journalist from the States, here to cover the vote."

He nodded, his face dead serious. Dropping his voice to a near whisper, he placed a sympathetic hand on my shoulder. "Be careful where ya bloody go."

The harder I tried to ignore it, the more the Gerry Adams Problem stuck to me like my own shadow. Walking down a street in heavily Protestant Belfast East, John and I passed two middle-aged women sitting on a park bench. I saw one staring straight at me as we passed and, nudging her companion, silently mouth the words, "Sinn Fein."

I soon stopped making eye contact and greeting passersby on the street with a friendly grin, figuring they wouldn't look at me if I didn't look at them. But that didn't discourage the double takes, dropped jaws, and quizzical stares in my wake. I could read the bubble captions over their heads: *"Gerry Adams? Lord above, a real man of the people, he is. And with no security whatsoever! Go figger!"*

We visited the home of a young Protestant woman who had attended summer camp in Maine as a girl with the Maine Irish Children's Program. Now eighteen, she was eager to cast her first-ever ballot. She quietly confided to me that she planned to vote "for peace."

Leave it to me to kill the mood. As I made small talk with the girl's mother, I forgot momentarily that this was a Protestant household and recounted how darned near everyone thinks I look like Gerry Adams. Weird, huh?

Rather than smile in wide-eyed agreement, the mother quickly folded her hands in her lap, looked down, and said, "Oh my . . ."

Again, the bubble caption: *"Dear God in Heaven, how am I going to get this man out of my house without the neighbors seeing?"*

I drove John to distraction, pondering my options, all bad.

Lose the glasses? I already had enough trouble reading the street maps, let alone my notes.

Shave the beard? I hadn't done that in twenty-three years. And what about my passport photo (beard) and driver's license (more beard)? What if, upon landing in Boston, U.S. Immigration took one look at my IDs, shook their heads, and sent me back?

Get a short haircut? Beneath all that hair, my scalp is a patchwork of scars from various childhood misadventures. Trust me, it's not a good look.

So, I kept my head down and soldiered on.

May 22, the day of the referendum, finally arrived. As predicted, the Good Friday Agreement passed by overwhelming margins throughout Ireland. Even in Belfast, the epicenter of the troubles that had plagued the region for decades, there was dancing in the streets.

Our final batch of copy and photos filed, John and I headed out late that rainy evening to find a pub and join the celebration before departing the next day. John drove the rental car while I sat back and exhaled a sigh of relief at a mission accomplished.

Then we hit a red light just outside Belfast City Hall. A half dozen young men, who had clearly started their celebration early, stood singing and cheering in the intersection, their bottles of Irish beer raised high above their heads.

One of them passed close by my window. Stopping suddenly, he leaned in until his face was but a few inches from the rain-streaked glass. I looked straight ahead, not even blinking.

"Gerry," he said in a low, incredulous voice, just loud enough for me to hear.

"Drive," I ordered John. "Go. Go! GO!"

John started laughing. "Nope," he said, pointing up at the signal. "Red light. No can do!"

The young man stood up straight and called to his buddies. "Mates! It's Gerry! In the flesh! Gerry Adams! Come look right here, mates—it's Gerry Adams!"

With that, they surrounded the car, jumping up and down and thumping on the roof, all the while chanting "Ger-RY! Ger-RY! Ger-RY!" until the light changed and John, beside himself by now, slowly inched his way through the lovefest.

We never made it to a pub. Much to my poor colleague's disappointment, I had no interest in taking this thing to the next level. Time to go home. My work here was done.

All these years later, I'm not sure I could still be mistaken for Gerry. But as I write this, my wife and I are planning a trip to Ireland sometime next spring and, just in case, I've come up with a simple strategy.

No, I will not shave off my ever-whitening beard. Not then, not now, not ever.

But I'll be careful where I bloody go.

AND HE LIKED THE LADIES
Paul Mills

THE CELEBRATED AUTHOR FRANK GRAHAM JR. IS PERHAPS BEST KNOWN for a variety of popular publications, including *Since Silent Spring*, and books on the New York Giants and Casey Stengel. He also wrote the first biography of Margaret Chase Smith. It came out in 1963, just as she was launching her trail-blazing campaign for the presidency. Early parts of the work are devoted to the remarkable career of Smith's husband, Congressman Clyde Smith, who, as a candidate for public office forty-nine times, died without having ever lost a single election. Worthy of a book in his own right, Graham makes this observation about some of Clyde Smith's personal passions:

"Though he did not smoke or drink, he put away enormous quantities of chocolate candies while engaging in another of his favorite pastimes, poker."

Growing up in Farmington—a community not far from the Smith family's Skowhegan roots—I had been aware of innuendos regarding one of Clyde Smith's less discreet interests. This awareness came to me, at any rate, while sitting in Frank Howatt's barber chair on Broadway in Farmington in the late 1960s. Howatt, then in his midseventies and the patriarch of a venerable family who followed in his footsteps in the same profession, had traveled throughout this area of Maine in his trade.

Howatt had spent time in Smith's hometown and was a repository of perhaps apocryphal but nevertheless entertaining conversation. I naturally asked him about Margaret Chase Smith. Part of his reply was that she had suffered from a husband with a wandering eye. At that time, I had relegated this story to the realm of spurious gossip likely originating from some disgruntled political adversary in Somerset County. I gave it little credence. How could any husband of such a mesmerizing, and during the time of his marriage to Margaret Chase Smith, highly attractive and engaging lady have had any interests elsewhere?

Fast forward to the late summer of 1990. "The Senator," the name to which she often responded, was now nearly ninety-three. She was as physically well-preserved and mentally alert as anyone half her age. The only disability was her failing eyesight, but her mind's eye and mental vision was as sharp as ever. Though on several occasions over the years I had been part of small groups that included her and her late aide and companion, Bill Lewis, the occasion now was her invitation to myself and my fiancé—who, like Smith, was also from Skowhegan—to dine out.

This was at one of the town's premiere establishments, the Heritage House. It being a Wednesday night and the only parties in our private corner being just four of us, who included the senator's close friend, retired Navy Captain Georgia McKearly, it was an occasion for candid interactions.

One figure about whom I asked, for example, was former Maine Senator and Governor Ralph Owen Brewster, a summa cum laude graduate of Bowdoin and mesmerizing if controversial political contemporary of the Senator and her husband. Based on his 1947 Congressional confrontation with Howard Hughes over the perceived limitations of Hughes's "Spruce Goose" flying ship, Brewster would by 2004 become the only twentieth-century Maine politician prominently featured in an Academy Award–winning movie *The Aviator*. The Brewster role was portrayed by Alan Alda.

I mentioned that the book on Brewster was the reason he dropped the "Ralph" from his name at midcareer in honor of his son, who died from an infection as a teenager. Not necessarily, the Senator claimed. It was also to avoid being mistaken for being Irish, something more likely if the name had remained "Ralph O. Brewster."

She, of course, also harbored understandable resentment against Brewster due to his association with Joseph McCarthy at a time when Smith courageously took on McCarthy over his witch-hunting tactics.

That resentment was not ameliorated when, a few days before Brewster died in 1961, he put upon Smith to borrow a rare book from her that he could not find elsewhere. His promise to "get it right back" to her remained unfulfilled at his death.

In the hours we spent that night over dinner and a tour of her residence afterward, I also mentioned her husband, Congressman Clyde Smith. In 1990, just a half-century after his death, still nurtured admiration and affection for him. She had worn with pride for years after his death in 1940 an engagement ring he had given her.

Smith recalled how, at a speaking engagement at a Midwestern university about 1954, she had briefly removed it to warm her hands. Somehow, in the hectic pressure of the moment, she misplaced it. A frantic search ensued, but she could not locate it. So upset by this, after returning to Washington, she hired a clairvoyant to ascertain where it might be. The clairvoyant reported that she saw a university groundskeeper had picked it up but could not nail down his identity with sufficient specificity so that the Senator was never able to retrieve it.

Her sentiments about her husband became somewhat tempered, however, when I mentioned his interest in chocolates. Her somewhat—to me at any rate—unexpected rejoinder was "Yes, he liked chocolates" and—with an added emphasis, *"And he liked the ladies."*

It was not a passage one finds in Frank Graham's book. It did, however, verify the more small-town anecdotal report of Frank Howatt. The credibility of your local barber should not be easily discounted.

Editor's Note: Let Paul Mills, Maine's unofficial political historian, provide some additional information about Clyde Smith:

Clyde was born in June 1876 and died in April 1940. In between those two dates, he won forty-nine elections, never losing one. Think of that incredible total with the breadth of experience that went with it. In roughly chronological order, he ran for and was elected as Superintendent of Schools of Hartland (this was an elective position back then) at age twenty; State Representative from Hartland at age twenty-one; Sheriff of Somerset County at age twenty-eight (when he moved to Skowhegan); Skowhegan First Selectman for sixteen years; State Representative from

Skowhegan for two more terms (1919–1923), then three terms in the State Senate from Somerset County (1923–1929).

In the Maine Senate, he was a notable champion of the interests of organized labor and an ardent—though at that time unsuccessful—advocate of "old age" pensions as a forerunning to Social Security at the state level was called. He served on the State Highway Commission in the late 1920s and early '30s, which was an appointive position, so he was probably not part of the Governors Executive Council 1933–1937 (which was elected by the legislature), and finally ran for Congress, winning in 1936 and 1938.

DATING HIGH JINKS IN DC
Dave Emery

MANY TV DRAMAS ARE REPLETE WITH STORIES OF CONGRESSMEN AND senators getting themselves embroiled in sordid affairs of one sort or another, leading to predictable storylines of international intrigue, crime, raw politics, and personal scandal. In reality, while these things have certainly happened, contrary to the usual barroom gossip, from my experience, most members of Congress are honest, diligent, and faithful to their wives and families.

For any married man or woman of less-than-perfect self-control, however, there are certainly opportunities to go astray, but for a young, single person, being elected to Congress is Nirvana. As one acquaintance of mine once put it, "Washington, DC, is where all the nation's most attractive, intelligent, and ambitious young people go after college."

In my case, I met Carol, the most spectacular young lady imaginable and now my wife of nearly forty-five years, within a few months of taking my seat in January 1975. As it happened, her boss, Henson Moore, was elected in a special January runoff election in a district that included the city of Baton Rouge, the state capital of Louisiana. Since Henson was the last member elected during that cycle, he was assigned to the last remaining office suite. That suite, located on the fourth floor of the Cannon House Office Building, was not deemed particularly desirable because its rooms were separated by a public restroom.

It was my great fortune that this particular office space was located next to mine, which was 425 Cannon. Henson and I became friendly rather quickly, and it took about *a microsecond* for the guys on my staff to discover the attractive Southern gals on his staff and vice versa. The staff from the two offices were close and remained close for the eight years I served in Congress. Several couples dated, but Carol and I were the only couple that tied the knot.

As I have often said, it was the best thing that has ever happened in my life, and I have the voters of Maine's First Congressional District (and I should add, those of Louisiana's old Sixth Congressional District) to thank for it.

Carol and I had been dating for a while when an issue of particular importance to Louisiana came up on the floor of the house for debate. Since Henson, as a member of the Commerce Committee, was heavily involved with the legislation in question, he was able to bring a member of his staff to the floor to assist in presenting charts and data while he was making his presentation. Since Carol was his legislative assistant responsible for that subject matter, she came onto the floor with him and took her seat in the front row on the Republican side, close to the lectern.

At that particular time, I was sitting in the back of the Chamber with several other members with whom I was friendly. As young men are wont to do, they immediately noticed the very attractive staffer who had just entered the Chamber.

"Wow," one of them said. "She's really cute!"

"I wonder if she's dating anyone," wondered another.

"I think I'll go down front and ask her if she would like to have dinner with me tonight," I said.

Of course, none of my buddies in the back row had any idea that we were already dating.

"Awww, you can't do that!"

"You don't dare to do that!"

"She'll shoot you down and you'll make an ass of yourself!"

"She'll never agree to a date just like that. She doesn't even know you!"

So I got up out of my seat and sat down beside her in the front row. We had already made plans to go out that evening, so my little scam on the back row crew was already fait accompli. Then a couple of minutes later, I went back to my astonished colleagues.

DATING HIGH JINKS IN DC

"What'd she say? What'd she say?"

"We're having dinner tonight at 8 at El Bodegón," I said matter-of-factly.

"Noooo waaaay!"

"I can't believe you really did that!"

So, I enjoyed my little scam for a while. Eventually, I let them in on the secret and we all had a good laugh.

For those unfamiliar with the DC restaurant scene during that time, El Bodegón was a very popular and romantic Spanish restaurant that featured Flamenco dancers as live entertainment and offered excellent Spanish wine served in an unusual—for Americans, anyway—manner. If you were brave enough to try it, a waiter would instruct you to hold your head back with your mouth slightly open and your eyes closed. He placed a precautionary towel around your neck and poured the wine from a spouted carafe onto your forehead just above the bridge of your nose, allowing the wine to run down either side into your mouth . . . all to the great amusement and applause of the other patrons. Sadly, El Bodegón is no longer in existence. With or without the wine facial, it was one of our favorite restaurants.

Carol and I have a great many friends in New Orleans as well as here in Maine, and we enjoy visiting "the Big Easy" about once a year, at least. Among our closest friends is a couple we have known all of our married lives. Marguerite (or "Muffin," as she is affectionately known) is from a large Franco-American family and was a high school classmate of Carol's; her husband, Charlie, grew up as a street-smart youngster of the variety known in New Orleans vernacular as a "Yat," as in "Hey Dave, where y'at? You comin' by my house for a crawfish boil this weekend?"

Charlie is one of a kind. He doesn't know a stranger, has an easy way about him, loves people from all walks of life, and will strike up a conversation with absolutely anybody, anywhere, on any occasion, and for any reason. He was once part-owner of a highly popular New Orleans nightclub named Forty-One Forty-One after its address on St. Charles Avenue. For years, I have loved touring New Orleans with him, especially the side-street restaurants and watering holes not necessarily frequented by Yankee tourists. This one particular day, we were heading back home across the Lake Pontchartrain Causeway, a twenty-four-mile-long bridge that connects New Orleans with communities on the north shore. We had spent the afternoon visiting his business associates and other acquaintances and had had our share of oysters and Abita beer in the process. Halfway across, Charlie says, "Man, I gotta pee bad."

A mile or so later, he pulled into a maintenance turnoff situated between the northbound and southbound lanes, got out, and proceeded to relieve himself against the side of the building. Thirty seconds later, a Louisiana Highway Patrol car pulled in behind our car.

"What are you guys up to?" demanded the officer.

"Nothing . . . just had to take a leak real bad."

"Well, next time, don't do it under the security camera!"

Whereupon I collapsed with laughter, much to the amusement of the Highway Patrol officer. With that, he let us go, and we have all laughed about it ever since!

THE LAST PATROL
Chris Potholm

ONE OF THE GREAT BENEFITS OF TENURE IS THAT IT SHIELDS THE PROfessor from political and ideological litmus tests and limits the intrusions of college deans and presidents. In fifty-five years of teaching at Dartmouth, Vassar, and Bowdoin, I can count on one hand any efforts of senior administrators who even tried to involve themselves with course content.

Over the years, this freedom has resulted in some exciting teaching experiences, and various courses could grow unfettered outside the hothouses of political correctness and groupthink—both very pernicious to intellectual growth and development.

One of the best illustrations of this was a senior seminar course that I taught at Bowdoin. The course—elegantly named "Conflict Simulation and Conflict Resolution" for the Faculty Affairs Committee, which had to oversee its initial course approval—soon became known to undergraduates as "War Games." It was a self-described "free speech island," "freewheeling" and a "judgment-free zone." The course syllabus stipulated that as long as students showed respect and goodwill, virtually any subject could be discussed with spirit and verve. Lots of action and outside-thebox thinking were included. Would-be censors on the Left and on the Right and in between were mocked with regularity.

This course was an elective and not required for government majors—much to the relief of many, no doubt—but sometimes, first-year students came to my office to sign up for it when they became seniors. They had been told you could be left out if you waited too long.

One of the highlights was a mock campus-wide election featuring media and competing teams. This proved to be quite frustrating for student government, as more students voted in the mock election for Congress than in the actual student class elections (at least until they could do so electronically). The Gov 3600 elections were more open and freewheeling, with few constraints on campaign practices, creating a genuine election atmosphere. Deans complained about the posters that emerged, covering the campus from one end to the other. Determining the authorship of the poster copy was often challenging for those most upset.

Another highlight was the outside simulations that taught basic lessons of war and combat (albeit at a very reduced danger and cost). Over the years, many service men and women came and shared with us their real-life experiences, including a chaplain who was at the battle of the Ah Shu Valley, one of the fiercest of the Vietnam War. Interestingly enough, when it came to presenting what combat was like in films, most combat veterans felt that the opening landing sequence in *Saving Private Ryan* came closest to giving an accurate presentation of combat in the moment.

Several veterans also took the course.

Peter Coffin of Brunswick was one of them. It should have been a piece of cake for this mature student who had done two tours in Vietnam as a Marine. Not only had Peter seen combat, he went on numerous long-range patrols into North Vietnam. His unit would be heloed into that country and spend a week or more observing and disrupting supply lines. On those patrols, he was never wounded or seriously hurt.

Peter shared with the class a memorable incident. After spending eight days in North Vietnam evading enemy patrols, his unit finally reached their designated pickup landing zone. Imagine that after a long, difficult patrol, they arrived at the landing zone only to see their pickup helicopter being slowly pushed over by an angry water buffalo! The helicopter toppled right into the mud of the rice paddy, bending its rotor blades and rendering it inoperative. Imagine how you would feel in a similar situation. The patrol assisted the crew out of the wreck and slipped back into the jungle until a rescue chopper finally arrived. "We were greatly relieved to finally get on board and up in the air heading south, for sure," Peter said. "Of course, the door gunner dusted off that buffalo on the way up and out."

Naturally, Peter was a leader in the class, and life's irony being what it is, on the first field effort, when the class was trying to duplicate some aspects of combat and teaching the importance of small group solidarity and discipline in action, he misfired. Leading his group, he jumped off a huge rock and broke his ankle. As no helo was available, he had to be carried from the field by foot soldiers. Can you imagine the chagrin of surviving unwounded from two tours in Vietnam only to be injured in a classroom assignment? He shook his head and laughed ruefully as the members of his squad carried him to safety. "Better here than there," he mused.

Another unexpected fiasco occurred when a young lady from New York disregarded the stipulation that troops carry their weapons, ammunition, and food on their backs, "humping" their supplies into the deep woods.

No, she thought she would use her parents' secondhand Mercedes for that purpose. She did okay on the wooded roads on the way to the battle site, but, of course, performed less well in the swamp where the battle was to take place. The tow truck she eventually summoned took over an hour to arrive and winch her vehicle out after her group was slaughtered by the opposing team, clustered as they were around the Mercedes, which was stuck up to its axles in mud.

Amazingly, she tried billing the Government Department for the cost of the towing service, but of course, that request was denied—with considerable glee, I might add. She did receive the "Attempted Con Job" award for that year. Charge someone else for your folly? Not on my watch.

War—even simulated war—punishes folly.

The class also provided a ready-made pressure group on campus-wide issues. When another dean came up with a speech code—which would have eliminated the words "dear" and "honey"—the "Joshua Chamberlain Anti-PC Brigade" got into full camo gear and warpaint to demonstrate their opposition on the campus quad. Whether in fear or mirth, another college dean then stepped in, and the speech code quietly faded from view and hence usage (let alone enforcement).

With regard to the lessons of Vietnam, simulations seemed to imitate historical reality. As one of the emerging patterns in the paintball-like simulations, for example, the women chose the role of Viet Cong soldiers; they avoided direct confrontation with the bigger, stronger, bolder, better-armed boys and took their time, hiding and waiting to ambush the loud and overconfident patrols. Most years, the women won. The men, assuming their superiority and stored-up aggression, got frustrated and eventually went where they shouldn't have—and made way too much noise when they did.

The classic example of this genre occurred one fine spring afternoon. The teams were tied for the semester, and the ultimate test—the struggle in the swamp—was next up. The distant Bowdoinham battle area had everything: rushing streams, thick vegetation, a bridge suitable for ambushes, and, at the center of a ten-square-mile area, a big swamp. A perfect open-air classroom for mock patrol action.

I remember both sides were really pumped and ready for action. I did notice, however, that as it began, the leader of the boys, "Jimmy," an all-American lacrosse player, was wearing a minimum of body armor and camo. He was so sure of a quick, early victory that he was only wearing a tee-shirt. I also noticed that he did not have a compass. "I don't need one," he told me. "I can tell by the sun."

Fighting went on for several hours, swung back and forth, and finally when the time was out, both groups came out of the woods within one hundred yards of each other. Both groups had brought their "wounded" and their equipment. Only Jimmy was missing. Nobody seemed to know where he was. His team was sheepish but only made desultory efforts to keep calling for him or looking for him on some of the nearby trails.

More time went by. Still no Jimmy.

By 5:30 p.m. the teams were hungry. Some team members insisted on going back to the college without Jimmy. Talk about the failure of small-group solidarity! Some went saying, "We'll be back"—and those who didn't return failed the exercise. But only several Marine cadets stayed through the dinner hour, along with one young woman who wanted a

THE LAST PATROL

"special" recommendation to law school. Most of those who went back for their dinner eventually drifted back, whether out of curiosity, concern, obligation, or fear of the instructor's wrath.

As you might imagine, as time went on, I became increasingly concerned. So reluctantly, we called the sheriff for help finding the lost platoon leader.

The students, who had initially welcomed Jimmy's embarrassment and found it quite amusing, were now worried themselves, especially the members of his team who had "lost him."

The sheriff wasn't worried, though, "We'll find him. Let's give him a chance to get out of the swamp when the moon comes up."

That's exactly what happened. At about 11 p.m., one of the deputies driving a perimeter road reported, "A half-crazed guy, covered in mud and foliage, came out of the woods waving his arms wildly around. Ran right into my headlights."

It was Jimmy who was indeed wet, muddy, frazzled, and crestfallen. But at least he had learned a valuable lesson, namely that when the sun goes down, it's hard to tell which direction is which and that deep in the swamp, dark comes earlier than on hilltops. Second lesson: The professor had recommended everyone have a compass for a reason (or two!).

The professor also learned an even more valuable lesson about risk-reward ratios, deciding, "Let's make that one the last patrol."

And so it was.

For all the subsequent years as well.

GUN RUNNING FOR A GOOD CAUSE

Jordan DeCoster

I walked into the Sportsman's Alliance of Maine, late for work one day in 2014. The door was still swinging shut a couple of steps behind me. I was thinking through everything I had to do that morning, deciding if I needed to reschedule anything. Maybe I didn't look like I was hurrying enough. A half-welcoming half-scolding shout echoed across the office, waking me up a bit: "Good morning Sleeping Beauty. Nice of you to join us." I thought I heard him right, but I needed to stop and think for a second. I wasn't sure, mostly because I didn't really sleep last night.

He was right to point out that I was late for work. Fair is fair. That's because I had driven four hours to Presque Isle and four hours back to Augusta overnight. Being called Sleeping Beauty was even funnier on just a couple hours of sleep.

That said, Maine's voters have surprised me over and over again with their generosity. I met people donating millions of dollars for wildlife conservation. I met thousands of Mainers giving what they could to put things right in our state. For many people that meant hour after hour making signs, knocking on doors, and talking about wildlife conservation with their neighbors.

In fact, Mainers are so generous that it can be a lot of work to deal with that generosity. The Sleeping Beauty race to Presque Isle and back was a part of just one day's work during the bear hunt campaign of

GUN RUNNING FOR A GOOD CAUSE

2014. It was easy to lose count of how many trips I made to Presque Isle, Brewer, Norway-Paris (the nice Paris!), Cape Elizabeth, Auburn, Scarborough, Lyman, Skowhegan, and on and on. I was driving up and down and across the state for most of 2014, picking up donations to Save Maine's Bear Hunt. That year, Question 1 asked Maine voters to restrict bear hunting. It was a rerun of the 2004 bear hunting ban when the anti-hunting campaign lost 53 percent to 47 percent. After waiting a decade, the same national lobbying organization took a second shot at Maine's hunting community, sending $2.5 million up from Washington DC. Voting YES on 1 would ban most bear hunting in Maine.

With twenty-four thousand to thirty-six thousand black bears, Maine has one of the largest bear populations in the United States. Maine's Department of Inland Fisheries and Wildlife (IF&W) has studied our bear population across the state since 1975. Maine's biologists regulate bear hunting to maintain the number of bears around the habitat's carrying capacity. Question 1 threatened big parts of Maine's outdoor recreational economy, especially some of our smaller, northern towns, and undercut the principles of scientific, research-based wildlife conservation. By 2014, everyone could see problems in states politicized hunting and banned parts of the bear hunt. Colorado was an unfortunate example. Human-bear conflicts forced wildlife officials to euthanize (i.e., shoot) more and more bears. From 2008 to 2013, these incidents doubled.

However, $2.5 million buys a lot of TV ads. What if Maine voters only saw anti-hunting ads for months? What if they never heard about IF&W's decades of research? Which way would they vote on Question 1? Mainers had to raise about as much money as the DC lobbyists to explain our side to voters. So we set out to do it.

Thousands and thousands of Mainers worked together to Save Maine's Bear Hunt. A lot of donations came in five or ten dollars at a time. Some guys kicked in much, much more than their fair share. Maine's sportsman's clubs, led by the Sportsman's Alliance of Maine, did a lot of the work. The U.S. Sportsmen's Alliance came up to help us. The Maine Trappers Association and Maine Professional Guides Association (MPGA), with their thousands of members, made some of the most impressive contributions.

We received tons of outdoor equipment donated to the NO on 1 Save Maine's Bear Hunt campaign so they could be turned into cash to buy TV commercials and time. I thought our best prize was one of Dale Tobey's hand-built Grand Laker canoes. Somebody won it in a raffle fair and square, but I'm still envious. That Grand Laker canoe was really the third prize in the MPGA Super Raffle. Somebody actually won a whole new log cabin on a ten dollar MPGA raffle ticket! Tons of outdoor equipment including donated hunting firearms had to be collected from all over Maine and brought to the campaign office in Augusta.

The Sleeping Beauty race was to pick up donations from Aroostook County and bring them to our office. I lost count of how many outfitters and sportsman's clubs were helping us. Their generosity was overwhelming. But there were lots of pressures, especially on me! We had to finish collecting those tons of donated gear by early August. I figured I could get the remaining firearms donations from Cumberland, Sagadahoc, and York counties and bring them back to Augusta in one day. But it was grueling. I drove through southern Maine, meeting at outfitters and sportsman's clubs to pick up their donations: shotguns, rifles, revolvers, and some high-tech bows. At each stop I got a few handshakes, some questions about our chances of keeping bear hunting, and more new-in-box firearms to pack into the cargo area of my SUV.

Once the growing stacks of boxes in the back got close to the rear seats, I started thinking about interior space as much as the traffic around me. Nobody had ever been kind enough to gift me a new hunting bow. I'd taken a few shots at targets with friends' bows, but I had never bought one myself. I learned that those new bow boxes are not small when people started handing them to me and I had to pack a bunch of them into my SUV. They were making me worry about running out of space. I drove to a few more clubs and picked up some more donations.

After packing most of the cargo area, I started stacking rifles and shotguns on the floor of the rear seat. It was a lot of work, and although I had faith in Maine's open carry law, I wondered from time to time if there was a bag limit! Then I was stacking boxes on top of the floor stacks, from the backs of the driver's and passenger's seats across the rear seats. I picked up more generous donations and I was packing the rear seats

GUN RUNNING FOR A GOOD CAUSE

mostly full, stacked tightly against the backs of the front seats. Eventually I took a walk around my SUV, with all of the doors open, looking for more space. Could I make room for another large bow box if I swapped that rifle into the cargo area and put some revolvers and a shotgun back into the rear seats?

I made two pretty solid blocks of gun boxes from the cargo door to the rear seats and from the rear seats to the backs of the front seats. This was a one-man job, not that it was easy or light work. I needed to pack the passenger's seat with guns from the floor up. As I picked up each gun box, I wondered, can I really fit every single one of these into my SUV? It was not just a question of space, the number of gun boxes and the size of the vehicle. I still had to drive a hundred miles, or so, and I would need to see my mirrors. I had to manage the large piles of guns in the cargo area and rear seats, along with the smaller pile in the passenger's seat, to keep the average height comparable to a person.

It was like ballasting a ship: Fill the spaces evenly. I had a roof rack and I did at times consider stacking a bunch of long gun boxes up there, but that seemed too flashy. After hours of driving, packing, driving, and repacking, I wedged the last few long gun boxes into the foot well of the passenger's seat. There was still room for my backpack and every single page of the firearms paperwork in the passenger's seat. There was not, however, much room for air inside the SUV once I got behind the wheel. If I rested my right arm on the center console my elbow touched the gun boxes in the passenger's seat.

I do not think I was legally required to buckle in that stack of boxes, but I did it to stop the pressure sensor beeping at me. After most of a day spent packing firearms boxes into every seat of my SUV except mine, I got back to I-95 headed north. I set the cruise control and imagined just how long I would have to spend explaining myself if I got pulled over. "Sir, I know that the law covers any amount of guns" would be my mantra! But how believable would that really be? I kept wondering.

Along with the donated firearms, I had stacks of paperwork documenting each donation, from each club or outfitter, and where it was going. We can be honest: I was not driving an SUV full of flowers and huggable stuffed animals. You could read Ruger, Remington, and Browning on the stacks of boxes through all seven windows and the windshield.

If I got pulled over there would be some questions asked no matter how supportive law enforcement officers might be. Supervisors would certainly have to be consulted for advice. Page after page after page of documentation verified every single detail, but how many hours would it take to review all of it on the roadside? What if they wanted to double-check the paperwork for one of the boxes underneath the rear seat? That would take me an hour to find, at least. My priorities were getting the firearms to Augusta, locked up, then convincing somebody else to review and approve all of the paperwork by close of business. I did not want to park this arsenal in my garage, not even for one night.

Would Maine's open carry law be solid cover? If I was doing anything that day I was openly displaying those firearms in pretty much the safest way possible. Many of the boxes were responsibly taped shut. While packing the boxes, I had even moved my seat forward several inches, to make all of the firearms more comfortable. It was a tight squeeze for the last hundred miles back to Augusta, but I made it safely and none of the boxes were crumpled! While a couple of our thoroughly responsible colleagues verified and sorted all of the paperwork, some of us immediately started opening the boxes, responsibly, to confirm that each firearm arrived in good shape.

We stacked so many brand-new rifles and shotguns on our desks that we needed to find somewhere else to work that afternoon. The hunting bows took up even more space leaning against the walls of our office. The revolvers were somewhere between the stacks of dozens and dozens of long gun boxes. The Taurus Judge .45/.410 makes a perfectly effective paperweight.

What does it mean to be generous? In some parts of Maine it means bending ash planks by hand for one hundred hours to craft a twenty-foot Grand Laker canoe, then donating it. In 2014 all eighty-five or so of Maine's sportsmen's clubs pulled together small donations to buy and donate hunting firearms so nice you'd have second thoughts about ever firing them. What if you scratched the gleaming finish or chipped the woodwork?

GUN RUNNING FOR A GOOD CAUSE

Maine's sportsmen's clubs, professional guides, and trappers did most of the hard work for NO on 1 to Save Maine's Bear Hunt in 2014. Some days I really had to hustle to keep up with them, and some nights I had to skip sleeping. It was all for a good cause, though. In the end, the DC lobbyists did have a little more money. But Mainers had more votes on Election Day and NO won again to defend Maine's hunting heritage.

As for the practical limits to "open carry"?

Still awaiting a definitive answer from some road stop in the future.

But thanks, no doubt, to Diana, the goddess of the hunt, I won't be there to get it.

ACKNOWLEDGMENTS

From Chris Potholm: This book owes a great deal of gratitude to many people. First, of course, to all those who shared with us the vignettes and word pictures of their lives, political and others. It was so much fun reliving Maine life from so many different perspectives and through the lens of so many Maine people. Our thanks to all who participated.

Kudos too to the hardworking and ever-cheery Jamie Jones and Guy Saldanha of the Bowdoin library staff for their fine help in getting necessary books and other background materials and to Carmen Greely who always has a bevy of books—on any subject—for us. We are all blessed to have the Bowdoin Library in our lives.

Working with Dave and Dennis on this book as well as *How Maine Decides* has been one of the major highlights of my authorship career. Not only have we worked on many campaigns together—sometimes on opposite sides—but over the years we have shared many, many happy exchanges and true, deep laughter concerning our many foibles and those of the myriad of others we have encountered in politics and outside of it. Those have been special, treasured moments. These are two very special people.

Gratitude also to Sandy Quinlan Potholm for her patience, forbearance, and all-around good humor in the face of our ongoing preoccupation with both ourselves and our feeble attempts at humor in this book.

The editors are also very grateful for the excellent and many contributions of the Down East/Globe Pequot Press team, particularly Felicity Tucker, Amy Paradysz, and Neil Cotterill. They were a joy to work with

ACKNOWLEDGMENTS

and their contributions were most substantial. A fine team in action and outcome.

And, as ever, a final and most formidable shoutout to Jed Lyons, whose contributions to this volume are legion and greatly appreciated. His abilities in the publishing field are considerable, and we as authors and editors greatly benefited from his participation.

From Dave Emery: This book was a lot of fun to write, or I should rather say, a lot of fun to assemble, as a part of this self-proclaimed quasi-literary triumvirate. I say that because in many ways, this book wrote *itself*! Each of us included within these pages has lived an interesting and event-filled life, so it was only necessary for us to kick back and remember all the wonderful, exciting, bizarre, and humorous things that have happened to us over the years. Our challenge was to share these events in a way that communicates our feelings of mirth, embarrassment, or consternation adequately with others. While this is not always an easy thing to do, from my perspective, there was great joy in remembering the people and events that have truly enriched my life.

Foremost among these are my wife Carol and our son Albert, both of whom have been present at some of the events related here (my weak stomach is a family legend), and have been regaled many times over with the telling and retelling of the others. I have had a great many smile-worthy adventures with Dave Sulin and George Smith, some of which (I hope) will never find their way into print. Sadly, George is no longer with us, but Dave and I continue to share our friendship and new adventures.

If it was not for Hattie Bickmore and her world-class out-sized personality, I could not have achieved the successes I managed to accomplish as a green twenty-something Congressman trying to break into the complex world of the Cumberland County political scene. Dennis Bailey and I have not always been allies; he was first a reporter for the *Portland Press Herald*, then the "flack" for Tom Andrews during my unsuccessful 1990 campaign. Dennis was always professional and competent, and I am very glad, finally, to have had an opportunity to work *with him* rather than *against him*.

ACKNOWLEDGMENTS

And finally, I must thank my good friend Chris Potholm for encouraging me to put these stories down on paper. On many occasions over the years, he had encouraged me to share my adventures and thoughts, an enterprise I had stubbornly resisted. Chris and I have been business partners and collaborators in many political campaigns and have hunted and fished together. Through his auspices, I was invited to work with his students on the annual Bowdoin student poll and still enjoy occasionally meeting with Bowdoin faculty and administration as we work on our next project, a more serious academic undertaking.

We are living in a cynical age, and if writing this book has accomplished anything, I sincerely hope that readers will appreciate that even political people are capable of laughing *at themselves*, and are all deserving, on occasion, of being *laughed at*. Humor is a great equalizer!

From Dennis Bailey: My memory might be hazy, but I think I first encountered Dr. Potholm when I was a press secretary for a 1990 Congressional campaign. Tom Andrews, then a progressive state senator, was running in the crowded Democratic Primary, and Chris would call me from time to time to offer advice and share polling data showing where Tom was doing well or not. I didn't know why he was calling; he was not on our staff or hired as a consultant. In fact, our campaign manager was very suspicious since Chris was seen as a Republican pollster, part of the enemy camp. I found out later Tom had been a student at Bowdoin and just liked him. I'm sure there was some bank-shot strategy involved in why Chris was offering free advice to the campaign of a liberal Democrat. But as a campaign newbie, it was over my head.

Years later, we ended up on the same team for real: the gubernatorial campaign of independent candidate Angus King. Chris not only brought his expertise to the battle but also his colorful stories and offbeat humor, which, in a tense, stressful 24/7 political campaign, are badly needed. He was a calming influence, like when he called me one day near the end of the campaign to tell me that he'd just got the results of a poll in Westbrook and Angus was trailing Brennan by 7 points.

"Oh no," I said. "That's bad."

There was a pause on the line.

ACKNOWLEDGMENTS

"Are you kidding?" Chris asked. "It's fantastic. If Brennan isn't beating Angus by double-digits in a Democratic stronghold like Westbrook, we're going to have a good night."

I learned that in politics, bad news can sometimes be good news—if you have the expertise around you who understands the data and can enlighten you. That's why I made a vow then that I'd never go into a campaign without Chris by my side.

Several campaigns later, my relationship with Chris has only grown stronger. Apart from his expertise with polling data, it's his generosity and good humor that keep me coming back. Even when we weren't working on campaigns, I'd usually call Chris the night before a big election just to check in and get his take on things.

And laugh.

Which is what this book is all about.

Living in Maine, it's so easy to take for granted the colorful, insightful, and enjoyable characters all around you, all of them with stories to tell. This book is an attempt to bring to life some of those everyday people and stories that, if we don't record and appreciate them now, will sadly disappear.

I also want to thank Dave Emery for his sage advice and many valuable contributions to this book. As the former Congressman will tell you, he and I were not always on the same side over the years. But I always believed that David was a real Mainer (you can tell by his accent) and a thoroughly decent person. And isn't it a sad commentary on our political times when pointing out someone's decency is considered a unique qualification?

Enjoy the book. If you have half as much fun reading it as we did putting it together, we've succeeded.

ABOUT THE EDITORS

Dennis Bailey is the author of the highly acclaimed *Pandemic Diary: A COVID Survivor's Tale* and *Ola Portugal*, as well as a major contributor to *How Maine Decides*. A native of Livermore Falls, he earned a bachelor's degree in journalism from the University of Maine and worked as a reporter for the *Lewiston Daily Sun*, the *Maine Times*, and the *Portland Press Herald*. He then worked on the Congressional campaign of Democratic state Senator Tom Andrews and became his communications director in the U.S. House and reelection campaign. In 1994, he joined Angus King's campaign for governor, serving as his press secretary, and later served six years as Governor King's communications director.

In 2000, Dennis launched Savvy, Inc., a public relations firm in Portland that represented businesses, law firms, political candidates, and state and local referendum campaigns. In 2003, he served as Casinos *NO!* public spokesperson and strategic advisor and went on to consult on anti-casino efforts nationwide. He has a master's degree in strategic public relations from George Washington University. Now living in Portugal as a digital nomad, Dennis continues to advise clients and campaigns.

Dave Emery is a native of Rockland. He served as a State Representative, U.S. Congressman from Maine's First District, chief deputy Republican whip of the U.S. House of Representatives, and deputy director of the U.S. Arms Control and Disarmament Agency, appointed by President Reagan, during which time he was Acting Ambassador to the UN Committee on Disarmament.

After returning home to Maine, Dave served as Interim President of Thomas College in Waterville. He then founded the consulting firm

ABOUT THE EDITORS

Scientific Marketing & Analysis, which provided polling and analytical services for Maine ballot measures such as widening the Maine Turnpike, Land for Maine's Future bonds, bear hunting, and several Forest Practices campaigns. He also provided polling services for Maine media, businesses, and municipalities and was the Republican consultant for the reapportionment of Maine legislative and congressional districts over four cycles.

A major contributor to the highly praised *How Maine Decides*, Dave is also the coauthor of the forthcoming book *Francos Ascendant: Their Rise and Continuing Relevance for Maine Politics*. Based on sixty years of election outcomes and census data, this work definitively proves Francos' decisive role in the Pine Tree State.

Chris Potholm was a registered Maine guide for twenty years and, for fifty-one years, a professor of government and legal studies at Bowdoin College specializing in African politics, Maine politics, conflict simulation and resolution, and war. He is the author of several books about Maine, including *This Splendid Game*, *The Delights of Democracy*, *Tall Tales from the Tall Pines* (fiction), *An Insider's Guide to Maine Politics*, *Maine: An Annotated Bibliography*, *Bill Cohen's 1972 Campaign and the Walk That Changed Politics* (with Bill Cohen and Jed Lyons), and, most recently, *How Maine Decides: An Insider's Guide to Ballot Measures in the Pine Tree State*.

ABOUT THE CONTRIBUTORS

John Baldacci served as Maine's seventy-third governor after his previous experience on the Bangor City Council, the Maine Senate (1982–1994), and the U.S. Congress (1995–2003), where he won reelection three times before seeking the governorship. A lifelong resident of Bangor, and educated at the University of Maine at Orono, his family restaurant in the Queen City, "Momma Baldacci's," was not only a gathering place for Maine political elite but for thousands of people over many years. It became a Maine institution known all over the state.

John's accomplishments during his two terms were significant for a variety of issues including Dirigo Health Care Act, school consolidation and the expansion and strengthening of Maine's community college system, and the historic promotion of gay rights and marriage equality. He also led the effort to streamline government service and expansion of healthcare and workforce training.

John received an honorary degree from Bowdoin College in 2011. He also served as Vice Chair of the board of the nonpartisan Northeast-Midwest Institute, a Washington-based, private, nonprofit, and nonpartisan research organization.

Robert Laurent "Larry" Benoit grew up a third-generation resident of Cape Elizabeth and graduated from the University of Southern Maine with a degree in education in 1971.

Larry began his career in politics and government working on a voter registration project with the Maine Democratic Party and Senator Edmund Muskie's presidential campaign (1971–1972). Thereafter he joined the district staff of Congressman Peter Kyros as a caseworker

ABOUT THE CONTRIBUTORS

(1972–1974) and went on to work for Senator Edmund Muskie as Senior Field Representative (1975–1980), Senator George Mitchell as Chief Field Representative (1980–1993), Sergeant at Arms and Doorkeeper of the United States Senate (1994), and Chief of Staff for Congressman John Baldacci (1995–2001).

After nearly thirty years of Congressional staff service, in 2001 Larry began a second career with the government relations division at Bernstein Shur Sawyer and Nelson law firm, retiring in 2012. He managed Senator George Mitchell's election campaigns in 1982 and 1988 and coordinated Congressman John Baldacci's reelection campaigns (1996, 1998, and 2000). He managed the Maine Democratic Party's media campaign in support of John Baldacci's successful runs for Governor of Maine in 2002 and 2006. He also served as chairman of Governor Baldacci's Transition Committees in the 2002 and 2006.

While at Bernstein Shur, Larry was the lead manager for several statewide referendum campaigns in opposition to citizen initiatives involving education funding and property tax caps, defeating the so-called Palesky 1% Tax Cap and two versions of the misnamed Taxpayers Bill of Rights, which would have devastated public education.

Keith A. Brown was born in Caribou in the late 1930s and moved to an old farmhouse in Harpswell in the early 1940s. The farmhouse had no electricity, no running water, and only the use of an outside privy. As a youngster, he dug clams and harvested sea moss and borrowed his father's John Deere tractor to prepare gardens and mow hayfields for pocket money.

Keith went to Brunswick High School and attended the University of Maine Business School, where he graduated with a business degree, majoring in accounting. He hung up his clam hoe and donned a coat and tie to work as an accountant for a local paper company before applying for a job at Bath Iron Works. When BIW received a development program to design and build a new FFG Oliver Hazard Perry class destroyer, Keith was assigned to open an office near Naval Sea Systems Command headquarters in Virginia and manage all financial matters. BIW was

ABOUT THE CONTRIBUTORS

eventually awarded the design contract, built twenty-six navy frigates, and provided lead yard services for the life of the class of the FFGs.

Keith moved up in the management of BIW to become controller and chief financial officer, but he yearned to start his own business. He and a fellow BIW vice president bought General Ship, a shipyard in Boston that overhauled destroyers. Over the next decade, General Ship overhauled more destroyers than BIW. Retiring from General Ship, Keith joined the board of directors at the Harpswell Heritage Land Trust and served as its president for seven years. As president, he led efforts to purchase two signature landmarks: Mackerel Cove and Scofield Shore Preserve. An avid skier, Brown owned a ski condo at Sunday River and took many ski vacations in Utah, Colorado, Wyoming, and the Italian high Alps.

Rob Caldwell has worked as a reporter and anchor for News Center Maine (WCSH in Portland and WLBZ in Bangor) since 1982. He has covered every major politician and political race in the state over the last four decades as well as interviewing George H. W. Bush, Bill Clinton, and Barack Obama.

Since 2003, Rob has co-anchored the evening news magazine *207*. His stories have been honored with Edward R. Murrow and Emmy awards, and he has been inducted into the Maine Broadcasting Hall of Fame and the Silver Circle of the New England chapter of the National Academy of Television Arts & Sciences.

In his spare time, he has visited the Truman, Kennedy, Johnson, Nixon, Bush 41, and Clinton presidential libraries. He hopes one day to see the rest.

Pat Callaghan began his broadcast journalism career in 1978 at New Hampshire Public Television. Then, beginning in 1979, he spent forty-three years as a news anchor and reporter for News Center Maine (WCSH6 in Portland and WLBZ2 in Bangor). Notable stories along the way included being on the air live at the Kennedy Space Center when the *Challenger* space shuttle exploded in 1986 and reporting from Belfast,

Northern Ireland, when former Maine Senator George Mitchell chaired the talks that culminated in the Good Friday Agreement.

Pat spent much of his time covering politics, reporting extensively reporting from both Augusta and Washington, DC. He also covered Maine's delegations at national political conventions and produced documentaries on notable Maine figures, including Ed Muskie, Bill Cohen, Olympia Snowe, and George Mitchell.

He is currently the host of *In the Arena*, a Maine politics podcast available on the WMTW TV website and all podcast platforms. He has a bachelor's degree in history from the University of New Hampshire and is a member of the Maine Broadcasting Hall of Fame and the New England Emmy Awards Silver Circle.

Don Carrigan has been a broadcast journalist for more than fifty years, starting when he was a student at the University of Maine (then UMO). His first break into commercial broadcasting came in the summer of 1973, when WBZ Radio called the campus radio station and asked him to cover a press conference in South Brooksville with former Watergate Special Prosecutor Archibald Cox, who had been fired by President Nixon in the infamous "Saturday Night Massacre" during the Watergate probe.

Don was hired by WLBZ-TV in Bangor later that same year, before graduation, as a reporter and late-night news anchor. That began a relationship with WLBZ and WCSH TV that continues to this day. He spent many years covering Maine politics, political figures, and state issues. He left television for three years to work for U.S. Senator Bill Cohen, though he kept a foot in the broadcasting door during that time by hosting an outdoors-oriented radio call-in program.

Don returned to TV at Maine Public Television in 1994 as Executive Producer of Public Affairs, moderating dozens of debates and hosting specials as well as the weekly program *Maine Watch*. In 2003, he returned to WCSH TV as State House reporter, covering campaigns, the legislature and the rest of State government. He has also provided extensive coverage of veterans and the program *Honor Flight Maine*. Don has

ABOUT THE CONTRIBUTORS

received multiple Emmy awards and Maine Association of Broadcasters awards for his work.

William S. Cohen served Maine as Mayor of Bangor (1971–1972), a Congressman from the Second Congressional District (1973–1979), and a U.S. Senator (1979–1997).

In Congress, Bill served with distinction on the House Judiciary and Senate Defense committees before being selected by President Bill Clinton to be the U.S. Secretary and Defense. He served in this role for four years, supervising, among many other ongoing problems, the American effort to end the war in Kosovo. As a first-term Congressman, Bill served on the House Judiciary Committee and was the first Republican on it to decide that President Nixon should be impeached.

In addition to his exemplary service to state and country, Bill is a prolific author. His books include the fiction titles *Collision, Final Strike, Blink of an Eye, Dragon Fire, Murder in the Senate, One-Eyed Kings,* and (with Gary Hart) *The Double Man* and non-fiction titles *Of Sons and Seasons, A Baker's Nickel, Men of Zeal,* and (with his wife Janet Langhart Cohen) *Love in Black and White.*

Bill is currently chairman of The Cohen Group, a worldwide consulting and policy company with many overseas outposts, including in China, India, and Australia. He is also a frequent guest commentator on the BBC, CNN, and MSNBC and has written commentary for the *Wall Street Journal, New York Times, Washington Post,* and *Business Weekly.*

Dana Connors was born and educated in Easton in Aroostook County and graduated from the University of Maine in 1965, where he also earned a master's degree in public administration. He was appointed City Manager of Presque Isle when he was twenty-three, making him the youngest city manager in Maine at the time, and held that position for sixteen years. Dana served as head of the Maine Department of Transportation under Governor Joe Brennan and as commissioner in Governor Jock McKernan's administration.

Dana also headed up the transition team for Governor Angus King and was appointed by the Governor King to serve on the Northern New

ABOUT THE CONTRIBUTORS

England Passenger Rail Authority and the State of Maine Governor's Business Roundtable for Early Childhood Development, among many other appointments across the administrations of five different governors. He has served as a key advisor to nearly every governor since Brennan, regardless of party.

Dana served for thirty years at the head of the Maine Chamber of Commerce and in 1997 led the successful effort to widen the Maine Turnpike despite its earlier defeat in 1991. After the 1997 defeat, as commissioner of transportation he created a diverse group of people and interests on both sides of the issue and inspired them to hammer out rulemaking for the Maine Sensible Transportation Policy Act. His widely acclaimed YouTube series *The Maine Take with Dana Connors* features a wide array of his interviews of Maine leaders in commerce, business, and politics.

Connors has also been inducted into the Junior Achievement's Maine Business Hall of Fame and received numerous lifetime achievement awards including the Maine Better Transportation Association's most prestigious award. In addition to his passion for transportation, improving Maine's business climate, and mentoring youth, he has also been a leader in many educational reform issues. He has received an Honorary Doctorate from the University of Maine.

Will Davis was born in Brunswick and currently resides in Harpswell. He has been a TikTok producer and influencer with over 1.8 million followers, engaging audiences on topics ranging from "The True Origins of COVID" to "Don't Touch My Truck" to the very popular "The Scenic Towns in Maine." In addition to his followers in the United States and Canada, Will enjoys significant audiences in India, Nepal, Taiwan, South Korea, Thailand, and Great Britain. The recipient of the Mount Ararat Honors English Award in 2024, Will is working on a major video project called "Up Close and Personal: The Towns of Maine" that highlights Maine people and places.

Jordan DeCoster grew up in Brunswick and began volunteering on political campaigns as a boy. In seventh grade, Jordan started making

ABOUT THE CONTRIBUTORS

trouble for his teachers by ditching school to join canvassing teams knocking on doors across Southern Maine. In his youth he reread *This Splendid Game* enough to learn to make something of himself and over the years he has worked on successful referendum and initiative campaigns, most notably NO on 1-Save Maine's Bear Hunt in 2014 and YES on 1-Regulate Marijuana Like Alcohol in 2016. Before and after work, he spends his time in Maine's woods, until his dog Hope gets tired, or boating between islands along the Midcoast, far enough beyond mobile phone range to sometimes worry clients and editors alike.

Kevin Delahanty was raised in Lewiston, Maine, by a family with decades of involvement in public service, government, and politics. A graduate of Bowdoin College, he also has an MBA from Rutgers University. Kevin was senior banker and then head of the large multinational corporate client segment for Morgan Guaranty Trust Company (subsequently JP Morgan) for the New England region and then at Security Pacific National Bank.

In 1991, he became regional president for Fleet Bank in Connecticut. He pivoted to the recruiting side of banking and capital markets, spending more than two decades with the Options Group, a premier executive search firm with a focus on global international banks and alternative management firms.

Kevin has been involved with Connecticut Special Olympics as well as with various business development groups in New York and New England. He maintains a keen interest in the Hudson River Valley and in historic preservation.

Says Kevin:

I had the great fortune of meeting Jed Lyons in August 1970. It was the first day of summer freshman football at Bowdoin College. He and his parents pulled into a parking space in front of a dorm at the same time my parents and I pulled into a space adjacent to theirs. We met and had a good laugh about how he had just driven all the way from Barrington, Illinois, and I had driven thirty minutes from my home in Lewiston. We bonded immediately, having similar strengths and weaknesses on the football field including good size and a desire not to get injured. We became great friends from that first day.

Two years later, Jed asked me to be in a political ad for Republican Bill Cohen's first Congressional campaign in 1972. Of course, anything for a friend, right? Well, I wasn't thinking clearly; once aired, I received a stern call from my father. Dad was a staunch, lifetime Democrat who had been a candidate himself for Congress in 1954, while Ed Muskie was leading the ticket running for Governor. Dad was later appointed by Muskie to the judiciary in 1958. He reminded me with that call which political party provided for my education, etc.

Jed's publishing success deserves recognition, first with Rowman & Littlefield and now with The Globe Pequot Publishing Group and Down East Books. With the publication of *Real Life, Real Funny*, he has a new star in his crown as he brings this premier volume of Maine's political humor to the reading public. I know my father would certainly laugh (as I did), add to the stories, and be immensely proud that I have forged years of friendship with such an extraordinary individual, even a lifelong Rockefeller Republican.

Bill Diamond grew up on a two-horse dirt farm in rural West Gardiner, with his grandfather, mother, and older sister (his father left town shortly after his birth and never returned—not the ideal confidence builder). Bill went on to become a teacher, thanks to President Johnson's Work Study program, and later became a principal and superintendent of schools.

Realizing that the most important decisions affecting education were made by state bureaucrats and elected officials, Bill ran for and won a seat in the Maine House of Representatives in 1976 as a Democrat. Later, he served eight years as Maine's forty-fifth Secretary of State. He also managed twenty nonconsecutive years in the Maine Senate from 1982 to 2022. Bill ran for governor in 1986 with a fistful of ideals and little else, but his presence in the race was highly regarded by voters for his honest engagement with our state's problems and proposed solutions.

ABOUT THE CONTRIBUTORS

Beginning in 1980, Bill founded or cofounded several successful small businesses in southern Maine. Long an advocate for Maine's most vulnerable citizens, his proudest accomplishment was founding the 501c3 nonprofit foundation Walk a Mile in Their Shoes, which is dedicated to preventing child abuse and the death of children in state care.

Spiros Droggitis was born and raised in Biddeford, where his family ran the WonderBar Steak House. Bowdoin professor Christian Potholm in his treatise *An Insider's Guide to Maine Politics, 1946–1996* called the WonderBar the "chief political hangout and eatery in Biddeford, owned and operated by the politically important Droggitis family." Spiros worked at the WonderBar at an early age, first as a host and cashier, then as a bus boy in his teens and finally as a bartender when he was of age. Upon graduation from Biddeford High School, he attended Bowdoin College where he was class president and graduated with a degree in government in 1974.

His first job out of college in the U.S. Senate and the office of Senator Edmund S. Muskie was extensively covered in his submission for this book. In 1977, after the reelection of Senator Muskie, Spiros worked in the Senator's office for another year. In 1978, he worked as a Washington representative for Fiber Materials Inc., a Biddeford company specializing in high-temperature materials and composites primarily used for defense purposes.

Spiros began his career in the federal government in the Office of Congressional Affairs at the U.S. Nuclear Regulatory Commission (NRC) two months before the worst commercial nuclear power plant accident in U.S. history—the Three Mile Island nuclear power plant near Harrisburg, Pennsylvania, on March 28, 1979. It was trial by fire with all the Congressional hearings in the year following the accident.

Later in his career at the NRC, Spiros was on the personal staff of two presidentially appointed NRC Commissioners and conducted liaison activities with state governments and federal government agencies. Spiros was the recipient of the NRC's Meritorious Service Award for his state liaison work. While working for the two NRC Commissioners, Spiros toured many nuclear facilities in the United States as well as in

ABOUT THE CONTRIBUTORS

Canada, Japan, Korea, Sweden, Ukraine, and Armenia, including Three Mile Island and Chernobyl in the USSR, the site of the worst nuclear power plant in history. Spiros served as a member of the Headquarters Fukushima Support Team after the 2011 accident at the Fukushima Nuclear Power Plant caused by an earthquake and subsequent tsunami in Japan. It was at that point and after thirty-five years of government service that Spiros decided to retire before being called upon to visit the site of that accident in Japan.

Spiros and his wife Ottilie raised their family of four daughters and a son in Bethesda, Maryland. Upon retirement, Spiros and Ottilie moved back to his hometown of Biddeford, where they live in a converted textile mill along the Saco River, a block and a half from where the WonderBar was located on Washington Street, and across Main Street where his grandfather, an immigrant from Greece, operated a shoe repair shop.

Ruth Foster was a longtime resident of Ellsworth. A former business owner of Ruth Foster's (a store for children and all who are children at heart) for thirty-five years, she was also a real estate broker and owner of Ruth Foster Real Estate.

Her list of community service is of longstanding. In addition to two years as Mayor of Ellsworth and four years as a member of Ellsworth City Council, she has been a director of Bar Harbor Bank and Trust, a trustee of the Maine Coast Hospital, board chair of Wood Lawn Historic Museum, and board chair of the Stanwood Wildlife Sanctuary (Birdsacre—a historic preserve and educational avian restoration facility).

She served ten years in the Maine House and four years in the Maine Senate, including two years on the Labor Committee, two years on the Judiciary Committee, and ten years on the Appropriations and Financial Affairs Committee. Foster is most proud of her landmark legislation: One removed divorce cases involving minor children out of the court rooms and into a mediation service—leading her to be called "the Mother of Mediation" and one that established the establishment of Living Wills.

Ruth is also the author of *Reason, Reality, and Humor: Stories of an Adventurous Life in Maine*. At the time of her death, she was writing

ABOUT THE CONTRIBUTORS

a book for children about Sammy, her highly educated (University of Maine) cat and his adventurous life in Maine.

Maria Fuentes earned a bachelor's degree from Boston University and an MBA from the University of Maine. She has been executive director of the Maine Better Transportation Association (MBTA) for over thirty years, a clear indication of how much she enjoys her work and the inspiring individuals she has been privileged to collaborate with in the transportation, construction, and engineering sectors.

At MBTA, Maria has worked on various funding and policy initiatives, including the 1997 turnpike widening campaign, numerous transportation bond referendum votes, and lobbying for passage of key legislation, including the fuel tax indexing proposal in the Maine Legislature, which won by one vote in the Maine House. Indexing generated over $300 million for transportation infrastructure projects across the state before being killed by the next administration.

Maria is a past chair of the Transportation Investment Advocacy Center and the Better Roads and Transportation Council of America and served as a director on the board of the American Road and Transportation Builders Association. She is also a past board chair of the University of Maine Foundation and the University of Maine Alumni Association and served as a member of the University's Board of Visitors. She is currently on the board of WTS-Maine and is secretary for the Hallowell Food Pantry and treasurer of the Capital Area New Mainers Project.

In her career, Maria has been honored with the Transportation Leadership Award by the Institute of Transportation Engineers; the Ralph G. Knowlton Award by the Maine Chapter of the Constriction Specifications Institute; and the Major Achievement in Construction Award by AGC-Maine. She was also honored by the University of Maine Alumni Association with the Pine Tree Emblem award.

In her spare time, Maria enjoys promoting the five regional hiking books written by her husband, Jeff Romano, and published by Mountaineers Books. She and Jeff have two (nearly) adult children.

ABOUT THE CONTRIBUTORS

Philip Harriman is a lifelong Yarmouth resident. He entered the financial planning profession in 1978, joining the agency of former Maine Governor James Longley. In 1983, he and Michael Lebel formed Lebel & Harriman, LLP, an independent insurance and investment firm. Lebel & Harriman is among New England's largest retirement advising firms today. Phil is also former president of the international financial services association MDRT and has served on numerous boards. He is currently vice chair of the board at Husson University.

Phil's public service began on the Yarmouth Town Council. He was elected to the Council twice, beginning in 1986, and served a term as its chairperson. In 1991, Phil won a surprising election to the Maine Senate, unseating an eighteen-year incumbent and Senate Majority Leader. He served four consecutive terms until 2000, when he was term-limited. Phil's notable legislative accomplishments include sponsoring the Child Support law, which motivated parents who were not making support payments to become current or risk losing their professional licenses. He was the only legislator to vote against electric deregulation, arguing it was merely reregulation, which has proven not to reduce energy costs as promised.

Phil has participated in several statewide referendums, including the Casino's NO initiative and efforts to cap property taxes. In 2006, he became one of the founders of *Inside Maine* on news radio WGAN. Phil's political analysis insights have been featured on NBC News Center Maine for over twelve years. He is currently a commentator on *In the Arena*, a Maine politics podcast on WMTW TV, and on podcast platforms.

Phil holds a bachelor's degree in business from Husson University and a Chartered Financial Consultant designation from the American College.

Corey Hascall became president and CEO of the University of Southern Maine Foundation in 2025, expanding her role since joining in 2017. She was instrumental in completing the $50 million Great University Campaign, the largest fundraising initiative in USM's history.

ABOUT THE CONTRIBUTORS

With over two decades of experience in political strategy, fundraising, and issues management, Corey has directed state and federal campaigns, overseeing paid and earned media, policy development, communications, and field operations, while raising record breaking multimillion-dollar budgets. She has worked alongside national organizations like EMILY's List, the Democratic Congressional Campaign Committee, and J Street.

In the private sector, Corey spent eight years leading community relations, crisis communications, and reputation management for clients in Maine and across the country. She earned her bachelor's degree in political science at the University of Southern Maine and an Alternative Dispute Resolution certification there in 2012. Corey is a graduate of Maine Development Foundation's Leadership Maine program. Her community involvement includes board service with The Ecology School, Nash Foundation, Maine Women's Lobby, and Maine AIDS Alliance. As former board president of The Ecology School, Corey cochaired its first capital campaign and now serves as emeritus board member.

Corey grew up in South Portland and now lives in Falmouth with her husband John, their two rescue dogs, and two cats. They have two adult sons, Max and Oscar.

Scott Hood joined the Bowdoin staff in August 1989. Prior to that, he was a reporter and news director for the Maine Public Broadcasting Network, where he cohosted *Maine Things Considered* and frequently contributed to National Public Radio news programs, including *All Things Considered* and *Morning Edition*. Throughout his career, Scott has interviewed notable figures such as Madeleine Albright, James Baker, George H. W. Bush, William Cohen, Henry Kissinger, and George Mitchell. He has received fourteen individual news awards from the Associated Press and the Maine Association of Broadcasters, including for his coverage of the 1989 Moody Beach case before the Maine Supreme Judicial Court and a 1986 visit to Portland by the Grateful Dead.

Born in Brooklyn, New York, and raised in Connecticut, Scott earned his undergraduate degree in English from Lake Forest College, located north of Chicago, and his master's degree in public policy and management at the Muskie School of Public Service at the University of

ABOUT THE CONTRIBUTORS

Southern Maine. He is also a graduate of the Leadership Maine program from the Maine Development Foundation. He lives in Topsham with his wife, Alison Bennie—Bowdoin College's associate vice president for communications and public affairs and editor of *Bowdoin Magazine*. They have four adult children.

Angus King is a U.S. Senator for Maine, serving his third term in that august body after being first elected in 2012. His reelection bid in 2018 was record-setting for a multiple-candidate election going back to the Civil War. Angus currently sits on the Armed Services Committee, the Energy and Natural Resources Committee, the Veterans Affairs Committee, and the Select Committee on Intelligence. He led Maine for two terms as governor, from 1995 to 2003, establishing, among other very important policies and projects, Maine's first-in-the-nation program to provide laptops for all Maine students. He was one of the first governors to recognize the importance of the internet as a teaching tool and turn it into public policy.

A significant accomplishment prior to holding public office was Angus' leadership in establishing the groundbreaking Land for Maine's Future program, which has set aside some six hundred thousand acres of special places to be enjoyed by Maine people and our visitors now and for years to come.

Although an Independent and centrist, Angus normally caucuses with the Democrats.

He was educated at Dartmouth College and the University of Virginia Law School. Early in his career, Angus worked for Senator William "Bill" Hathaway, was a staff attorney for Pine Tree Legal Assistance, and worked in renewable energy development, forming an energy company called Northeast Energy Management.

Angus is the author of *Making a Difference: A Leadership Agenda for Maine*, *A Senator's Eye* based on his popular Instagram posts, and *Governor's Travels,* which chronicles his family's RV circumnavigation of America after he left the governor's office. Angus has also taught courses as a guest lecturer at Bowdoin and Bates colleges and has toured the

ABOUT THE CONTRIBUTORS

entire State of Maine on his trusty Harley Davidson, meeting all manner of interesting people, some of whom are profiled in this work.

Juliana J. L'Heureux began writing about Franco-Americans when the *Portland Press Herald*'s York County edition sought a columnist to replace a French language writer who had taken a position in Paris. Starting in 1992, she authored columns centered on her husband's large extended Franco-American family. Reader interest prompted Juliana to broaden her focus, leading to the publication of hundreds of articles and blogs that included interviews, cultural reporting, religion, political reports, French language content, regional and international travel experiences, and book reviews.

Her articles have also been published in the *Portland Press Herald*'s statewide edition, *the Sanford News*, the *Bangor Daily News*, and *Le Forum*, a journal published by the University of Maine in Orono. As a member of the University of Southern Maine Franco-American Collection, Juliana cohosted and participated in seminars and receptions for Franco-American dignitaries, artists, political leaders, and writers. She also served on an academic panel about Franco-Americans hosted by the college president, Barry Mills.

As a professional registered nurse, Juliana is the former president of the American Nurses Association of Maine (ANA-Maine) and coauthor of the book *Maine Nursing: Interviews and History on Caring and Competence*, which discusses the state's nursing history from 1912 to 2015. She was appointed to serve on the governor's task force on Franco-Americans in 2011, and in 2016, she was inducted into the Franco-American Hall of Fame by the Maine Legislature.

Janet Mills is currently the seventy-fifth governor of Maine. A moderate Democrat, she became the first female governor in the history of the state in 2018. She won reelection handily in 2022, receiving more than 373,000 votes—a Maine record.

Janet was born in Farmington and educated at Colby, the Sorbonne, and the University of Massachusetts (Boston) and earned a law degree from the University of Maine. Her groundbreaking political career included being the first female criminal prosecutor in Maine (appointed by Governor Joseph Brennan), the first female district attorney in New England, serving in the Maine House of Representatives from 2002 to 2009, and becoming vice chair of the Maine Democratic Party in 2011. Janet was subsequently elected Maine Attorney General in 2013, serving until 2019. She was the first woman in Maine to assume that role. She cofounded the Maine Women's Lobby and served on its board of directors of the nonpartisan Climate Alliance. A widow with five stepdaughters, Janet has made improving the lives of Maine people her top goal.

As governor, Janet Mills has championed balanced budgets on the state level; fought for individual rights, including the rights of the LGBT+ Mainers; and improved Maine government's relationship with its Native American Wabanaki Nations in Maine, the Maliseet, Micmac, Passamaquoddy, and Penobscot tribes. In the feisty manner of Margaret Chase Smith (one of her childhood idols), Governor Mills has boldly taken on such political figures as Governor Paul LePage and President Donald Trump on issues of importance to Maine.

Paul Mills is a Farmington attorney and Harvard magna cum laude in history who is well known for his historical understanding and analyses of public affairs in Maine. He has been a regular columnist for many Maine newspapers such as the *Sun Journal, Franklin Journal,* and *Morning Sentinel* over the past twenty-five years. Prior to his sister Janet's election as governor in 2018, Paul was the election-night analyst for WGME Channel 13 in Portland. Many insiders regard him as Maine's unofficial political historian.

When not practicing law in Farmington, Paul also regularly wields the gavel at town meetings in the Franklin County area, having presided at nearly 250 of them in some fifteen municipalities and school districts over the past forty-five years.

Bill Nimitz retired in 2022 after a forty-five-year career in Maine journalism, including as a columnist for the past twenty-seven years for the *Portland Press Herald* and *Maine Sunday Telegram*. His work has taken him to every corner of Maine and five times to war zones in Iraq and

Afghanistan, where he reported on the Maine Army National Guard. He also followed Mainers as they responded to the aftermaths of the 9/11 Manhattan attacks, Hurricane Katrina, and the 2010 earthquake in Haiti.

Bill is a member of the Maine Press Association Hall of Fame. His other honors include Maine Journalist of the Year in 2004, a Distinguished Service Award from the New England Newspaper Press Association in 2007, the Shalom House Hope Award in 2007, and the Intelligence and Courage Award from the Frances Perkins Center in 2015. He is a former chairman of the board of trustees for the Salt Institute of Documentary Studies and former president of the Maine Press Association, and he served for many years as an adjunct faculty member at St. Joseph's College of Maine.

After retiring, Bill served as president of the Maine Journalism Foundation, which assisted with the transformation of five daily newspapers and sixteen weeklies throughout Maine to a nonprofit model under the Maine Trust for Local News. He serves as host of Maine Public Book Club.

Tony Payne is a native of Maine, a graduate of Hobart College, and a longtime business executive. He served as a field representative for the Monks for Maine U.S. Senate campaign, was the Maine GOP Executive Director, chaired the Portland Republican City Committee, was a delegate to the 1988 Republican National Convention, ran as a candidate in the 1992 Republican primary for Maine's First Congressional District, and chaired the Falmouth Town Council. He and his wife are now retired and reside in Yarmouth.

Tony's seminal article, "I No Longer Recognize the Republican Party," published in the *Portland Press Herald* on May 30, 2024, is regarded as a classic by political followers in the Pine Tree State. Drawing on his vibrant political sense of place and personality, he contrasts today's party with those of Presidents George H. W. Bush and Ronald Reagan, concluding that both the party and the country need to return to their principles and values.

ABOUT THE CONTRIBUTORS

Bobby Reynolds grew up in a small farming and factory community in central New York State. Immediately following graduation from high school, he enlisted in the U.S. Navy. After four years in the Navy, he came to Maine in 1980 to attend what was then called Southern Maine Vocational Institute (now SMCC) to receive training to enter the US Merchant Marines. Twelve years at sea was enough for Reynolds to seek a career change; for a short time he hammered nails as a framing carpenter, worked as a mason tender, and milked cows for a local farmer before becoming a full-time professional firefighter in Portland. His involvement with the local firefighter union led him to a life in politics.

Nearing the end of his twenty-year stint with the fire department, Bobby returned to school with the intention of becoming a lawyer but was saved from that fate when offered a job with Senator Susan Collins. His role included advising on both military and homeland security issues as well as working on two Collins campaigns as her political director. Bobby left the Senate life to join Maine Street Solutions, the government relations group at Verrill, where he gained consultant work on numerous referendum campaigns as well as advising varying advocacy groups on tax reform, court nominations, and candidate campaigns.

Bobby has been a senior advisor to Congressman Jared Golden since 2018 and is a Mainer living in exile on Capitol Hill in Washington, DC. He is an avid outdoorsman and has written numerous articles for the *Maine Sportsman* magazine. He has three adult children, none of them (thankfully) involved in politics.

Edie Smith grew up in Winthrop and graduated from Bowdoin College in 1981. Politics was in her blood from an early age as she tagged along with her older brothers George and Gordon, volunteering on campaigns. Edie worked alongside her brother George on the two gubernatorial campaigns of Angus King and worked at Eaton Peabody Consulting Group for healthcare, education, and forestry clients. Edie really dug deep into the fabric of Maine by working on referendum campaigns, including the Big Bird Campaign at MPBN (winning the YES vote), Sunday Sales (winning the YES vote), then as Campaign Manager of three hard-fought campaigns where a NO vote was required: NO campaigns against physician-assisted suicide, casinos, and a very tough campaign in 2004 defeating efforts to stop Maine's bear hunt. Edie was Field Director for Angus King's campaign for the U.S. Senate in 2012 and has served on his federal staff in Maine for the past twelve years. In her spare time, she was a counselor at the Dirigo Girl's State program at Husson University for thirty years.

For her superb track record doing ballot measures in Maine, as well as for The Nature Conservancy in Florida and Virginia, Edie was called "Queen of the North—and of the South" in Christian P. Potholm's book *How Maine Decides: An Insider's Guide to How Ballot Measures Are Won and Lost.*

Ethan Strimling served for ten years as Portland's Democratic Mayor and as its State Senator. He also spent nineteen years as the executive director of LearningWorks, a social service agency that assists at-risk kids, low-income families, and immigrants in breaking the generational cycle of poverty through education.

Currently, Ethan is a community organizer for progressive causes around the country while pontificating on politics in print, on radio, and on WMTW TV. He is also one-third of the podcast *In the Arena* with host Pat Callaghan and Republican Phil Harriman, the only bipartisan podcast on politics in Maine. Ethan earned a bachelor's degree in history from the University of Maine and a master's in education from Harvard University. In another life, he also attended the Juilliard School as a theater student.

Bob Whelan graduated from Bowdoin College in 1962 with a degree in English and as an ROTC student. He entered the U.S. Army as a 2nd Lieutenant in Infantry. Bob completed Infantry Officer Basic Course at Fort Benning, Georgia, then attended Jump School for paratrooper training, followed by Ranger School, where he learned land navigation and patrolling techniques. He subsequently served in Korea on the Demilitarized Zone overlooking North Korea. After returning to the United States, Bob was assigned to the Seventh Special Forces Group and completed the Special Forces Qualification Course.

ABOUT THE CONTRIBUTORS

Bob was then reassigned to the Fifth Special Forces Group and deployed to Vietnam in 1965. There, he served on two different A Teams in the foothills of the Central Highlands. He served a second tour in Vietnam in the Mekong Delta from 1968 to 1969. Other assignments earning a master's degree in English and teaching English at the U.S. Military Academy at West Point for six years. His miliary decorations include the Legion of Merit, Bronze Star with First Oak Leaf Cluster, Meritorious Service Medal, Air Medal, Army Commendation Medal with First Oak Leaf Cluster, Vietnam Service Medal, Vietnamese Cross of Gallantry with Palm, Civil Action Medal (First Class), Combat Infantry Badge, Parachutist Badge, and Ranger Tab.

Bob retired from the U.S. Army in November 1982 as a Lieutenant Colonel and began a twenty-seven-year second career as an English teacher and administrator at the University of Maine, where, from 1985 to 1997, he served as assistant to four university presidents.

www.ingramcontent.com/pod-product-compliance
Ingram Content Group UK Ltd.
Pitfield, Milton Keynes, MK11 3LW, UK
UKHW041938210426
5322IPUK00016B/236